ARCHIE MOORE...
The Ole Mongoose

THE

AUTHORIZED BIOGRAPHY OF

ARCHIE MOORE

Undefeated Light Heavyweight

Champion of the world
by
Dr. MARILYN G. DOUROUX

Branden Publishing Company, Inc.
Boston

Library of Congress Cataloging-in-Publication Data

Douroux, Marilyn Green.
    Archie Moore : the ole mongoose : the authorized biography
of Archie Moore, undefeated lighheavyweight champion of the
world / by Marilyn G. Douroux.
        p. cm.
    Includes bibliographical references and index.
    ISBN 0-8283-1942-1 : $19.95
    1. Moore, Archie, 1916-
    2. Boxers (Sports)--United States--Biography. I. Title.
GV 1132.M75D68   1991
796.8'3'092--dc20
    [B]   90-2417A
                                                        CIP

Special limited edition--signed, dated and numbered:
    0-8283-1944-8 $39.95

BRANDEN PUBLISHING COMPANY, Inc.
17 Station Street
PO Box 843 Brookline Village
Boston, MA 02147

CONTENTS

To:

BOXING, WOMEN

and

JAZZ

ACKNOWLEDGEMENTS

This author gratefully acknowledges the opportunity given to me by Archie Moore to write his story; to interpret its meaning within the context of other histories; to shed light on his contributions and those of his contemporaries.

Special thanks to Arthur Abrams for graphic displays, to Ira Needleman for locating resources, to Mary Ann Pentice of Coyote Junction Studio for the photographs appearing on the cover of the book, and to family, many friends and lovers of boxing.

THE BIBLE OF BOXING
Founded 1922

STANLEY WESTON
Publisher
Chairman Of The Board

STUART M. SAKS
Associate Publisher

STEVE FARHOOD
Editor-In-Chief

KENNETH MORGAN
Art Director

KENNETH J. GUDAITIS
Executive Vice President

ROBERT J. THORNTON
Senior Adviser

JEFF RYAN
Managing Editor

ROBERT CASSIDY
JOSEPH C. TINTLE
Associate Editors

BILL APTER
Photo Editor

55 Maple Avenue
Rockville Centre, NY 11570
Phone: (516) 764-0300   Fax: (516) 764-4370

ARCHIE MOORE ISN'T JUST ANOTHER MAN-- HE'S A NATIONAL TREASURE

I recall the day in Archie's suite at Montreal Mount Royal Hotel. It was two days before he was to defend his world light heavyweight title against local idol Yvon Durelle and the king was hosting a press conference. Although he graciously answered all questions, as was his style, he seemed more interested in plugging his friend, a veteran but little known comic named Redd Foxx, who was still years away from his smashing success in the role of Fred Sanford in the critically acclaimed TV series *Sanford & Son.*

Archie was convinced that all Redd needed to make the big time was the right exposure, and what better place to get it than in Montreal where the world press had gathered to see the legendary champion defend his title. Archie made sure Foxx was right there at his side every time a reporter or press photographer was in range.

That's the kind of person Archie Moore was and always will be: never failing to put the interests of others before his own.

In the more than half century that Archie has been a national treasure a few million words have been published documenting his fabled career as an immortal boxing champion, movie star and humanitarian. I didn't think it possible to capture the whole story between covers of a single book. I was wrong.

Marilyn G. Douroux has accomplished the impossible, and in so absorbing an artful a way that I challenge anyone who begins reading *Archie Moore... "The Ole Mongoose"* to set it aside before devouring each and every word.

STANLEY WESTON
Publisher

FOREWORD

This biography chronicles the accomplishments of Archie Moore, a man who became a boxer; yet it goes beyond boxing. It deals with the family and the struggles of a people; with love and music; racism, politics and newsmen; with education and values; youth and old age - all significant themes in the life of one of the most colorful champions of our times. It is both tear jerker and humor, written in an historical mode for fans of boxing as well as for those who are not fans of the sport.

It is a story about living, of how one man's triumph over adversity propelled him into a position of dignity among his contemporaries, among kings and presidents, but most meaningfully, among the poor from whose midst he sprang.

Archie Moore is an anachronism, a far cry from the stereotypic idea of what a boxer is and becomes. He lived by his wits.

In moves unprecedented in the boxing world, he personally garnered support to pave the way for his ascent to the championship, regaining the respect of even those who had counted him out as "too old" for the ring.

Moore's story needed to be written, especially now when the public is desperately in need of a success story; when it searches for answers to the problems of youth and society in general.

Celebrate the life of a man whose fight connection has stretched into almost three decades since retirement from the ring; but "Ancient Arch" - the "Mongoose" - has just begun to fight. This time, he fights for America's youth with drug abuse and gang violence as his opponents. This book explores how he got to this point.

PROLOGUE

The Shaping of a Fighter: Early Episodes

After reflecting on the whole thing, he decided that he had indeed made a terrible mistake; but it was a little late for regret. Archie Lee Moore, now all of fifteen, had finally landed himself "three hots and a cot" in the St. Louis, Missouri, Detention Home for Boys. Being part of the crowd now seemed quite foolhardy by comparison to what he had given up.

As he readied himself for bed in this austere setting, he made a mental contrast between this and the comfortable home which his aunt and uncle had provided. The bread and milk which had served as his most recent meal seemed an insult to his stomach, considering his usual fare of hot buttered cornbread, fatback and cabbage which Auntie Willie prepared on her wood-burning stove.

Sitting on the bed assigned to him, he began to miss the soft feather bed and billowy, soft pillows which he had left behind. The quilt coverlet, a maze of colorful patches sewn together by Auntie Willie, jarred his sense of appreciation for what he had somehow taken for granted. He tried to reconstruct his own room as a means of comforting himself in this strange, prison-type holding place into which he had been thrown along with about twenty other Negro boys who had been accused of violating the law.

In his own case, he had graduated from taking small items, usually edibles from the Boulevard Market Place, to the crime which had landed him here. Archie and several other boys had decided on a whim to "hijack" the trolley which ran along Chateau Street. Their "MO" was that one boy would divert the attention of the stone-faced conductor while another disconnected the trolley from the electric wire throwing the car into darkness. It was then that agile Archie, who had been stationed at the front of the car, swooped up the plunder of about seven dollars and had run with it. As he ran at a cheetah-like speed along the street, he heard the word, "STOP!", then a "pi-yow" which traveled skyward; but it was the sound of silence after the shot which said that the next one would not be over his head. With a final release of

energy, the cat came to a halt and put his hands up as he had sometimes seen it done in the movies. He was just a kid; but without the
male guidance backed up by the towering six feet of Uncle Cleve's
muscular body, Archie had become a leaf which had literally fallen far
from the tree.

He remembered having silently wished that the judge before whom
he went could have had that same realization when, after about twelve
days in the Children's Detention Home, he was brought to court for
sentencing.

As Archie approached the bench, he remembered with disdain
having been brought before the same judge for a fighting incident.
"Archie," said the judge without looking down at the face which peered
up at him, "you came before me once before. I'm going to give you
three years because of this last incident."

Instead of fear, the knowledge of what the judge had said sparked
utter surprise in Archie; for use of his first name, "Archie," as well as
the tone, had suggested a more clement decision on the judge's part.
"It just doesn't fit!" reasoned the prisoner; not when he had known the
sentences given other individuals for the crime of *murder*. As a matter
of fact, some such crimes had drawn no punishment at all. "Just a kid,"
he mimicked softly, as he was led out of the courtroom, "Just a kid."

This statement had pierced his consciousness as nothing else had
done in the three years since his uncle's death.

Auntie Willie had been as strong as anyone could have been, and
though she had preached and taught from the Bible, mandated Sunday
School and "whipped his ass," as the saying went, she could not compete
with the love of excitement and challenge which lured him away from
home and her guidance.

From the first night in this miserable place until this night, he
had lain in the darkness opting to think and not sleep, to purge himself
and recap his burning love of challenge against the backdrop of a short
but eventful past.

As far back as he could remember somewhat whimsically, he could
pinpoint some of the episodes which he felt had led him to this point.

Episode One: "Back to His Corner"

When he was but seven years old, his Auntie Willie had saved
enough money to take him and older sister Rachel back to spend the

summer with their mother in Benoit, Mississippi, the place of their birth. Their mother, Uncle Cleve's sister, had her first child at fifteen and Archie at seventeen, judged as too young by Auntie Willie to do a decent job of rearing.

Now, the two Moore children could enjoy the fresh air and open spaces of Benoit, a welcome change by comparison to the colorless confines of city life in St. Louis. The family had made its home there in one of the rows of duplicate shot-gun houses built by absentee owners on Gratiot Street on "the Negro side" of St. Louis.

"Country life is so wholesome," promised Auntie, as they rode the train into Benoit. And so it was, with early breakfast of corn meal and milk that had been warmed by the cow herself. And after small but enjoyable chores of feeding the chickens or feeding the hogs, there was the adventure afforded by the open-spaced environment.

One morning after chores, Archie decided to re-live one of the stories from a book that had been given to him by an old woman who owned a dry goods store downtown. It contained stories about knights and dragons and fighting for honor.

"Forward!" bellowed the seven-year old as he charged across the pasture on his mighty steed, an old, faded-brown plow horse. Archie had climbed gallantly aboard by using the porch and railing of the "castle" to get a boost. His sister Rachel and cousins trailed behind "Sir Archie," leader of the "Crusade?" Their skinny arms bore shields and swords (lard can covers and broomsticks) which flailed about as they made the noises of an advancing army. Just as they entered the "forest," a lad of nine or ten darted out from behind a tree, struck the gallant steed on his rump, causing the proud knight to fall on his own royal rump.

With almost no hesitation, the furious knight jumped to his feet, found the boy, grabbed him by his shoulders shaking him viloently. "Why did you do that?" Archie shrieked. But all that could be heard were the clicking of teeth and the sounds of dead leaves rustling beneath the shaking and struggling of "knight and foe."

As both foe and frightened crusaders ran their own separate ways, Archie remained behind, disgustedly throwing pebbles at the ground, unmoved by what he had done in retaliation against the dastardly deed of the evil lad who had ruined his fantasy. Ultimately, Archie had been more embarrassed because without aid, he had been too short to remount the old horse so that he could continue on his mission to save the damsel in distress. In any event, the horse had run behind Rachel and the others, causing him to have to walk back home alone.

"Couldn't you have done something other than shake a white boy?" was what jolted Archie as he returned to the railing and porch which had earlier given him his boost onto the plow horse. Both horse and cousins had heralded his return and news of his confrontation with little emphasis on what the other boy had done. He resented the accusation.

Realizing the danger inherent in even that child-like antic, Archie and Rachel were whisked away by Auntie, back to St. Louis and safety. The seven-year old could not have known the perils that might have grown out of that incident; for but two weeks later, Mother had written Auntie Willie an account of the lynching of a Negro man who had been dragged by his heels behind a car and then set afire by something called the KLAN. It seems the Negro had turned in fourteen bales of cotton to the owner's wife who had been helping her husband. At the time of payment there was a difference of four bales. Consequently, when the Negro insisted on payment for the amount turned in, it was interpreted as an insult to the white woman's integrity and the word had spread like wild fire.

Though too young to understand, Archie had found the look on his aunt's face quite disturbing at the mention of the word KLAN. "They must be bad people," he mused, as he skillfully shot his marbles across the worn out dining room rug, a habit which Rachel found quite annoying.

"That's all you know, Archie Lee!", she said, while "rolling her eyes" (lowering her lids slowly as she turned her head away mechanically). It seemed the mannerism of some little Negro girls which let you know they were truly resentful of something, as was Rachel of Archie's noisy game.

"Never again can I visit Benoit," said Archie regretfully, still not understanding the whole matter.

Even Archie himself realized, however, that there was something within him that was different. His reflexes were fast, too fast to stop and think about rules and laws that justified less than human treatment of one man by another.

Episode Two: "The Underdog"

It was like the time when he took a shortcut through an alley on his way to the library on Eleventh and Olive Streets. He had gone to get a book that had been assigned him by his fifth grade teacher.

Suddenly, something had dropped from above, narrowly missing his head and splattering juice and seeds onto his pants and shoes. A cantaloupe had been dropped by three boys who leered at Archie from a window three floors above. "Nigger!" they laughed, with the same look that he had seen on the face of the boy who had frightened his horse on his visit to Benoit a few two years earlier.

His feeling was one of rage and helplessness as he ran with tear-filled eyes back to the safety of his home. That night as he lay wide awake analyzing what had happened to him, he was driven to remember something else which he had seen, something which impressed him greatly.

Episode Three: "Roar of the Crowd"

It had happened on Gratiot Street as he was on his way from the ice house, pulling ice in a wagon which he himself had built. In it was a large block of ice which Auntie would wrap with a cloth before putting it into the icebox. This would slow down the melting of the ice thus saving a few pennies. Auntie was thrifty that way.

As Archie walked along, he could hear strange noises coming from behind a tall, wooden fence. "Hit the son of a bitch!" a voice said. "Grab him!" Archie heard. "Step back, duck, dance around him!" "Knock him on his ass!"

He was drawn by the thuds and grunts to a knot-hole in the weather-beaten fence. His single, squinted eye rolled from one end of the knot-hole to the other, taking in with amazement the huge black, sweaty, bodies that punched away at each other with muscle and might.

They could not have known the impact they would make on this outside observer who, oblivious to all else, egged them on with clenched fists. In his excitement, he was oblivious to the warm urine that had begun to trickle down his legs. It formed a rivulet which joined the puddle of water formed by the melting ice in the wagon.

As he stooped to grasp the handle of the wagon, it was with no embarrassment over wet pants or the pennies wasted by the ice which had melted. He was more impressed by what he had seen and even more proud that he, Archie Lee Moore, had been the only one on the other side of the fence to see it. This back yard match represented the self-styled entertainment of urban Negro dwellers who, removed from the mainstream and limited by poverty, had to create their own recreation as it were.

As he moved regretfully away from his one-eyed vantage point, Archie also remembered the excitement on the faces of that crowd. The awe and reverence for the fighters were in sharp contrast with the looks that he had seen on the faces of the pranksters who defiled him. For the first time he felt something very decisive stir within him, a feeling which received reinforcement from having heard his uncle and other men who hung around after work speaking with excitement about powerful men like Jack Johnson and Kid Chocolate. While such fighters had his uncle's admiration, Archie felt that knowledge of his own involvement in fighting would have been discouraged. So he filed away the fighting experience in the head which held the eye, which peered into the knot-hole and beheld the big, black, sweaty bodies that punched and grunted at each other. He sank peacefully into sleep that night and dreamed of cheering crowds full of reverence and admiration for young Archie Moore. This zeal for boxing grew as did Archie into a determined young man.

Episode Four: "A Foul Blow"

Miss Garnetta Mosby had been the very reason why Archie had not missed a day as a ninth grader. He guessed that even Auntie wondered how one boy could have changed so much over a summer. The extra care he took with his grooming and insistence on being on time should have alerted even the least suspecting on-looker that Archie Lee Moore had developed a crush on a female.

He arrived early in the morning before anyone else, just to help her and be alone with her. He even discouraged the company of his best friend and play brother, Arthur "Knox" James, for fear that Knox might want to linger at the corner to watch certain girls pass by. Archie couldn't risk being late and having his teacher, Miss Mosby, let someone else help her.

He loved the wavy black hair which framed her russet brown face and fell to her shoulders like a cascade of rain. He had even convinced himself that the impish smile which revealed her white, even teeth was just for him. Whenever she smiled at him, he felt a little ashamed at his innermost feelings as his gaze traveled from her full mouth, down to her erect breasts, tiny waist and hips which appeared molded into her dress. "What if someone knew," he thought, "that whenever Miss Mosby walks across the floor, I imagine that she is a dancer moving to some easy blues." He had heard the music of trumpet master, Charles Creath (a well known local who plied the muddy Mississippi on the Riverboat

Streckfus. It featured the bass of Singleton Palmer and the guitar of Beady Baskerville). Such music gave Archie the same warm, satisfied feeling. as Miss Garnetta Mosby's walk.

Archie's private thoughts were suddenly interrupted that day. For no apparent reason, Webster, a clown from across the aisle, jabbed him in his thigh with a needle used for stitching softballs.

"Oww-w-w!" he hollered with pain, bringing Miss Mosby, who had her back to the class, face-to-face with his own. This time, however, hers was distorted with anger as she admonished an already injured student.

"Moore, why did you yell out that way?" she asked resentfully. The question was more an accusation and this time, there was no love in her voice. As she walked over to him, she lacked her usual grace and rhythm. As a matter of fact, he didn't know how she had gotten over to him so quickly since he had noticed no legs or feet, only the right hand as it went back and came forward, landing a flat, stinging, blow to the side of his cheek.

"How could she?" he languished. "I've never been a cut up, always was a good student! Why couldn't she have asked me or someone else why I yelled before embarrassing me the way she did?"

These were questions that were never quite answered, because Archie never communicated with her much anymore or liked school after that day and it wasn't so much because of the embarrassment. It was more because he did not want to see or be taught by the Miss Garnetta Mosby who had shattered his dreams. Despite his being "just a boy," he had secretly decided that he would eventually grow up and marry her and plant kisses on those lips that had given him the special smiles. Though the dream had died, that episode was to follow him long into manhood and he had already begun to take on the trappings of a man.

Episode Five: "The Knockdown"

One night after everyone had gone to bed at the Moore home, there was a knock on the door. When Archie heard the door open, he assumed Auntie had let Uncle Cleve in after his return from a lodge meeting. He had not, however, returned under his own steam and was carried by two of his lodge brothers into the small bedroom.

Amidst Auntie's tears and clandestine talking about what had transpired, Uncle Cleve lay limp on the bed, paralyzed from the neck down. It was an accident that had happened during a lodge initiation and it had involved some horse play.

As the two men left at about 2:30 A.M., it was with a promise to return in the morning to take Uncle Cleve to the hospital. It was Archie who let them out, eyeing them suspiciously as he smelled the strong scent of alcohol. Just as he closed the door, he could hear Uncle Cleve call in a strange voice, "Archie Lee, come here!" There was a note of urgency in that voice, as though something could not wait. "Give me your hand," he said, trying unsuccessfully to close his own hand over Archie's. "Listen, son," he whispered, "I want you to promise me that you will take care of your Auntie."

"Yes sir, you know I will ," assured Archie, who seemed suddenly forced into manhood, a tenure that was to begin with the death of his uncle on the following morning.

To make matters worse, just one year later, Rachel, all of seventeen years of age, had become pregnant, bore twins and died in childbirth of a hemorrhage. She was survived by a young husband, Elihu Williams and one twin, June Marie, who would become Auntie's charge.

Not until Rachel's death had Archie realized just how much he loved her. His life would know no more of her prodding and bossing which he remembered now with painful, melancholic longing. He and younger brother Samuel slept under her casket in Auntie's living room the night before the funeral as though to hold onto her for a few more hours.

Thus with the death of his uncle, then Rachel, tuning out on school in the ninth grade, eventually leaving school in the eleventh grade and the lure of the streets, Archie had begun a new love: a flirtatious affair with Miss Juvenile Crime, which was to culminate in apprehension by the law.

Rachel, Samuel and Archie Moore (about 12 years old).

Rachel, age 14,
and Uncle Joe Wright

CHAPTER I

The Price of Error: Loss of Freedom

Tonight, as Archie Moore spent his last pensive night in the detention home before transfer to a reformatory, he knew the decision he had made to become a boxer would be a little harder to achieve. As the sound "Lights Out!" was heard, he could see the boxing gloves which he had intended to buy with the plunder from the trolley, fade as did the glow of the tungsten wire in the globe until all lay in darkness.

Not even the knowledge that he was to be taken away from St. Louis that next day was enough to strike fear into this determined boy of fifteen; yet had he known the tactic to be used, he might have tried escape or resorted to some other drastic measure. If there was fear at all, it was that Auntie Willie would be embarrassed by the whole badly handled set of events which were to follow.

As though a three year sentence were not enough, Archie and six other youths, some younger than fifteen, were hooked together along one long stretch of chain which clanked as they walked along the street. They were then marched to the train behind adult prisoners, some of whom were hardened criminals, rogues and murderers, held in submission by handcuffs and leg irons. They walked stiff-legged for four blocks which, to Archie, was the most dehumanizing, ridiculous part of it, and it was in public view. Instead of the admiring faces seen in his dream of the big black boxers, he saw the faces of local folks, some of whom could tell his Auntie what they had seen. He prayed this would not happen. And for the first time he said, "Oh God, please help me to be strong, and please take care of Auntie Willie!".

It was .with good reason that this utterance came forth; for in the early thirties at the peak of depression, families were doing well to survive with everyone pitching in. Who would help his family with Archie being one hundred sixty miles away at the Boonville, Missouri Reformatory? While he realized he had shamed his family and himself, he now called to mind one of the teachings given him by the person he cared about most. Auntie Willie had taught him this:

When a task is once begun
Never leave it 'til it's done
If the labor is great or small
Do it well or not at all.

Well, he had no choice in the task about to be begun, but he had made up his mind to make the best of it.

As the train signalled its departure, some onlookers stood in the station to gape at the "criminals" who were leaving St. Louis. As they left, the familiar chug-a-chug sound was replaced, at least in Archie's ears, by "Just-a-kid ..., Just-a-kid ..., Just-a-kid ..."

The trip to Boonville was rather uneventful with small talk among Archie and the other boys about whom they'd see once they arrived; for each boy knew someone who had been "sent up." His thoughts were not much with the boys, however. With only water and no food, his painfully empty stomach growled its displeasure as the trip dragged for approximately five hours.

When the train pulled into Boonville, there would be another bumpy ride for the half dozen boys chained in the back of an old grey truck with high framed sides. Upon the 4:30 PM arrival, they were taken to a holding room and ordered to strip and shower in a trough which was angled into the floor. In the ceiling above their heads were shower pipes.

Each boy was given blue denim pants, a pin-striped shirt and a pair of socks and shoes. All were then assigned to "C" company, "probably C for colored," thought Archie during briefing. "C" company sat together, separated from "D" through "F" which were all white companies. All sat in the same dining hall to eat and the newcomers were probably first to finish.

After supper, each company was led by a drill instructor, and all marched in lock-step back to the barracks where some played dominoes, checkers, or talked quietly. At 7:30 p.m. the boys heard, "Bedtime!," a signal to strip, hang one's clothing on a nail in an assigned spot, line up and pass a guard on the way to the second floor. At the second level, each naked boy was accounted for by the trustee. Each then put on a gown which was kept under his pillow. Such an involved procedure was ostensibly to guard against the concealment of weapons or the carrying of food into the sleeping quarters. Ultimately, there was little or no room for monkey business and the boys knew it.

As was the practice with new boys, Archie and the others were assigned to the brickyard, a place least likely to prove successful for beginners since it required special skill to mix the clay, pour it into forms and remove and stack the finished bricks. This took strong backs and some of the boys were young and not fully developed.

After only a day, however, Archie had to be transferred to the laundry and a less demanding job due to an injury to his hand suffered in a fight before leaving the detention home. In the laundry, he could do a job more familiar to him; for under Auntie Willie's tutelage, he had learned to iron his own and his uncle's pants and shirts with a cast iron made searing hot by a small furnace of hot coals.

Here, it was one of Archie's tasks to iron the uniforms of the administrators and guards, but he didn't mind it. Even at this early age, he had developed a way of fantasizing such that difficult situations were made manageable. He did not merely pull down on the ironer as the other workers did. He did it in a rhythmic fashion so as to concentrate the energy to build the muscles in his hands and arms. "Oh, this feels so good," he said, as he held his breath until the hot steam cleared, bathing his body in sweat, yet increasing his ability to hold his breath. He smirked silently as he felt the stares of other workers. He was purposely building an aura of mysticism which was later to serve him well.

Recreation at Boonville, though a relaxing time for most, was a cautious time for the administrators and guards as well as for Archie; for situations of competitiveness often bred or accelerated hostility among individuals or groups. Add to this the vast age differences among the boys. There was Tank, a natural-born trouble maker who was all of twenty years old and six feet tall, who would challenge even the trustees. He spewed out profanity, purposely calling names to draw them out. Archie wondered why Tank had not been placed in an adult facility; yet intuitively he realized that Tank's presence served to keep younger boys in tow as well as to make the trustee work harder to keep his place. Natural leadership was not encouraged.

Then there were the younger boys, some of eleven and twelve, and one little tyke, Jack, who was but eight years old. He had been orphaned at age six and sent to the reformatory as were some others who had no other place to go. While they were watched over by Archie and some boys who had the paternal instinct, the young boys were considered by some of the vultures as "fresh meat." This dichotomous situation found young boys imitating the behavior of older boys, while falling prey to their very strong-arm tactics which stole an earned place in line or food or some other rightful due from them. This built toughness in the young victims who steeled themselves against tears or snitching to avoid a chain of backlashes. Challenges to older inmates like Archie were usually over some personality conflict or territorial right.

It was during a checker game that Archie's first open confrontation occurred: "King me!," he said for the fourth time to his opponent who had become trapped in an angular fashion with few "men" left to get him out of the corner. With an action calculated to add sport to the game, Archie announced that he was getting up to get some water, knowing that his opponent's position was too obvious for him to cheat by altering his checkers in any way. As he turned his back to drink, "Fat Jaw," a hyena-type predator, jumped into Archie's seat left warm by the already lengthy game of which Archie was the obvious winner. As he walked back from the fountain, through a cautious calm could be heard a warning made up of five very short words: "Get out of my seat!" he ordered. Since Archie had already anticipated the encroacher's refusal to give up the seat, it is doubtful that anything could have prevented what was to follow. With calculated speed, a well-aimed right uppercut lifted the thoroughly padded though vulnerable Fat Jaw from his seat, knocking him out cold. "It's your move," said Archie, as he reclaimed his territory opposite a mesmerized opponent.

Not even the checkers which had been rearranged by the skirmish were enough to urge him to take advantage and get out of the hole formerly made inescapable by Archie's four kings. In any event, the throngs which had converged on the "three-man checker game" had foiled Archie's declaration as the official winner. Thus to the reputational repertoire of this laundry room mystic had been added yet another dimension - that of FIGHTER! And without a doubt, he would fight if challenged!

Life in the reformatory was not so bad for boys like Archie who had never intended to make it his permanent home. He played by the rules and made friends cautiously. It was not long after his stay began at Boonville that his trusted friend, Arthur "Knox" James, was also "sent up" for some reason that Archie knew had been calculated by Arthur himself. Even Mrs. James, who had been like a second mother to

Archie, had anticipated that the two would find some way to be together.

"Man, why'd you do that?" queried Archie, in a tone that could have been misunderstood only by someone unaware of the bond between the two. And as the friendship grew, both gained in awareness and courage.

The biggest temptation for Archie was to be drawn into fights; for by this time, he had quite a few and being the victor had given him added impetus. "You know, I like to fight," confessed Archie to Arthur James one day after one youth had curled up his pinkie finger and had given a wink at him. This was reformatory sign language for homosexual intent which Archie had heard about but never paid much attention to. It said, "I want you!"

"Well, he got you all right," chided Arthur James, after Archie retaliated by a punch to the jaw which literally uncurled the pinky finger. Contrary to popular belief, however, there were little such outward manifestations of homosexuality, partially because it was culturally frowned upon by the inmates themselves. It was on the list, however, of those infractions which would result in severe punishment as did stealing and fighting. In the latter case, Archie had escaped punishment because his fights had been over before anyone, even the guards, had heard about them. Besides, the code among the boys was never to inform on anyone.

Only once had Archie himself been "switched" by one of the guards for a minor skirmish, though it hadn't been a severe switching. Tactically, he had crowded the whip so as to shorten its length and not get its full thrust. It was the end which stung enough to make the mouth grow dry as it tore into the flesh. He had seen this happen to young Walter Mays, a slightly built youth of nineteen. For some minor infraction, Walter had been beaten by a guard with eighteen strokes beyond the limit of six. With each blow, the guard would say, "So you ain't gon cry, huh?" The determined youth had refused to cry in front of his peers who were made to watch to see if he could "take a few." As the larger mid part of the whip cut the thighs, the end wrapped round his buttocks opening his flesh. The blood seeped through the thick denim and it stuck to his body. The gory sight caused some of the boys to turn away and little Jack fought off the urge to vomit. Since the infraction had been rather small and not very widely publicized, Archie knew the severe beating was to set an example for all to see what would happen if *anyone* had done *anything*! As a matter of fact, the beatings had occurred with some predictability.

With his time for release getting short, however, Archie did not plan to be used as an example. All he could dream of now was getting out and seeing his beloved Auntie Willie from whom he had gotten only a few notes periodically. Though not always legible, Archie had cherished them all, knowing that they sent the warmth, encouragement and love of the mother that she had always been.

In one of his own letters to her, he had set down the following thoughts, as much for himself as for her:

October 2, 1934

Dear Auntie,

In just one more month, I'll be able to see you again.
It's been a long time and I've learned my lesson. You know, I can't wait until I can taste your food again. It's ok here I guess, but not nearly as good as yours. We get a lot of potatoes and rice and vegetables seasoned with "essence of meat." I hope you'll understand that I mean its hardly there at all (smile).

I have something to tell you and I know you will understand as you always have; but if Uncle Cleve were living, he probably wouldn't. You see, I've decided to become a boxer. You know how much I always enjoyed the fights when they showed short subjects at the movies in Fox News. Remember the time I told you about the Tiger Flowers movie and about the big house he lived in? The money he earned from boxing was enough to buy the things that some white people couldn't even afford.

Tiger was wonderful, Auntie. He even had a gym in his house with punching bags and showers and everything. I'll never forget the kitchen either. It did not have a wood stove like we do. It was a modern stove on which his pretty wife cooked him a steak as big as both of Uncle's Cleve's hands. And Tiger put his arms around his wife, hugging and kissing her for fixing his steaks, just like in the movies. She was a pretty lady too, as brown as a tea cake and almost as pretty as my old teacher, Miss Mosby. I wonder, Auntie, what ever happened to her?

One day, Auntie, I will become Champion of the World and have a pretty wife too, a big house and a big kitchen and you will come to live with me. I want to buy you all the things you never had and make up for the hurt I've caused you. Until then, Auntie, I hope you will be able to "make do" as you always have. Tell Mrs. James hello for me and that Arthur also will be home soon.

Your nephew,

Archie Lee

He knew that by now, Auntie would be crying as she usually did when she was happy. What he had not told her, however, was that he would not be staying with her in St. Louis for very long. In any event, he was anxious to get there.

"Ya-Hoo!" he yelled uninhibitedly, as the day for release had come; yet he knew, despite his love of freedom, he would miss this place. Unlike Little Jack and Cecil and some of the homeless, he had a place to call home. He would, nevertheless, miss the comradery and the constant challenge that institutional life had provided. While he knew that he and others had been set apart, had been given the lesser skills to learn, he felt that giving up the skills of shoe making and tailoring afforded the white boys in the reformatory was well worth it when he considered his own needs. Perhaps he was selfish, he thought, but the kind of readiness provided by an all-Negro environment was what he had needed to toughen him up for what was ahead.

Only a Negro boy could understand the invigorating experience of "playing the dozens," in which case a verbal bantering about a boy's "mama" would provide fun as well as an exercise in quick reflex on a mental level. This would not have been possible with white boys present, Archie had rationalized. Missed would also be the harmless punching and wrestling which both separated friends and brought them even closer together after they made up. Yes, it had all been a learning experience, but one which Archie was ready to leave because it was "done." Even Auntie would agree with this.

CHAPTER II

Rehabilitation: A Painful Reality

There was indeed something special about this morning of November 4, 1934, as Archie marched into the mess hall with "C" Company. Though the grits were warm and buttery, toast just right, he didn't wolf down his food as he usually did. He didn't want seconds this morning on the day of his release; for he was full of good wishes from his friends, full of longing to see Auntie, and bursting to the brim with plans to pursue boxing.

Before leaving, he received a flannel suit, a pair of Brogans and a bundle containing his old clothes and shoes which no longer fit after his two-year stay at Boonville. He felt good about cutting his time by one year for good behavior, a feat not easily accomplished under the social and psychological constraints imposed by institutional life; but his zeal for boxing had somehow always illuminated the right path, and being the winner had served to spark new determination for a stronger goal. This was the stuff that Moore was made of, starting from his obscure birth as Archie Lee Wright in a southern town in Mississippi, through one of the longest seasons in the fight game.

On this crisp winter morning, Archie looked around as though surveying the land, but really savoring freedom. The recapturing of it seemed to act as his own barometer for SPRING and a new chance at life.

As the 1934 Ford Sedan state car sped away carrying Archie and three others, he gave a final wave to his friend, Arthur James, who would also be released shortly thereafter.

The six-hour car trip was quiet, much like the train trip which brought the boys, though without the shackles and the embarrassment. Archie, optimist that he was, thought back to Boonville, the place which had surprisingly provided the basic training ground for a budding athlete: discipline, three square meals, proper rest, peer respect through competition, and development of the work ethic. He realized also that there would be some who would remain at Boonville much longer because they had not used the environment to develop a skill, to replace a bad choice with a better focus. (Though not consciously, Archie had also already begun to formulate his approach to the training of youth.)

Other than for pit stops, the trip was uninterrupted and the passengers were left to their thoughts about home going. Hours later, as the car made a left turn onto Leffingwell from Easton Avenue, Archie had almost forgotten that prior to his leaving, Auntie and he had moved to the North Side on Leffingwell Street. It had been Auntie's intent to get Archie into a better environment with better schools; yet "better" had deteriorated even since leaving home two years ago.

As he alighted from the state car, Archie paused for what seemed to him an eternity as he wondered what Auntie and the neighbors would think of him. "I look a little like penitentiary," he reflected, as he gazed down at the big Brogan shoes which plopped to the ground ahead of him; but it didn't matter to him as he walked up to the porch. He held his head erect and made enough noise on the wooden steps to bring Auntie to the door.

"Archie Lee, come on in!," she smiled, as she reached to put her arm around his neck. The other was covered with flour, a sight which conjured up fond memories and filled his head with delicious anticipation.

He had clean forgot to say anything to the state officer. As both he and Auntie went to the kitchen, he could hear the car make its way up Leffingwell on its way to deliver the rest of the boys.

As Auntie floured the rest of the chicken, they talked of old times, of who had married and who had died and on and on. "Funny," he thought to himself, "how Auntie always knows what to talk about. She hasn't asked me if I've suffered or stayed out of trouble or anything like that." This realization sent a gush of love through him. Add to this his fond appreciation for the sacrifice he knew she must have made in this time of Depression to prepare the crusty, golden fried chicken, greens and cornbread which he would soon devour.

As they both waited for the chicken to fry, Auntie and nephew stood beside each other at the sink, he the dishwasher, she the dryer. For some odd reason, he loved to wash dishes with the yellow lye soap which was used for everything from bowls to bodies. As he meticulously cleaned the wooden drain board and hung the dish rag on the sink to dry, he became a little misty-eyed as he thought of Uncle Cleve. Were he alive, he would be first to sit down at the table and wait with his fork and knife in hand as would a surgeon, ready to slice into whatever miracle Auntie managed to prepare.

"Now," thought the new man of the house, "it's all up to me." And before they both sat down to eat, Archie threw his arms around this aproned angel and hugged her to him. He hugged and said nothing. He didn't have to.

After a few days of homecoming bliss, he set out to fulfill two of his commitments: one, to become the bread winner and "man of the house," and two, to adhere to the conditions of his parole. His early release had been predicated on good behavior as well as upon securing gainful employment. He knew that without this, there could be no real concentration on boxing.

It had been arranged for him to work for Mr. Frazier who owned a wood and coal business on Leffingwell Street not far from his home. "I will do well," he thought, "supplying customers with the fuel that everyone needs during these severe St. Louis winters."

Mr. Frazier had promised to pay Archie one dollar a day to carry the heavy, eighty-pound bushel baskets to the door of each customer, sometimes up three flights of stairs, and return the money to him. As he did so, Archie felt a sense of power; for so many thirty-five cents had entered his hands that day, more than he had ever touched. The truck held about forty bushel baskets and they had made three trips that day, a grueling job for an ordinary young man; but he saw it as yet another way to build himself up for boxing. It was mind over matter, and some matter it was; for by now, the snow was coming down and his feet were numb from the cold.

Through his own generosity or stupidity, he had allowed himself to be talked out of the state-issued Brogans by an uncle who had given him two dollars in exchange. Even the boxing gloves purchased with the money seemed questionable by comparison to what he had to endure. Each time he stepped into the gutter or into a puddle, the rain and slush bathed his feet in a painful, biting cold. On his feet were shoes two years too young, the shoes which he had worn before Boonville. He had to split the seams at the back of the shoes to make them fit his feet, taping them across the back and around his ankles to keep them from coming off. The sight would have been enough to evoke sympathy from any onlooker; though it evidently seemed Mr.

Frazier was a disinterested party. He looked only at Archie's hand as it traveled to his, depositing the constant stream of thirty-five cents into his change bag.

"Just look at the selfish son-of-a-bitch," thought Archie vexedly, "as snug as a bear in his lair;" for Mr. Frazier sat in the cab of the truck, warmed by a little furnace which sat on the floor. It doubled as a cooking stove on which he warmed coffee and beans and biscuits, none of which he offered his well-iced, indentured servant. To add insult to injury, Archie was also forced to advertise the approach of the thriving coal business by singing out the words in a voice that literally cracked from the cold, "Wood Man ..., Coal Man ..., Get your kindling and coal!" And as he did so, some needy customer three flights up would say, "Over here, boy!"

When the day ended, Mr. Frazier drove the truck back to his home and led Archie down to the basement which was a maze of junk - old car parts, furniture, and rags. This he felt had little to do with Mr. Frazier's financial status and more to do with pride, or lack of it. It was a far cry from the order of his own home or that of the Boonville reformatory.

With almost the same carelessness as his environment reflected, Mr. Frazier flicked out a fifty-cent piece to Archie and said in a half-hearted, unconvincing tone: "Look, boy, we didn't do too well today, and you know, I do have the overhead, and ...." Suffice it to say that at this point, Archie's indignation was equalled only by his aching shoulders, numb feet, and unpleasant-looking countenance made worse by the freeze-dried mucous which formed flakes beneath a running nose.

"No, you keep it," he lashed out with a simultaneous flicking back of the coin to the miser. "You need it more than I do!" With that, he turned on his make-shift shoes and tromped past the piles of junk, his face a flush of dark crimson as his eyes focused on an ice pick stuck in the crude door which served as both entrance and exit to that dungeon.

"I need to take that ice pick and plunge it over and over into this cheap-assed bastard!" he said aloud. But as he thought of his goal, his Auntie, and his love of freedom, he fought back the urge and exited just as he had come in - cold, wet, and penniless.

Auntie's reactions to his account of the experience was, "Well, Archie Lee, there will always be people like Mr. Frazier; but what goes around comes around. He'll have to answer to a higher power. Come on," she soothed, "take off those wet clothes and I'll fix you something to eat." Archie looked at Auntie with admiration and pride in the knowledge that his determination had come from this great woman. She had exhibited the strength and courage of women like Harriet Tubman and Sojourner Truth, giants in the annals of history. Though not his natural mother, Auntie was no less committed, no less nurturing than one who bore him could have been.

She stuck by him, encouraging him, when after a day of searching for work, he returned to announce dispiritedly that he had found none. He combed the streets looking and asking from Leffingwell and Franklin to the Pullman yard on Chateau and Compton Streets, trying to land a job.

Evenings were spent at the gymnasium with notable, Monroe Harrison, a light heavyweight, all around sports champion from St. Louis. As a boxer-coach at the Pine Street YMCA, he was looked up to with admiration both by his peers and boys from the neighborhood. He was regarded by Joe Louis as one of his best sparring partners, so difficult was he to hit.

What a thrill it was to spar with his idol, "Munchy," and hear him say, "Archie, you're going to be a champion. The only difference between you and Joe Louis is weight and size, because you punch just as hard!" If that claim was meant to flatter, it did the trick, because he grew in confidence and strength with Munchy's constant reinforcement.

Then too, the gym virtually provided the arena for young fighters to enter into quality competition and move up to the Golden Gloves, the apex of amateur boxing.

It was from George Porter, also an amateur at one hundred eighteen pounds of dynamite, that Archie gleaned a wealth of boxing lore. He studied the matches and the stats, breezed through the YMCA competitions and was drawn ultimately to attend as a spectator, the Argus Boxing Tournament. It was promoted by a Negro weekly newspaper by the same name. Attendance was made possible by Mrs. James who had purchased the sixty-cent seats up in the "roost" for herself, her son, Arthur James, now back from Boonville, and for Archie.

"I'll bet you didn't know Mother James was a fight fan, did you?" she chided, as she waved three tickets above her head. She had been spurred on by the Joe Louis rage then sweeping the country. In addition to his obvious superiority, Louis was a more "acceptable" champion to whites and to race-conscious Negroes; for unlike Jack Johnson, he had a more subdued temperament and no known affiliation with white women.

As the audience watched Julius Kemp win yet another tournament, Archie literally wished he could have been in those shoes; for still taped to his ankles and gaping at the backs were the shoes he had worn before Boonville. They had put blisters on his heels and had prevented his beating Kemp in the trials before the tournament. Embarrassment had kept him from asking Arthur to borrow a pair of his shoes; though Arthur's knowledge about Archie's condition of poverty, as well as his friendship, would have made him more than willing. And though this hand-to-mouth existence lasted through the lean summer of 1935, Archie's zeal for boxing remained and the chance for pay-back finally came.

Again it was George Porter, perennial opportunity seeker, who walked into Auntie's kitchen one morning and announced, "Hey, Arch, there's a card on the latter part of the month that the Kessler brothers are promoting. Let's get signed up!" And so they did; but this time, as he walked the three miles to the Kessler offices in downtown St. Louis, it was in a pair of new tennis shoes he had purchased with the dollar ninety-eight cents given to him by Mrs. James for doing odd jobs around her rooming house on Garrison Avenue. It was a fine house by comparison to most in that area and was adjacent to the house where Victoria and Al Sanford and nephew, Elroy resided. (Elroy was later to become Redd Foxx of comedy fame.)

As the two challengers entered the office, they were met by Harry Kessler himself. (Ironically, it would be the same Kessler who would later figure even more decisively into Archie's future in the fight game.)

The bold George Porter promptly asked if there were any fights left on the card. Coincidentally, there were two: George, himself a flashy bantam weight, was matched against bantam weight champion, Hugie Epperson, while Archie was slated to meet his old rival, Julius Kemp. What an honor it would be to share the same card with champion, Monroe "Munchy" Harrison!

After three hard fights, each challenger emerged the victor and Archie sensationalized his bout by stopping Kemp in the third round.

Dawn of the following morning found the proud winner of the Kemp-Moore match searching for the "Bulldog" (earliest edition of the *Glove Democrat*). He couldn't believe his eyes nor his bad luck when heread: "KEMP KNOCKS OUT ARCHIE MOORE IN THE THIRD ROUND."

His indignation mounted as he realized that until he could clear up this gross error, he would be embarrassed by questions from those he had told of his victory. "George will take care of this," he assured himself, knowing of George's smarts in this area. And as it turned out, the correction in the next edition netted Archie a two-inch space in the news. Like a town crier, he walked up one block and down the other, showing off his delayed victory.

Soon, however, it was back to business again, the business of earning a living, since Auntie's earnings of five dollars a week at Beamish's Bag factory were hardly enough for two.

Acting on a tip given him by a friend, he headed for the Pullman yard for a job as a dish washer only to be beaten by a few steps and another boy who had just entered the side door before him and had landed the job. "Damn it," he cursed! "What have I done to deserve all this bad-assed luck?" But "down on luck" was a sign of the times.

Though cities had their own personalities then as now, St. Louis being no exception, those Depression years saw cities across the land take on a single identity. Even Chicago, a restless, undaunted giant in the 20's, now found itself gripped in an ever-tightening vise which mercilessly clutched at its throat. It was indeed the worst of times.

1933 had seen a nation and President Roosevelt virtually bankrupt in both money and spirit. Unable to find work, hungry people could be seen rifling through refuse piles at public markets in an attempt to salvage food. By pitiful contrast, farmers, unable to sell their grain, left it in the fields to rot or burned it because it was a cheaper fuel than coal. What with wages averaging $18 per week for men and $9 for women, every penny was needed to fight off the wrath of Depression.

Roosevelt, a conservationist in theory (and even in practice when Governor of New York), sent to Congress a message on unemployment relief in which he proposed putting people to work in the precious forests across the United States.

Within days after the request, Congress passed the Emergency Conservation Work Act (ECW) which gave birth to the Civilian Conservation Corps (CCC). It was to sponsor some 300 differing types of work projects enlisting over 250,000 youths. They had to be between the ages of 18 and 25, physically fit, unemployed and unmarried, have dependents and be willing to allot $25 of their $30 earned per month to them.

It was during one of his searches for work, a daily endeavor, that Archie first learned of the CCC. He had seen a flier which outlined the requirements and procedure for enrolling. With boxing gloves slung over his shoulder, the eighteen-year old walked along home holding the paper before him, making a one-to-one match between the list of requirements and his own qualifications. To his list, he could have added yet another qualification - hungry!

After talking over his plans with Auntie, Archie secured permission from Sergeant Thomas Moran, his parole officer, to waive parole and allow him to leave St. Louis to join the CCC and Camp 3760 F [for forestry] unit at Poplar Bluff, Missouri.

During one week of waiting, he proudly passed the physical, received shots and instructions on personal hygiene and was sent to an Army post for processing. As an enrollee, he was furnished with clothing suitable to work and weather of Poplar Bluff: heavy woolen clothes, a work jacket, gloves and mittens, and heavy shoes and over shoes. As he clutched the shoes, he recalled his former unhappy experiences with his old make-shift shoes and promised himself aloud: "You can bet I won't part with these sons of bitches if I can help it!" He wore them quite proudly and boarded, along with about two-hundred youths from St. Louis, a troop train bound for Poplar Bluff, bound for battle in the war on poverty.

This time, the rhythm of the train engine reverberated all over the countryside (or so it seemed to Archie). It announced ... "Not a kid ..., Not a kid ..., Not a kid anymore!"

Chapter III

The Civilian Conservation Corps:

Solution to Survival

When Archie's group arrived at Poplar Bluff in the fall of 1935, their quarters had scarcely been finished. Tent camps had preceded the large wooden, barracks-type structures that would shelter them. So new were the barracks that the army cots had not yet arrived, forcing the new arrivals to sleep on the floor temporarily. None seemed to mind, however; especially not Archie to whom this freer environment seemed heaven by contrast with the barracks of reform school.

The camp site included a main building and about four 50-man barracks, a mess hall, a recreation building, quarters for Army and technical personnel, an infirmary, educational and library building, small garage, tool shed, and machine shop.

Since Archie and the other young men housed at this facility had never used axes or other tools in the ways required by this project, they had to be taught by local experienced men (LEMS) who provided on-the-job training. It was primarily in conservation, general forestry, road building, construction or development of camp sites, beaches, or picnic sites.

Educational experiences extended from fairly simple reading and writing in traditional school subjects to typing, mimeographing for the camp newspaper, photography, leather, wood and metal craft, auto mechanics, safety, cooking, canteen management, forestry, and a host of other subjects.

Ultimately, the Educational Adviser had to use considerable ingenuity and resourcefulness and, in the face of short money, secure a great deal of help from forestry personnel and the camp Commander in charge of its administration.

The camp to which Archie was assigned was an all-Negro camp where one of the greatest problems was the elimination of illiteracy. As an eleventh grade dropout, he might have attended formal classes to complete his education; but he chose athletics instead and used the library to forage for knowledge as he had seen it done by his friend George Porter. Consider also that Archie was advanced intellectually compared to most of the boys in his unit and his aggressiveness in boxing would prove a help in becoming a leader, both in recreation and at work.

The work schedule in the camp was as follows:

6:00 AM - Rise
8:00 AM - Report to the technical work agency, where
each enrollee was assigned to a group of six
to twelve, under a LEM as an instructor.
1:00 PM - Lunch delivered to work site.
4:00 PM - Returned to camp.
5:00 PM - Supper from 5:00 to 5:30.
Following supper, the enrollee had the choice
of athletics, attending classes by the Educational
Adviser, or reading in the library.
10:30 PM - Lights out.

Each enrollee was required to spend part of his time at camp, cleaning up the barracks, policing the grounds, aiding the cook, and assisting in the maintenance of equipment and structures. Others were selected as clerks, both for the Army and for the technical service.

The task of boys like Archie, of clearing out roads for the engineers and surveyors, was hard work; nonetheless, it was the kind of work needed to toughen up his body. He set a pace for himself viewed even by his peers as a bit crazy; but no one did anything to discourage him.

Each morning, a large stake truck piled with equipment would transport the boys to their work locations. While the other boys sat in the bed of the truck singing, tapping out rhythms or telling jokes, Archie stood directly behind the cab of the truck for a reason by then quite familiar to the boys if not to the officials.

As the truck wound its way along the forest trails, there were low hanging branches which either skimmed the top of the cab or were lashed back with such swiftness that the riders would be showered with a rain of leaves and small branches. In a split second, just as a branch would come at him, Archie would duck and bob and weave, much as he had done in his "championship" fight with Julius Kemp, much as he had seen it done by his idol and mentor, Monroe "Munchy" Harrison.

This make-shift training, though dangerous, developed a technique which was to become part of the ring style of Archie Moore. His ingenuity and determination had also begun to attract the attention of "Captain" Ralph Parks, a former U.S. Army colonel and camp administrator who was not only a sports enthusiast, but ardent believer in competition as a morale builder and an outlet for the drive and restlessness of youth. There was already an orchestra, swimming and basketball teams and now, to Archie's thorough delight, the go-ahead by Captain Parks to have a boxing team. It was to be organized and taught by the forester turned boxer who would learn even more by teaching and beat all comers in competitions arranged by the camp.

By 1936, the boxing team from Poplar Bluf, Missouri, had entered the Golden Gloves and, with one exception, had won all of their bouts over the Southeastern, Missouri and Illinois boxers. Though one of the winners, Archie was beaten in the final competition in St. Louis by Courtland Shultz; but he bounced back later by winning the tri-state sectional tournament. This victory and the good showing made by the team served to spread the fame of the camp, to the sheer delight of Captain Parks, the sports buff.

"Hey Archie," he called one morning as he passed by the chow line in the mess hall, "I'm going to take you and the team to town tomorrow evening. There's a local boy down there whose supposed to be pretty good. Let's see what you can do with him." Archie's wide grin was all that both needed to seal the agreement and the next evening's event seemed too slow in arriving.

Finally, Captain Parks and the boys eagerly boarded three trucks and headed for town and a bout between Archie and the "hometown favorite." He could detect the hostility even as they met in the center of the ring; yet Archie was careful to focus his attention on what he was about to do. He wanted to make Captain Parks and the team proud of him.

Early in the first round, Archie heard the referee bellow that his brother was fouled. "Shit," the challenger complained to himself, "does the referee have to be hometown and family too?" The referee even stopped the fight to give his brother time to recover from the beating he was getting, a delay which was clearly unfair; yet Archie resumed his former advantage over the opponent, knocking him out in the second round. What with the "boos," "hisses" and "kill that Nigger" threats of the angry crowd, Archie had neither time to raise his gloves in victory nor even to get out of his boxing gear. He and the team were spirited away by Captain Parks who had previously alerted the men to be ready for quick get away by removing the governors from the trucks so they could go at maximum speed.

Three tired trucks arrived at the camp with a caravan of angry and sore losers in hot pursuit. When the venomous group attempted to enter the gate, Captain Parks, armed with a machine gun and a guerrilla-type stance, shouted, "Ok, you Mothers, you are on government property. I warn you, I will do my damnedest to defend it!" Well, the sight of the sub-machine gun and an unmistakably determined warning by Captain Parks cooled the mob down to a mere grumble and a reluctant retreat.

Encouraged by the support and enthusiasm of Captain Parks and his friends, Archie increased his record of wins and was fast becoming the camp's hero.

During one weekend, he and several of the boys decided to use their time off to visit friends and relatives in St. Louis. Having no money to get there, they hopped a freight train which seemed an adventurous thing to do. While several boys rode inside one box car, Archie rode aside a tank car containing molasses. With one hand, ne clutched the rail which ran around the car while the other held a bag containing his boxing equipment. "You never know," he reflected, "I might luck up on a fight when I get to St. Louis."

"Look out!", he heard from the boys in the box car as he was attempting to climb the ladder to get to the top. "Look out!"

As he whirled around, he came face-to-face with the brakeman, his face contorted with rage. "Get off this train, nigger," he said, as he rushed at Archie with a club raised over his head. "I'll teach you free-loadin niggers not to hop my train!" he snarled. As the club came down, Archie weaved past it such that it hit the side of the car and smashed into smithereens.

"... as my brains would have done," fretted Archie, struggling desperately to get to the catwalk. Falling once, he straddled it, his foot hitting the spinning wheel of the train. In his struggle to get up, he lost his bag; but he succeeded in running across several box cars to catch up with the others and safety.

Without the benefit of his club, however, the brakeman did not follow, though Archie wondered why he had taken his mission so seriously as to attempt to club a man's brains out in the first place.

Even if hopping a train was not entirely honest, it was a common occurrence during Depression.

That experience, that face, was to haunt Archie for years thereafter. He would see it in the news on the faces of Nazi soldiers as they persecuted the Jews. He would see faces of sheriffs as they clubbed and hosed down non-violent protesters who were led by Martin Luther King, Jr. in the Civil Rights movement of the '60's.

He wondered if the brakeman would have pursued with such vengeance had he been white. Though he never accepted the whole incident, his faith in human nature was somewhat restored when some good Samaritan found the bag containing his equipment and took the trouble to look him up and return it to him in St. Louis.

"Well," he convinced himself, "it seems I ain't gonna get a fight, so I'd just as well not waste the rest of my time." With that, he decided to test the waters at the local restaurant where Gladys Williams worked; but this was no casual visit. Archie had met her when he first returned from Boonville. Then he went in to buy a cup of coffee just to see Gladys during each of his few weekend visits (and each five cent cup of coffee had been a sacrifice).

Gladys really confused him too. "Last time, she winked at me," he confided to George Porter, "then told me we could be 'just telephone friends'. She also said, 'You know I'm Shuck-Eye's woman, anyway.' It's like an opponent dropping his guard to lure you in and then knocking you out with a left hook," he conveyed to George, the therapist.

"Well," added George, "I know your problem, 'cause she done filled out, man, as fine as a brick shit-house! You got to watch out for Shuck-Eye, though. He's slick!" With one good eye and one "shuck" or phony eye which remained half closed as the result of a brawl, this character had built himself an effective network of customers. As a cab driver, he was dependable, reasonable and, most of all, he kept his mouth shut. He was both match-maker and lover and a cheerful giver. This was especially welcomed by Gladys who needed help to make ends meet. It mattered little that his "shuck" eye made him less than handsome. What mattered was that HE WAS THERE!

"Well, man, he wasn't around when you went there this morning," reminded George Porter. "Maybe they've split."

"I doubt it," countered Archie, "but I've thrown my best punch. I've asked her to a dance tonight."

"Man, are you punch drunk or something? Shuck-Eye will find out. Then what?"

"He's on the ropes, George, he's on the ropes," chuckled Archie, leaving his inquisitive friend to figure it out for himself. (Archie had known that Shuck-Eye was married and probably not eager to make too much of a public fuss about Gladys. Besides, that kind of publicity would be bad for his business.)

That evening, Archie took the fifteen-cent ride by trolley to pick up his date and then they went by trolley to the Castle Ballroom on Olive and Euclid Streets about eleven or twelve miles away.

The dance was live. The Jitterbug was just coming in and though he was a pretty good dancer, Archie preferred the two-step or slow drag with Gladys for obvious reasons. "Oh, you're so soft," he whispered to her, while drawing her closer, now feeling what he had admired from afar. During intermission, he walked around proudly with her. "It feels almost as good as when I win a fight," he told himself.

He truly hated the thought of leaving as he heard the band leader announce that they were playing the last selection (The band was Chick Finney and His Saint Louis Crackerjacks, featuring Harold and Winfield Baker on trumpet and trombone. Trumpeter Clark Terry of St. Louis would later join the band).

As Archie and Gladys stopped at the coat check to pick up their coats, a sobering thought hit them and they voiced it simultaneously: "It's one o'clock!" But it was Gladys who asked, "How will we get home, Archie? The trolleys have stopped running!"

After what seemed an eternity of Archie's silence, Gladys had the last solution he wanted to hear. "I'll call Shuck-Eye," she announced in a tone which Archie deemed to sound just a little too gleeful; but there was no alternative. He had spent what little he had on the trolley fares, thirty-five cents apiece for dance tickets, and twenty cents to check the coats. They'd also had a couple of cokes at five cents and Archie had about twelve cents in his pocket.

"No problem," said Shuck-Eye, seeming not to mind the trip nor their date in the least. He even made small talk on the way home about plans to one day own a fleet of cabs and eventually go into the limousine business. To make matters more unsettling, Archie could not see Gladys to the door or perhaps go in for a spell and kiss her passionately as he had planned. He had, much to his chagrin, no way to get home.

But good old dependable Shuck-Eye was there. "He'll drop you off," assured Gladys, in a way which made Archie feel like the baggage which Shuck-Eye regularly picked up in transporting passengers to and from the train station.

To add insult to injury, Archie had to pawn his over coat to Shuck-Eye to pay the fifty-cent fare he charged to take him home and had to borrow the money from Auntie to retrieve it next morning before going back to camp. He had to steel himself against hitting Shuck-Eye in his good eye as he matter-of-factly accepted the fifty cents and handed over the coat. He was even "noble" about it! "Let me get my ass away from here," said Archie disgustedly as he headed for the railroad tracks.

If the trip to St. Louis was life-threatening, the trip back seemed a close second as he caught a faster train back carrying perishables, but one which landed him in Poplar Bluff at midnight, just in time to see the rear lights of the camp truck. It had just picked up the guys who regularly visited the city and had begun the fifteen-mile trip back to camp. "Dog it," he cried out, "only five minutes more and I'd have made it!"

By this time, and based on an already staggering record of bad luck, Archie knew he shouldn't stop to question his luck.

He began the fifteen-mile trek, walking briskly in order to make camp before the bugle sounded on Monday morning. He knew the area well and thought of a way to lessen the distance by taking a short cut; though first he had to cast aside his inhibitions about passing through a cemetery.

As he walked past the white grave markers, he felt a little uneasy at first and even bumped into a few as he groped along in the dark. After awhile, however, he was convinced that the dead could certainly do no more to him than some of the living had attempted to do. The latter notwithstanding, the silence of the night was a little unnerving and he was more than relieved when he stepped out of the cemetery onto a gravel path to continue on his journey. At least the gravel road would break the monotony of walking in silence since he could hear it "crunch, crunch" as it moved to the rhythm of his gait. Momentarily, he thought about a Negro tap dancer dubbed Howard "Sandman" Sims, known for using sand to enhance the rhythm of his step. This creative thought was suddenly interrupted by a "crunch, crunch" that was not like the sound of Sandman, nor was it even the sound of his own feet; for Archie had begun to quicken his pace by now, only to hear the crunch behind him quicken. When he slowed, it slowed and he wondered had someone followed him out of the graveyard.

"If its a ghost," he joked half-heartedly, "it damn sure isn't following acceptable ghostly practices. They're supposed to wail and groan and moan, or so they say."

It was an eerie feeling to say the least; but there was little he could do besides walk on. The night was so black that he could scarcely see his own feet beneath him; yet he knew instinctively that someone was there.

Suddenly, the sound caught up to Archie and was punctuated by a flickering light which illuminated the chalky white face of a man who lit a cigarette, gave out with a diabolical chuckle and just as suddenly disappeared into the night. Though nothing else happened, it conjured up questions as to who the man was and what he was doing out there. Well, he wasn't going to find out and he even tried not to think as he struggled the last mile home.

With dawn breaking, there were a few cars on the road but none would stop to give him a lift. Eventually, with blistered feet he arrived at camp 3760 with time to spare but no energy to answer questions like, "Man, what happened to you, Archie?" And on the job that day, some of his buddies covered him with leaves so that he could grab a few winks of much-needed sleep while they raked the leaves and fallen branches in the forest.

He couldn't have been asleep for more than ten minutes when the order rang out. "OK... clear out, we're going to burn the brush!"

"Oh, God," yelled Connie Thompson to his brother Walter, "Archie's back there!" They ran frenzied from one leaf pile to another, poking and feeling to find their sleeping friend before he would become an incinerated, former friend.

Not any too soon, they finally found their "Rip Van Winkle" and swiftly carried him away from his leafy bed to safety. "Man, you're hard luck," said Griffin Young in utter disbelief that one human being could have so many mishaps in his life.

This was Archie Moore; yet he was not always the victim of circumstance. There were times when his natural instinct as the challenger took over, especially in the face of some social inequity. He knew the army-type discipline discouraged involvement in violent or controversial activities which could mean a strike against him. He had already incurred a couple; but this one was close to his heart or, more specifically, to his stomach.

What with the noon meal having to be taken at the work site, the boys often found themselves eating cold stew, beans, or sandwiches which were not exactly palatable nor fortifying for hard workers, especially in the wintertime. Complaints to the supervisor of the crew saw no change, nor did those arising out of fines of fifty cents for a rule infraction such as being tardy for camp. Fifty cents was, after all, ten percent of each boy's monthly allowance.

Tensions mounted to such a state that one boy, Sam, refused to work until he got hot meals. "Oh, so you're going to lead a rebellion!" jeered the supervisor. "Well, let's see how many of you are just as crazy! Line up on Sam's side if you feel the way he does!" And what a can of worms was opened that day as Archie and his crew filed behind the lone dissenter, all save one. A huge hulk of a boy named Charles stood alone. "Damn, we've got a strike breaker!" Archie sneered.

In a split second, Archie had crossed back over to the side of the anti-striker and delivered a right hand to his jaw. Instead of hitting the ground, he stood there glaring woefully with tears in his eyes. Had he decided to retaliate, Archie might well have lost one of his early fights because his hand had become useless. He could still feel the shot of electricity as it traveled from the iron like jaw, through his fist, into his wrist. An injured hand was well worth the pain, however, when Charles moved meekly to the other side, making the protest unanimous.

By this time, Captain Parks had arrived and announced with the authority of a true Army man: "I'm not going to have this kind of behavior in my camp. If anyone of you wants to leave, I'll make out your papers now!" Needless to say, lean times dictated the course of action and no one budged; yet the fairness of Captain Parks evoked a change. Cast iron kettles formerly used to transport the food were replaced by kettles heated by means of kerosene burners. Soon, hot food flowed to the outdoor workers and the victory was a clear indication to all that justice had been served rather than that the administration had gone soft. Archie, more than most, had known the strength of Captain Parks, a strength which he absorbed and now longed to test in the world outside camp 3760. He felt confident after his nine-month stay that he was ready to join the pros.

Moore worked out during early years at the Pine Street YMCA gym in St. Louis, Missouri.

CHAPTER IV

Out on His Own: Turning Pro

It was in the fall of 1937, with approximately twenty two fights under his belt predominantly won by knock-out, that the plucky challenger boarded a bus for Indianapolis to join his first, official manager, Cal Thompson.

Cal was a barber by profession, well-off for the times, an industrious owner of one of the finest barbershops in the Hume-Mansure business complex in Indianapolis. He had spotted Archie when he won a decision over Sammy "Kid" Slaughter during September of '37. It had been a proud moment for Archie, almost as proud as what he was about to do: ride as a paying passenger on a Greyhound bus to Indianapolis.

"Do it well or not at all," he repeated prayerfully, as the bus motor revved up and drowned out all but his visions of being a champion. He relaxed totally and proceeded to read the advertisement on a sign above the rear seats assigned to "colored passengers only." The sign advertised Conkaline, a lye-based product for straightening the hair, commonly used by Negro entertainers and boxers (also called "process" or "gas" in various regions of the country). As his gaze travelled along, it fell on the seat, rather on the passenger in the seat across the aisle, two seats up. Her slender ebony leg stuck out into the aisle as she swung her right arm as though it were a pendulum.

"Interesting," he thought, "how some Negro girls are made - small calves and big thighs. They're nice." His mind then drifted to his one sexual encounter with a girl he had met in Boonville. She was an inmate at the Tipton School for girls.

Theresa also had dark, slender legs. He had initially seen her at a dance arranged by the Boonville Reformatory with the intent of bringing boys and girls together in a social setting. As he thought in retrospect, he laughed at the dance music rendered by Songbird Butch and His Royal Syncopators performing on a piano, drum, guitar and kazoo. This was a far cry from the jazz he would grow to love, especially when it featured a saxophone.

He had looked Theresa up on his return home; for she too had finished her term and had returned to St. Louis. Archie had not known how to approach her on the dance floor let alone approach her for a sexual encounter; but it had happened. He spent all day with her at the home of her aunt who had left early that morning for work.

In this his first intimacy, he had numerous, unbelievable explosions of passion urged on by Theresa's own insatiable love making, deferred much as his had been after two years of reform school and isolation from the opposite sex.

He had not since this sexual initiation allowed himself to dwell on it, not even now as he admired the limbs across the aisle. "It's tempting," he told himself, "but I have to concentrate on boxing. Besides, women need attention and I don't have that kind of time." So he leaned back on the pillow of the seat, ruminating about his fighting escapades and speculating about his new manager and his future.

The bus rolled to a stop in the Greyhound Station and gave out a final belch of air which signalled the opening of the doors. One eager passenger was up and out of the door before everyone else, even before the "ebony legs" across the aisle had a chance to stand.

"Welcome to *Nap Town*, Archie," chimed Cal, in an unmistakably flamboyant manner. He put his jeweled hand on the shoulder of his prospect, eyeing him up and down as would a referee or a coach.

He then ushered Archie rather swiftly into a 1937 Dodge which had scarcely a thousand miles on it. Its sleekness and newness evoked from the young boxer the kinds of expressions which Cal appreciated.

"Wow, Cal, this is some car! When did you get it? You sure have a lot of class!"

It was a style to which Archie would soon get accustomed, because Cal was used to high living. He thought big and exemplified it.

"Now Archie," he advised, as he inspected his seedily dressed passenger who wore a combination of brown and blue, "you'll have to wear a fresh shirt and tie each day, pressed pants and shined shoes. You've got to look, think and act like a champion!" These words would become a litany as the months passed and Cal groomed his fighter and made bountiful promises for the future. He even moved him into his own tastefully furnished, modern house, an arrangement which was to be short-lived.

Early rising to do road work and his having frequently occurring mishaps were to prove too much for Cal's wife, Alberta, to handle. His country kitchen approach to preparing food would also prove disastrous as he tried making breakfast as he thought he had seen it done by Auntie Willie. He buttered the toast, put it in the toaster and ruined his first exercise in mechanized cookery, not to mention Mrs. Thompson's toaster. It was the last straw and his first experience at living in a boarding house; but the food was good and the boarders were supportive of his boxing endeavors.

Cal secured the services of Hiawatha Gray, an ex-fighter turned trainer who had a penchant for using half-hearted anger to get a fighter to work hard. His manner suggested that he was never quite satisfied with even a good job. But it paid off; for 1937 unveiled an unbeaten knock-out artist. Only Sammy Slaughter had lasted through a tough ten rounds before giving up the struggle. He had been a rugged contender for the middleweight championship and had lost to Gorilla Jones. Only his skill in sharp shooting, however, had sustained Slaughter against Archie's merciless pounding. This bout was also characteristic of the bouts which Archie had already fought. They were not, much to his disappointment, the quality fights which would move a man up the fistic ladder.

Thus by the end of the year, an aspiring champion walked the few blocks to the barber shop and, with some trepidation, advised his manager of his well-thought-out decision.

"Cal," he hesitated, though not from lack of decisiveness, "I'm going home! The fights I've had are not getting the kind of publicity I need, and the fighters I'm beating only make the rated fighters fear me more." (Most were hard-hitting, experienced, Black fighters that no one, especially the champions and top contenders, wanted to fight. They were destroyers, men to be avoided; so being at the top of that heap made Archie "anathema," a curse.)

Cal's reaction was an admixture of let-down and hurt inasmuch he had boasted outrageously about his up-and-coming champion as well as invested some money. He had borne the living and training expenses almost totally, mainly because the purses, ranging from $50 to $250 (the latter only once), had hardly been enough to cover it all.

"Well," Cal lamented almost inaudibly, "if that's what you want to do." The sight of Archie's small valise which held his few belongings indicated his resolution to delay no further. Cal said no more, even though he found his remorse hard to conceal as he drove Archie to the bus station, listening to all the reasons for the decision.

"You see, Cal," he explained, "I've already spent two years in reform school and nine months in CCC Camp. I'm twenty-one, and I should already be established as a national contender." Though Cal listened, it was with the ear of the entrepreneur, still convinced that he could pull it off even as they waited in the bus station.

Though having no doubts about his decision, Archie's appreciation and admiration for this self-confident man who seemed before his time, made him even more uneasy about turning his back. A mutual, "Good luck... Keep in touch," was, nevertheless, the dissolution of an unwritten but well-intentioned agreement.

It was only the sight of George Porter in St. Louis that lifted Archie out of his doldrums as he always did. "Everyone should have a friend like George," he often told himself.

"Man, Archie, I've been reading about you. You really amazed me! Makin' a big name for yourself, ain't you!" Yes, that was typically George Porter.

After a sandwich at Auntie's and a lot of pugilistic palaver, Archie laid out his dilemma with an almost immediate solution provided by George.

"Why don't you talk to my Uncle, Felix Thurman, Archie. He's going back to California where all the good middleweights are. He'll steer you right. I'm sure he will." Archie looked at George, half-amaz-ed, half-envious of his resourcefulness and decided to take the advice.

The introduction of Archie to Felix established the groundwork for mutual respect and each man liked the other immediately. Felix, like Cal, was a businessman but without the flamboyance. He owned a garage and could repair anything, a skill which Archie had not developed; so he felt it would strike a good balance as they made the way to California.

It was Felix Thurman's sincerity and confidence in Archie's ability that would make up for his lack of experience as a manager. He even sold his garage which was his living, an act which strengthened the level of his commitment to the task.

As though an additional nudge were needed, George, the all-knowing psychologist, needled Archie...

"Man, you don't stand a chance on the West Coast. The Bandit Romero will make dog meat out of you!"

"Ok, friend," Archie chortled, "I'll make you eat all the dog meat he makes!"

With that, the old Plymouth pulled off on its long haul to California and each time it needed repair, Felix used his precious tools to do the job. It seemed he never ran out of tricks. They had left St. Louis with $37, two cases of Coca Cola, and a bag of peanuts between them to eat along the way.

Dusk of March 30, 1938, was to signal a gloomy fate as they drove along a two-lane highway headed west. Suddenly, they spotted an oncoming car attempting to pass another in its lane. Unable to get back into his own lane in time, the driver entered their lane.

"Lookout!" Archie yelled to Felix who had already braced himself and held his right elbow up to keep his panicky passenger from grabbing the wheel. In a split second, Felix turned off the road with such force that the car flipped and landed top-down off the highway.

They blacked out, both men victimized by the driver who sped along, uncaring that they had probably saved his life by running off the road and sacrificing themselves. First to return to consciousness, Archie could hear a steady dripping which he just knew was gasoline.

"My God," he panicked ... "Felix, Felix, come on, we've got to get out before this thing blows up!"

His body was sort of crumpled in his seat and there was a bump on his head; so Archie knew it was up to him to act fast. When he tried the door handle, the door of the overturned car would not open thus punching through the glass seemed his only alternative. Warm blood began to ooze out of a gaping cut in his wrist and dripped like thick, red paint down the side of the car. As he went around to the other side and tried to open the door, he discovered his mistake.

The door of the overturned car could not have been opened in the conventional way and he had not thought to try the other way before punching into the window. He had panicked in a crisis; but he would learn from this (and later tell other young boxers: "You see, the real danger in any crisis or contest is panic,"... and further, "many a guy will rush in for a knock-out early in a fight and risk being knocked out himself. A good boxer realizes that well-aimed body punches can wear an opponent down gradually but effectively").

As he gave serious thought to his discovery, he carefully pulled Felix from the car so as not to injure him further. His own blood covered Felix's shirt too as he struggled to free him from the car which never blew up, because the "drip, drip, drip," proved to be water from the spinning car wheels which had picked it up from the irrigation ditch.

Just when he thought he would bleed to death, Archie looked up to see a 1938 Oldsmobile pulling up. Inside proved to be an intern and three other people.

"Is this some miracle?" he asked aloud. It was uncanny to have experienced such a paradox in so short a time.

Gone was one driver who caused hurt and had chosen to ignore it, and yet another who sensed need and volunteered to assist.

Both were white men, a realization which seemed to say, "There's hope for brotherhood!"

All that mattered to the intern was stopping the bleeding, the likes of which he said he had seen end in death in a matter of minutes if not checked. As he tied the tourniquet, Archie could see Felix being revived by the other intern and two nurses. "He'll be all right," the intern promised. "Just a bump on the head. Come on, we're taking you both to the hospital.!"

"But what about your car," Archie warned. "We're all blood and dirt!"

"Never mind that. What's important is getting you two treated," the intern assured. Though his wrist pulsated with pain, the solicitousness of the medical team sent a gush of good feelings through Archie, seeming to make the pain secondary.

As it turned out, the physician who attended them upon arrival at the hospital was quite a fight fan and Archie invited his awe by being able to describe Joe Louis and Jack Johnson in the most graphic terms. This seemed to Archie to compensate for their inability to pay for the care, though the intern had said payment was not a condition for treatment.

"Will I be able to hit hard with this hand, Doc?" queried the anxious patient.

"You'll be ok," he advised. "Just change the bandages and keep it clean. Go to a doctor when you get to California."

"Somehow, we will get there," asserted Felix as he later turned the car upright and made minor repairs to get it running; but it was to be a trying trip. It seemed as though the two men were leaving markers, bleak markers on a map of the west.

By New Mexico, they had run out of money and were hungry; so Felix's wife responded to a call to La Jolla where she was employed. She wired ten dollars which lasted until Flagstaff, Arizona. There, Felix pawned most of his tools which advanced them closer to San Bernardino, California. In a final act of desperation, Felix sold his prized possession, a spray gun, which obtained enough money for the final trek to La Jolla.

Following much-needed baths and a night's sleep, Felix and Archie arose new men, undaunted by the sequence of bad luck they had endured.

"Come on Archie," Felix urged, "we've got to see Linn Platner. He's a San Diego promoter and I think we can get him to give you a fight." Now the law of averages might have dictated that their share of misfortunes had been experienced, but this was no average duo.

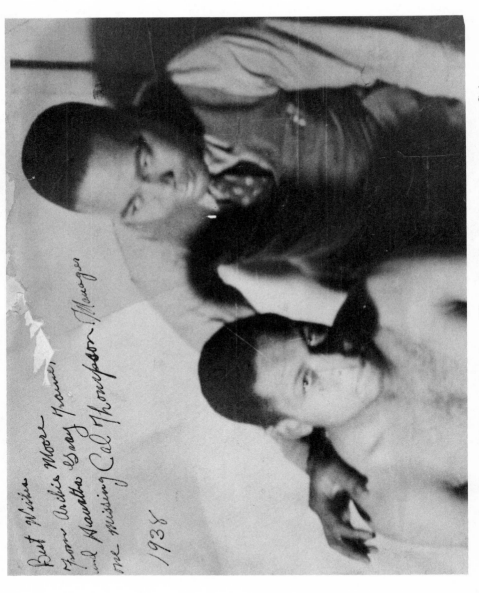

Archie Moore and trainer, Hiawatha Gray, hired by manager Col Thompson, 1938.

UNCROWNED Middleweight CHAMPION

Archie Moore

St. Louis, Mo. -- 160 Pounds

Do Not Overlook This Big Box Office Attraction!

Most Spectacular Fighter in the World Today
34 Kayo's out of 48 Fights

LOOK!

READ!

LARRY ATKINS of St. Louis
Matchmaker and Promoter
February 1, 1939

I regard Moore as one of the most feared challengers. He is the hardest punching middleweight in the game today and is ready for a shot at the crown.

St. Louis Globe Democrat
February 6, 1939

Archie Moore is the most outstanding fighter developed in St. Louis since Henry Armstrong.

BILLY STEVENS
New York Enquirer
May 17, 1939

They say Archie Moore, St. Louis middleweight, is the best looking 160-pounder of the whole lot, and his local gym workouts have proven so.

JOE WILLIAMS, New YORK
June 18, 1939

Watch this latest threat to the middleweights, Archie Moore. He's sure to wear the crown if given a title shot.

Los Angeles Examiner
September 28, 1938

Al Hostak, newly crowned middleweight champion, is dickering with the Olympic Auditorium for a fight in Los Angeles, but he definitely does not want to meet Archie Moore, sensational negro. Highly significant is Hostak's attitude. Evidently the Seattle blonde has heard about Moore's knockouts over Frank Rowsey, Johnny "Bandit" Romero, Ray Vargas, Jimmy Brent and Johnny Sikes.

RAY ARCEL, New York
March 20, 1939

A dynamite punching youngster of whom Ray Arcel said after the Yarosz fight: Quote: "Moore? He's a great fighter."

Has Defeated:

"BANDIT" ROMERO *
SAMMY JACKSON *
SAMMY SLAUGHTER *
DOMINIC CECCARELLI *
LORENZO PEDRO **
MARTY SIMMONS **
RAY VARGAS *
JOHNNY SIKES *
FRANK ROWSEY *
TOM HENRY *
BOBBY YANNES,* Etc.

* Won by Knockout   **Won by Decision

W. J. McGOOGAN
St. Louis Post Dispatch
March 18, 1939

Teddy Yarosz showed all the respect in the world for Archie Moore's punching power and would not give Archie a chance to hit him. One round went to Yarosz because of a low blow struck by Moore, and so close was the verdict that the low punch might well have decided the contest.

San Diego Sun
August 11, 1938

Archie Moore, whose name strikes fear into the hearts of the leading middleweights, added Frank Rowsey to his list of victims last night, winning by K. O. in the third round of their scheduled ten round battle.

RAY SMITH, St. Louis Post
June 12, 1939

Why don't they bring in Solly Krieger or better still, Fred Apostoli to fight Archie Moore. He's an even bet to win.

KID REGAN
St. Louis Star-Times
February 7, 1939

Archie Moore set himself in the king row of middleweights with a decisive ten round setback of Marty Simmons, a Saginaw, Michigan, battler with a stocky frame and a savage glint in both optics. It was a most thrilling scuffle with Simmons staging a late rally to be met by a well conditioned Moore who literally punched Marty's ears off.

St. Louis Post Dispatch
January 5, 1939

Italy's light heavyweight champion Dominic Ceccarelli, who has stayed the limit with John Henry Lewis, Billy Conn, Buddy Knox, and other top notchers, was kayoed by Archie Moore, great 155-pounder, last night in 2 minutes and 24 seconds.

Young Archie Moore was in the "King's Row" of Middleweights.

CHAPTER V

The California Scene: Boxing, Women, and Jazz

Consider the let-down when after their arrival in San Diego, they learned that the Coliseum had just burned down. "Good God!" whispered Felix, not wanting to lower Archie's morale; but Archie was too stunned himself to hear.

"Shit!" he winced in disbelief, as he pounded his fist on the side of the truck causing his wrist to bleed again. Instinctively, he used his other hand to apply pressure to the bleeding wrist, with his gaze affixed to the still smoldering ruins of the Coliseum, once magnificent and proud landmark in San Diego. But gazing didn't get it!

Acting on a tip, they decided to try their luck in Los Angeles, the base of operations for Babe McCoy, well known for his influence and shrewdness at the financial end of the fight game. They found him with little difficulty and approached him with caution.

"Mr. McCoy, sir, I'm Felix Thurman and this is my fighter. This is Archie Moore," said Felix, in his most polite tone. "We heard you are always looking for good fighters and Archie is one. He's won every one of his matches and he needs a fight now."

With scarcely a glance at either of the petitioners, McCoy began leafing through some papers and casually made a neat pile on one corner of his desk.

"Naa," he sneered sarcastically, "we got too many colored boys up here now. Central Avenue is full of 'em. (Central Avenue was in 1938 and into succeeding decades, the "main drag" for Negroes in Los Angeles, especially for Negro entertainment.) If we opened up anymore cards to colored boys," McCoy went on, "we'd be letting ourselves in for trouble!"

"But Mr. McCoy," Felix petitioned earnestly, "just let him fight anybody. If he turns out to be no good, we won't even accept the money!"

"Wow," thought Archie disgustedly, "where does that leave me?" Despite his awareness of Felix's intent, the offer had killed his spirit. It was as though he was a thing and not a man; yet men more notable than he had been stripped of their dignity. Even the great Jesse Owens, wonder of the '32 Olympics in Los Angeles, had been made to race against a horse for the sport of sick-minded men.

Yes, McCoy was correct about one thing; there were too many Negro fighters on Central Avenue, mainly because of greedy men like himself. He only promoted Negro boxers if he could get his claws into them. Thus many capable fighters never reached the forefront, especially if they were a threat to "boys he had built up." There were good punchers like Cannonball Green; brothers, Chalky and Lee Wright; Turkey Thompson; Hut Thompson; Richard Green; and John Thomas. (The latter two became referees of note.)

"No," McCoy repeated even as the two had moved toward the door, "just too many colored fighters. I'd go broke... be out of a job. Come to think of it," he offered, as though throwing one more punch at a man already on the canvas, "it would be better to go on and get the boy a job!... and if you find him one, get one for me too!"

As both men walked out of the door and even out of earshot of McCoy, neither could say anything, so stunned were they by the blatant flurry of put-downs.

Their old Plymouth couldn't carry them fast enough, away from the Olympic Auditorium at 19th and Grand, southeast to the Negro district, to Central Avenue, Harlem of the West. Few Negroes lived on the far west side due to a subtle Jim Crow, and though theoretically free to travel anywhere, they converged on Central Avenue for a sense of belonging.

Archie and Felix stopped at 43rd and Central amidst a hive of consumers patronizing shops run by small-time peddlers, renters and a few owners. Nestled together were barber shops, shoe shines, clothing stores, pool halls, greasy spoons and barbecue joints, each of which had its own regional flavor and name (not to omit fried catfish which penetrated the air, giving the streets a distinctively crisp odor). It seemed the greasier the food, the more were the customers.

Most prominent along Central Avenue was the Dunbar Hotel where Negro name bands played, changing up usually every two weeks. Other big names often passed through and sat in, performing with more zest than they would for the elite. There was Jimmy Luncford, a great director and writer, leading the likes of famed trombone player, Trummy

Young, and trumpet player, Gerald Wilson. The Lionel Hampton Band was a popular hit band, including Illinois Jacquet, famous for his solo on "Flying Home."

Those eager to see the stars could see them come out in their finest galaxy - an array of singers, actors, dancers and other hopefuls. There were actresses Louise Beavers; Hattie McDaniel; Ethel Waters; the one-of-a-kind, Bill "Bojangles Robinson"; and dance artist Catherine Dunham; also Canada Lee, former boxer of the '20's turned actor. Whenever Satchmo came through, the place blazed with his Dixieland flavor and unique guttural solos, as it would with the jamming of Duke or Basie. There was not a Negro personality around, including boxers such as Joe Louis, Ray Robinson and Archie himself, who had not passed through the portals of the famous Dunbar Hotel.

Archie was on hand the night Ivy Anderson crossed Lena Horne with a subtle challenge. Ivy, then main vocalist with the Duke Ellington Band, had become revered for her rendition of "Stormy Weather"; but Lena was much more. Having recently completed "Cabin in the Sky" and with rave reviews from performances at the Cotton Club in New York, she was the envy of most. She was escorted by her protective father.

When Ivy insisted that night that Lena sing "Stormy Weather," Lena, diplomat that she was, steered skillfully away from it, choosing another favorite instead. She was without her own piano player, as she politely pointed out, and was backed by Billy Kyle, another piano player of note. In any event, each singer preserved her dignity, reigning supreme as an artist in her own right.

The undisputed king of all personalities along Central Avenue and its environs was a smooth, black, intelligent street bureaucrat, respected, and aptly dubbed "Black Dot", his given name being Elihu McGee. He was a gambler of the chanciest type, apt to bet on rain in the Sahara Desert in mid-summer. Not ordinary by any sense of the imagination, he ran three businesses simultaneously - one night club, a pool hall, and a booking operation carried in the inside pocket of his Hickey Freeman suit. He literally stepped on $5,000 each day, keeping his bankroll in his sock or in the band of his Stetson hat. He willingly gave to those in need, peeling from his "Michigan Roll" (a wad of bills of various denominations). There was nothing that one wanted to find or procure that couldn't be arranged through Dot, and not always for a sum.

His nightclub, Casablanca, honored the presence of various and sundry potentates including Mickey Cohen (for whom he was later a pallbearer) and George Raft. He regularly reserved a table for Orsen Welles and Rita Hayworth, reigning royalty of Hollywood. Lena Horne was his "pet" and he thoroughly enjoyed feting her as he did the great Dinah Washington, yet unparalleled as a song stylist. Crooner Bing Crosby and news mogul, George Hearst, were also among his guests. This after hours haven bridged both social and racial gaps, bringing together people who would not otherwise have had the opportunity.

Dot was drawn to Archie because of his love of sports, a subject about which he never tired of talking. His skill extended to the game of pool, as much a player as a bettor. He made bank shots with ease, handling his stick with much dexterity and a kind of grace. He was a fair man, a real sportsman, kind enough not to draw Archie into a betting situation, especially since he was undisputedly the more skilled of the two. To be most admired about Dot, however, was his skill in human relations. He thoroughly understood the human animal and all of its motivations... and there were not too many who crossed his path that didn't like or respect Dot. To many, he was the unofficial "Mayor of Central Avenue".

As they left Los Angeles, Archie felt fulfilled, his thoughts now turning to Linn Platner in San Diego. He hoped they could bank on what they'd heard... that he was a man of principle, a lover of the sport and not money alone. Subconsciously, Archie was hoping for an individual with some of the qualities of his trusted friend, Black Dot.

They found Platner at the Coliseum surveying the ruins and planning the renovation of the charred edifice, a place in which he had ownership and pride. As Felix approached Platner, it was with a pitch that focused on Archie as a local talent. (It is in the promoter's financial interest to build local talent to attract hometown fans.)

"My name is Felix Thurman, Mr. Platner... I'm from St. Louis and I've got a boy who can really fight. He's had about eight fights and he's won seven by knockout. We'd like to fight some of the top middle-weights." Now, a skilled manager would not have wanted tough opponents. He would opt instead for less formidable fighters to allow his fighter to build a reputation of wins to boost his confidence.

With an all-knowing grin, Mr. Platner continued surveying the ruins with the two men following in hopeful pursuit. Platner, like Babe McCoy, had enough local talent; unlike McCoy, however, he used foresight. He knew that he needed a new face on the card to keep local interest alive.

He stopped in his tracks, causing Felix to stumble onto him and Archie onto Felix. If not for their anxiety, both stumblers would have been embarrassed. Turning to Felix, Platner asked thoughtfully, "Can the boy fight?"

"Yes, he can do that, assured Felix, "and he's cooperative and respectful too!" (He had not forgotten McCoy.)

"I like that," Platner answered. "Come on, we'll go over to my office where we can discuss this in private."

This meeting placed Archie in a preliminary bout matched against Jimmy Brent, a local middleweight. More importantly he was to be on the same card with Maxie Rosenblum vs. Odell Polee, the main event. Maxie was also known as "Slapsy Maxie" because of his delivery of slap-type blows. He was, nonetheless, former light heavyweight champion and it was a fortunate first for Archie to be on his card in this his first West Coast fight.

Platner moved the fight to Lane Field, the 10,000 capacity city ball park, and though not filled to capacity, the cheers of fans at Archie's first-round K.O. of Brent would have seemed so. Those cheers also indicated that Archie was a fighter to be reckoned with.

A few weeks later and the knockout of Ray Vargas brought him to the brink of the challenge he had received from his old friend, George Porter, when he teased: "Johnny the Bandit Romero will make dog meat out of you!" Well, not quite; for he managed to last ten rounds against the more experienced twelve-year veteran rated number seven in the world.

Two more fights and two victories later had earned Archie a second shot at Romero; but this time it would be accompanied by confidence from the reputation he had built. It wasn't difficult to detect that Romero had also begun to respect his image when on the night of the fight, they had to share the same dressing room in the renovated Coliseum.

"You know," said a smiling Romero, "I have a very warm feeling for colored people ... a lot of my close friends are colored."

"Well , that's fine," commended the challenger; "but I'd try to knock my own brother out if I met him in the ring, just as I'm going to do to you!"

"I wonder what George Porter would say about the great Romero if he heard that?" he snickered. "I wonder does George still relish dog meat?"

As Archie moved through the crowd, he thought back to the cheering fans of the backyard match that he had witnessed when but small boy - the vigor of it, the admiration for the big, black boxers who punched and grunted at each other. He had always kept this in the back of his mind, even moreso now, as he knocked out Romero in the eighth round. And the ecstasy was complete when fans crowded the dressing room to get his autograph and shake his hand. This too was a first. "Humm," he smirked, "a little more dog meat for George."

Several of the fans hung around longer, recounting the victory and touting the champ for his fistic abilities. They were locals who seemed real fight fans, three of whom were a young man, a friend and his sister, Mattie.

"You fought real good," Mattie said, as she curiously watched the champ place his gloves, tape, liniment, mouth-guard and scissors into his bag.

"Glad .you enjoyed it," blushed the champ... "how's about going out for a soft drink or something," he offered. And the realization hit him that not since taking out Gladys in St. Louis and his embarrassing misadventure with Shuck-Eye had he been able to ask a girl out and treat her. He guessed he was a hopeless romantic, as quick to love as he was to jab, because by the end of the evening, he knew that Mattie had gotten next to him.

He could not, however, pursue Mattie seriously because of a true commitment to boxing which netted him his next three consecutive victories. Then, it was back.to St. Louis for five more consecutive knockout victories. More importantly, Archie Moore had become a main-event fighter, a hometown champ. Everyone in St. Louis knew it ... even Gladys.

He headed toward the restaurant one evening half thinking that by now, Shuck-Eye had hit it big and set Gladys up in grand style; but there he was, sitting outside the restaurant in his cab just where Archie had last seen him, waiting for his next load. Nothing had changed, not even Gladys... still waiting tables and being subsidized by gratuities from Shuck-Eye; but her eyes were different this time as Archie entered the door of the restaurant and got a special wink which stirred him passionately.

"You done good, Archie," she smiled. "Sorry I couldn't see you fight, but I heard about it. Everyone has!"

"How's about picking you up at your place tonight," he asked. "We can take in a club or something."

"O.K.," she agreed anxiously as she poured a root beer for the champ, not looking for an instant at the cab parked outside, just in front of Archie's Oldsmobile.

They went to a bar owned by Jourdan Chambers, a mover and a shaker, a local politician. Appearing there by pleasant coincidence, was Clark Terry on trumpet, backed up by bassist "Singy" (Singleton Palmer), a tuba player of note, and Harold "Shorty" Baker on trumpet. (Both trumpet players were later to become twelve-year veterans of the Duke Ellington Band.) Their smooth rendition of "Stardust" seemed to make Gladys even sweeter. "California really agrees with you, Archie," she complimented. "You look great. I've really missed you." (She was definitely scoring points!)

"What about Shuck-Eye," recoiled the champ? "How do things stand between you?"

"Look, Archie," she confessed, "I've loved you all along... I've stuck with Shuck-Eye only because I've needed his help. I didn't really want to."

Though those were words about which Archie had long fantasized, he was quite unsettled about the heightened ardor exhibited by this one-time, hard-to-get woman; nevertheless, he was caught up in the spell.

Later, after several hours of love making, wildly passionate laments and soulful kisses, Gladys had evoked a promise from the champion to return with him to San Diego.

"What have I gotten myself into?" he rebuked himself as he drove home. It was an empty feeling, not to mention being a puzzle. Was it the string of victories which had worked its magic, or had Gladys really loved him all along?

Finally in desperation, he called and told her he had received a telegram and had to leave for an out-of-town fight. "Boxing, after all accepted me when she wouldn't", he convinced himself. "It's my last chance and my first love!"

It was Auntie who would assist him in grappling with the guilt and second-guessing that he still harbored because of what he had done.

"Well, Archie Lee," she advised, stressing his middle name, "there are times in life when you have to make a choice. Sometimes this is hard to do and sometimes even harder to live with. Can you live with your decision, Archie?"

He knew intuitively that Auntie did not require an answer, but that she was encouraging him to search his soul, to make his own decisions. He watched her intently as she began to rock rhythmically in her chair and open her well-worn Bible to the page she wanted to him read. She moved the red, tasseled string to the page and handed him the book, directing him to read aloud a passage she marked in the Old Testament, Ecclesiastes 1:10, which said:

"Whatsoever thy hand findeth to do, do it with all Thy might."

"Yes, son," she whispered softly, "it's all here. There's no lesson for life that can't be found in the Bible. It's much like the little poem I taught you... "When a task is once begun, never leave it til its done...."

While Archie had not known the origin of the poem, it was as sound as what he had read in the Bible and it would later serve him well. (Had even Ralph Waldo Emerson been so original when he wrote: "The manly part is to do with might and main what you can do?")

As he handed her the Bible, he swallowed hard to fight back the tears welling up in his eyes, and made a mental note to replace Auntie's well-worn Bible with a new one as soon as he made enough money.

Main Eventers in Coliseum's Opening Tonight Await the Bell

ROMERO		MOORE
27	Age	21
165	Weight	160
5-11	Height	5-11
15½	Neck	15½
76	Reach	78
39	Chest	35
40	Chest Exp.	38
12¾	Biceps	13
12	Forearm	11½
7	Wrist	7
12	Fist	12
33½	Waist	31½
18½	Thigh	22
14¾	Calf	14½
9½	Ankle	9

ARCHIE MOORE　　　　　　　　　　　　　　　**JOHNNY ROMERO**

Above are the two really great fighters who clash in the headliner of the first boxing show to be presented in the newly rebuilt Coliseum Athletic club this evening. They went 10 rounds recently, Romero taking a close decision by virtue of a pair of knockdowns, but Moore finished strong and game. They go the same distance toni ght. Both are confident of winning.—(Tribune staff photos.)

Archie vs Johnny "The Bandit" Romero in the San Diego Coliseum.

Top photo: Archie Moore and Elihu "Black Dot" McGee--Unofficial Mayor of Central Avenue, around 1938. McGee was recently honored by Mayor Bradley of Los Angeles.

Bottom photo: Playful times at Club Casablanca. Among those pictured are Mrs. McGee (white dress), "BlackDot", Dinah Washington and Duke Ellington, 1938.

QUEEN OF THE BLUES IS DEAD AT 44

Jazz World Mourns Lady Day

By JAMES DONAHUE

From Baltimore to New Orleans, from Kansas City to Chicago, wherever jazz hold reign, the blues rose and fell in a mournful wail yesterday.

Lady Day was dead.

Jazzdom's queen of queens, Billie Holiday, the girl with the tortured soul and the incomparable voice, would sing no more.

And the trumpets moaned, the trombones sighed, and the drums rolled out in disconsolation throughout the jazz world.

FOR, WITH BILLIE, a magnificent part of that would died.

"A tragic, tragic loss," said Benny Goodman, with whom Billie cut her first record in 1933.

And his words were echoed in jazz chambers throughout the land as musicians, who knew her, played with her and, best of all, heard her sing, fumbled for words to express themselves. Behind the unspoken words it was there for all to feel—the sense of irreplaceable loss.

For them, there was only this: there would never be another Lady Day.

For, her passing—at 44—in the early hours yesterday at Metropolitan Hospital, was tragedy compounded on tragedy.

There were those that remembered her, not as the shriveled, tormented shadow of a woman whose fast life had finally caught up with her. They remembered her as she was—the very heart and soul of the blues, the woman who, above all, could capture and hold enthrallingly the spirit of all jazzdom.

BUT PERHAPS it was her life, one of sordidness, bitterness, ignominy and defeat, that made Billie great—that put the vibrance of suffering, the world of tortured feeling into the blues in which she drowned herself when she sang.

Perhaps it was all that that made her voice, in the very words of the song she herself wrote, "Fine and Mellow."

Billie was born in Baltimore on April 7, 1915, of a father who was a jazz musician and a mother who took in washing—and she later described her home as "just another one-night stand."

At 14, she was on marijuana.

Continued on Page 5

BILLIE HOLIDAY . . . mourned by jazz world.
(UPI Photo)

She made Jazz happen in those days. Her influence is felt today. Moore knew her well.

CHAPTER VI

Management Decision: Sacrificing a Marriage

Tougher decisions were in the making as fights got harder to come by. What with Archie's growing reputation as a classy boxer and two-fisted puncher, managers of champions and top-rated boxers steered clear of him. The moguls of boxing ignored him just as they did other tough Negro boxers, considering them spoilers. Thus boxers like Holman Williams, Charley Burley, Lloyd Marshall, Eddie Booker, Jack Chase, and Archie himself at the top of this cadre of "raging bulls," had to fight each other "round robin" over the years in order to remain active. (Archie, for instance, eventually boxed Jack Chase six times; Billy Smith, six times; Jimmy Bivins, five times; and Lloyd Marshall and Eddie Booker twice each. Needless to say, the fights were colossal; yet beggars or panhandlers might have fared as well on a good day.)

With Felix in California, Archie had been more or less hustling his own fights and, as formerly stated, meeting the same opponents repeatedly. With no shortage of publicity, it was not surprising that he was known by Edley Shipman, a St. Louis insurance man whose interest in boxing included the upward mobility of his son-in-law, Paul Duke, an unseasoned amateur boxer. He wanted Archie to train Paul and for himself to become Archie's manager. The offer of $500 for starters being "big money" to Archie, he contacted Felix in California and obtained his permission to fight in New York.

Not even Robert Ripley would have believed Archie's proneness to mishaps as the Oldsmobile he drove to New York was rammed from the back by a truck. By this time, however, Archie had almost begun to prepare for trouble, and had minutes before reinforced the need to be careful. Did this type him as paranoid? No, not if one knew his past.

Once in New York, it took some doing to find quarters to accommodate their Negro-white mix, but they finally found a hotel which rented them separate rooms overlooking Central Park - one for Shipman and his son-in-law, and one for Archie and, who else but George Porter?

Archie looked good, too good in his gym workouts with Eddie Madler who had fought Joe Louis and Tony Galento; but it was a lesson he learned too late, due to his own indiscretion, as well as Shipman's lack of astuteness as a manager.

The only beneficial thing to come out of that arrangement was that Archie got to fight an exhibition with Paul Duke at the New York World's Fair and he relished the fact that his friend, George Porter, fought on the same card. Following this, they returned to St. Louis.

It was well-timed luck, therefore, to have Felix arrive in St. Louis to attend to the liquidation of his small taxicab business. "I can use the money more profitably in California," he pointed out. "There's Jim Crow there too, but it seems that my wife and I are not as hindered in what we want to do. Here in St. Louis, we're huddled together and there seems to be no out. At least the weather's good in California."

"Tell me about it," laughed Archie, remembering hard times during St. Louis winters. He had never been able to get meaningful work there, although he had been willing to work even before the stealing incident which sent him to reform school. "And had I stayed here," he added, "I might have resorted to a life of crime like some of our buddies did. Without boxing, I'd be in worse shape than I am now. At least there's hope."

"Speaking of which," advanced Felix, "I'm not yet for certain, but I should know by Wednesday if it's a go on a fight with Shorty Hogue in San Diego. He's tough, but I think you can take him."

"One thing I can say about you, Felix," injected Archie, "you're on you J.O.B. Just get'em, and I'll take 'em," he laughed.

After confirmation of the match with Hoague, Archie and Felix prepared for the long road to California and again along for the ride was the signifying, George Porter. To have heard them along the way would reveal their genuine admiration for one another and their mutual reverence for boxing. They literally fed off each other, but in the most positive sense.

Not even the inability to use public restrooms where they bought gas nor lack of places to get decent food deterred them. They settled instead for raw vegetables, fruit, stale bread and pop. It was just as well; for with three drivers, there was no need to stop for rest.

Once in San Diego, Archie began preparing for his fight of December 21, 1939, with Shorty Hogue, a tough and scrappy puncher. Archie had, however, beaten tougher fighters than Hoague and had won some ninety percent of his fights, mainly by knockout. Though he lost this six-round competition by decision, he felt he'd actually won, a conviction which helped him feel better about the loss and made him train even harder.

"This sure ain't St. Louis," quipped George Porter, as he and Archie ran along a scenic San Diego road, perspiring in the warm weather... "kind of hard to get the Christmas spirit with no snow," he puffed, as he admired breathtakingly beautiful foliage and blooming plants in the month of December.

Archie was not thinking about the season, however, nor the flowers or their beauty. He was caught up in the youthful excitement and rekindling of his love affair and eventual marriage on January 4, 1940, to pretty Mattie Chapman, the girl who came to his dressing room after his stunning upset of Johnny Romero.

"I've got a place for us to live downtown on Market Street, Mattie. It's only one room, but it's all we can afford right not, honey," he told her as he lovingly embraced her and ran his big palm down the small of her back.

The ecstasy was to be short-lived, however, as the opportunity for challenge reentered through Jack Richardson, a car dealer in downtown San Diego. Though he touted himself as a former fighter of note, Richardson had been but a pug of scant skills; yet he had maintained his contacts and had literally pestered Archie after every fight in San Diego to let him be his manager.

"Moore," he boasted - "why, I can promote you into matches that will land you the championship. I know the fight game and I know the politics. Now your manager is an O.K. guy, but he doesn't know the right people." Well, Archie nor even Felix could argue with this. Despite all of his victories, Archie was still not moving any closer to a championship fight; so for $400, he was bargained for and purchased much as would one of Richardson's used cars.

"Australia, here we come!" Archie announced as he entered their one-room love nest that evening. "What a great place to have our honeymoon, Mattie." She looked at him strangely as he picked her up and swung around like a whirling dervish with her in his arms.

"What on earth are you talking about, Archie? We can hardly afford one room let alone Australia!"

"Well," he joked, "it's not exactly your everyday vacation spot; but its where we're going for my next fight, and soon." And as he made love to her that night, it was with a tenderness promoted by freedom from worry about where his next penny was coming from; for the fights were to net him $2,500. And they talked far into the night, mostly questions from Mattie that Archie couldn't answer; but he asked her to trust him.

Jack had painted a vivid picture of the life "down under". "We'll be leaving in just a week; so get everything ready and say your good--byes," he instructed. "The Australia experience will be a good one for you. It'll charge you up for a world championship back here in the states."

In his state of euphoria, Archie had never remotely considered that Richardson had not included Mattie when he said "we'll be leaving in a week." The excuse given for not taking her along was that sex with a woman tended to weaken a boxer such that he would not perform at his peak.

Since prior to this time he had had no consistent engagements in sex, this seemed logical in the light of his performance; yet Richardson's statement had been made from a purely selfish standpoint.

"If it is the promoters who are paying the passage," Archie reasoned, "why can't I take Mattie anyway? I'd be able to control my own actions as I've always done."

While he later realized that he should have demanded that Mattie go, he had not been in the habit of questioning too much; not even Felix whose experience in boxing had been far less than Richardson's.

To discover later that Richardson was taking his own wife and son vexed him to no end, making it extremely difficult to break the news to Mattie. He felt like a heel, despite their mutual awareness of a boxer's having to go where the fights were; yet actually having to do it tore at his insides. "Leaving here is painful... like failing to tense my stomach before a belt to the middle. I wasn't prepared for this, Mattie, but somehow, I will send for you!" he vowed to her. And he repeated this at the dock in San Pedro, California, after embracing her one last time, savoring the now familiar scent of the perfume she wore on her ear lobes. He kissed her all over, not caring about who on the dock stared at him. And as he walked up the gang plank, he stamped the vision in his memory; for he would need to retrieve it often during the twenty-one day trip to Sydney, Australia.

Though Archie would have a lot of time to think and regret and admonish himself for not taking a stand, he displayed no hostility toward Richardson; though it was difficult, especially when he saw Richardson strolling with his wife on deck or sharing dinner with her and his son. Though he fraternized with them at times, he was often isolated by "white folks talk." It seemed they would go on and on about trivia. Without the interest and inclination to concentrate, he often fell asleep, much to the irritation of Mrs. Richardson.

"Well," he concluded, "there's one thing I know about cruises; they're meant for the rich. You've got to work hard at doing nothing!" So with little else to do besides listen to the trivia, eat, (and he knew he'd have to watch his weight), and sleep, he began on his first night aboard ship to do something he liked doing.... It was writing:

January 7, 1940

My Darling Mattie,

How can I explain my feelings when I'm a whole day and already hundreds of miles away. I can't even explain why things turned out the way they did. The only thing I can explain is my feeling for you, Mattie. My leaving you, my wife of a few days, doesn't mean I don't love you, honey, because I do; but boxing is also part of my life. I guess I'm a little like a mountain climber. Because I know the top is there, I want to reach it even if I have to strain every muscle and fall a few times. But I want you to stay in there with me, Mattie, just as we were on our last night together. Help me dream, Mattie, and I know it will come out all right.

Yours always,

Archie

He wrote to her almost every night of the trip and was prompted to write others near and dear as he experienced things which he wanted to share with them. After Pago Pago and Hawaii, he wrote to Felix since he didn't feel Auntie would like hearing about women who went around bare-breasted, covered only from the hips by the traditional lava-lava.

"Well Felix, I'm on the way to the "continent down under" and, as you know, it's my first experience aboard a ship. At first, it was a bit boring, but stops in between have begun to make it interesting. We docked in Hawaii, Pago Pago and the Samoan Islands and, boy, is it hot and humid!... drizzles every five minutes with sun after every drizzle. It kind of makes me have highs and lows because I see happy people together and I miss my wife and friends.

Boy, these Samoans are really big people and they don't leave much to the imagination either. They dress lightly for the weather. The muscles in their legs and arms are something to see. I'd hate to meet one of them in the ring (smile).

Give my regards to your wife. I'll keep you posted.

Archie

By the Fiji Island, he was prompted to write the impressionable George Porter:

Hey George,

It's me - Archie, coming to you from the Fiji Islands and wishing you were here to see this. The people here look so much like some of us Negroes, it isn't funny; but they are called Melanesians. They have a language of their own and they also speak English quite well.

At first they looked odd to me because of the way they fork their hair with a little comb causing it to stand straight up, making a six foot man with two feet of hair look gigantic. It's a sight to see a hairdo resembling a huge ball of black cotton candy... and even the kids are a smaller version of the "giants" - hair and all. But I guess I must have looked funny to them too with my combination of "gassed", straightened hair and dark skin. It's funny George, how we often follow suit, trying to look and act like what we're not; but I guess the real me came through even with my "gas." As I think of it now, George, boxers who have worn the "gas" in their hair might have received eye injuries if the stuff from the hair ran into their eyes when they perspired. I have nothing to prove it, but I often wonder why, aside from being hit in the eyes, quite a few Negro boxers have lost their sight. In any event, boxing should look at the whole picture to make it a safer sport.

Now, as I was saying, these people worship Joe Louis and when they found out I was a boxer, they made a celebrity out of me. They took only me to their village and I ate and danced with them and enjoyed every bit of the attention.

You wouldn't believe this, George, but there was one man in the village who had both arms bitten off at the shoulders by a shark and he still managed to swim ashore. He was one of the great shark hunters as are many of the Melanesian men. And he still shows courage. He feeds himself by eating directly from a dish and makes his feet and legs double as arms and hands. It convinces me even more that anybody can succeed if they have the guts. It's only when a man considers himself handicapped that he becomes so. What about "Wingy" Mannone, a New Orleans musician who first played kazoo and then a trumpet with one arm? As I think back, I read where he lost his arm at nine years old, trying to hitch a ride on a trolley; but by age twelve, he had become famous, playing on the streets of Storyville, red light district where jazz was allegedly born. He later became widely known on records, in films and books. Now, I ask you, was that guts?

I haven't the slightest doubt that it also takes guts for Melanesians to hunt sharks with just a knife; also it takes real determination to shinny up a tree to get a coconut and slit it open with that same knife just to give me a drink. Their effort honored me, not to mention giving me the tastiest drink I've ever had. You'd never believe it, George, to see the hard muscle-like callouses which have developed on the sides of their large feet as a result of climbing the rough trees; but they wouldn't remove them since they actually aid in climbing. They also fed me a paste from taro root which they prepared in large caldrons. And you know me, George, I wondered whether they had boiled some of the white explorers in those same pots (smile).

Before leaving, they made me dance with them to a kind of native music played on stringed instruments. It sounded a little like some of the Dixieland jazz (minus brass) and lively rhythms we used to hear played by Negroes along the railroad tracks in St. Louis.

As the length of my letter should tell you, I experienced a lot in two hours and I hated to leave when it was time for me to return to the ship. You know, George, when you look at it, people are not really so different after all.

Your friend,

Archie

At Auckland, New Zealand, the last large port stop before Sydney, passengers disembarked and tried to duck the raindrops as they souvenir hunted in the shops patronized mainly by tourists. Here, Archie purchased small trinkets for Mattie and for Auntie Willie to whom he wrote:

Dearest Auntie,

I know you've been worried about me but I'm in good hands. Here on my ship, the Monterey, I've become quite a celebrity. Though not a Tiger Flowers yet, I'm getting there (smile).

We just stopped in a place called Auckland, New Zealand, where the natives are called the Maori people. They were here before the coming of the white men, but are now dominated by them. This situation is a little like the lesson you showed me from that old history book of Uncle Cleve's, about Columbus and how he found people he called Indians, living in America when he discovered the land.

You know, Auntie, I don't know if I ever told you this, but my fifth grade teacher really thought I was smart when I was able to tell her all about the Indians before she even taught it to the class. As a matter of fact, I also told her that you had taught me about how our state got its name and about the Missouri Indians who lived along the river at one time. They're all gone now though.

I think about you often, Auntie, and it makes me feel proud to have you as my mother and teacher. You did a good job!

Your Nephew,

Archie Lee

P.S. I bought a little Maori basket for you today in a New Zealand shop. I'll bring it when I return to the states.

Moore aboard the Monterey, bound for strange lands.

Archie Moore, Elusive Customer—
Weaves, Ducks And Parries Punches

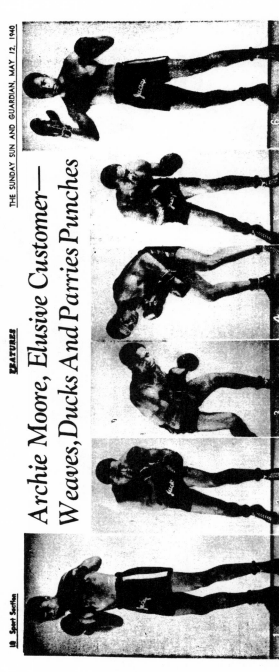

Put yourself in the place of fellows who fight Moore. Supposing you were sparring up to him, what would you do in this case?

(1) He has both gloves cocked for a punch. Is he going to lead with a left? Or, maybe, he will whizz over his right? (2) Huh! Tricked you that time. He didn't lead his left, and he didn't whirl his right. He bobbed to get a shot at the body. Looks like a left shooting for the old solar plexus. What are you going to do about it?

(3) Here it comes. Yell for the police. It won't be long now. That one made you gasp like a stranded swordfish. Flash back a right cross counter. (4) Too late. Archie has weaved over to the right. Now have a cut with your pet left hook, and make sure you don't miss. That right hand looks like doing something terrible if you don't time your punch. What difference, anyway. If you land it Moore doesn't mind. He says it's fun taking a punch.

(5) So now, what? Archie's coming straight at you, crouched. Bang a straight left at him. Hit him between the eye, with a straight right. That ought to knock him back on his heels. And then cover up your body, because if you don't, you're going to feel as ill as a kid after a Christmas party. You can see that those two arms bent for a body attack mean business. (6) Get Joe Wallis to give Moore a i.k.o. win. What's the good of fighting a man whom you think is going to weave all the while and then stand up like this and nearly bounce your head off your shoulders with a left jab. No good honking at him. That rigid right forearm will catch your glove. Throw in the towel and call it a night.

Archie Moore, early recognized as a great Scientific Boxer. Photographed in Sidney, Australia.

CHAPTER VII

Jack Johnson's Australia: The Proving Ground

As the Monterey entered Sydney Harbour, Archie took note of the identically red-tiled roofs of houses which dotted the land. As he beheld this impressive sight, he readied his passport for the walk down the gang-plank to meet the waiting promoters and matchmakers. Absent, however, were the "Members of the Fourth Estate" or newsmen who had no knowledge of the existence of Archie Moore.

"Hmm," he thought in response to a deflated ego, "they should have seen me on that island!" He fully realized however, that he was to the promoters a little like cargo as they delivered him to King's Cross or downtown Sydney. His hotel was in the shopping district near the center of town where there was a busy hive of people - whores, thieves, hustlers and seamen - all feeding off each other in this sin city.

"I wonder," he thought with a tinge of sarcasm, "how Richardson and his family are enjoying Bondi Beach?" It was miles away from where Archie lived, away from urban stress. The location of his own abode did have its merits when he thought about it. It was not too far from the gym; but more importantly, it was located a few blocks from historic Sydney Stadium where the great Jack Johnson, first Negro heavyweight champion of the world, knocked out Tommy Burns (also known as Noah Brusso). This nearness to greatness gave an ambitious Archie Moore a stimulating feeling of warmth and pride.

"Let Richardson watch the sharks," he quipped, as he left the window of what he sportingly called his "historic hovel." "Everything seems to be falling into place," he reflected, "except for this cold I've gone and got." He guessed it might have been due to walking in the rain at his last port stop before Sydney. As a result, the scheduled fights had to be rescheduled while he recuperated from his severe cold, resting and thinking of Mattie. He wondered if she had received his letters.

When he got better, he began to venture out and decided to tour the city, a place in which he least expected to see familiar faces. But there across the street from him were two suavely-dressed Negroes. He recognized them instantly, not to mention happily. They were two fighters from the states who had been in Australia for a year - one Johnny Hutchinson, an accomplished little featherweight out of Philadelphia and Al Brown, a bantamweight and stablemate of Johnny's. Though a division apart in weight, they were sparring partners and also shared an apartment to which they invited Archie.

"You fellas are like Fric and Frac," Archie teased, as Al cooked a down home meal, dancing even as he peeled potatoes.

"... you ever try any of that in the ring?" Archie joshed as he watched this slightly built man exhibit the grace and moves of a Bill Robinson or a Fred Astaire. "This is the trouble," he thought, "there are so many Negro hopefuls whose greatness is never realized" (or like Bojangles, realized long after he had drunk himself to death, having danced prior to his tragic death in honkey-tonks and taverns throughout southern counties and towns in America).

Archie's contributions to the festivities with his new friends were a few records he had brought with him, one of which they played and enjoyed well into the night. It was "Jumpin Jive" by Cab Calloway and it was an unusually hilarious sight to behold the three pugilists, jabbing and punching at air, bobbing and weaving to the rhythm of the great master of song.

Luck later found Archie moving to another apartment nearer to Al and Johnny thus abandoning with some nostalgia his lonely abode. It was good to have the collegial support which the three boxers enjoyed, because it was a racist Australia to which they had come; yet they were no strangers, given the prejudices and isolation experienced back home.

To have read headlines in Australia or back in the states that, for instance, the Mills Brothers or great tenor singer, Bob Parish, were well received promoted a false image of Australian policies. In fact, acceptance of Negroes into Australia had to do with the fact that they were celebrities or dignitaries. This resulted in a distortion at both ends; for Australians were led to believe the status of Negro visitors was indicative of the respect and privileges accorded most if not all Negroes in America.

Archie had thus begun in this his first visit to a foreign country, to extend his eleventh grade education with the world as his classroom, delving deeply into fields of sociology and psychology. He thoroughly understood if not accepted why Danny LaVerne, another boxer who worked out daily at the gym, had refused to identify with the three Negro boxers and join in their bull sessions; especially since with a Negro father, he was by social definition, a Negro.

"I'm hardly Negro at all," he said one day when they were in the shower room and had gotten into a conversation having racial overtones. "My mother was Hawaiian, and that makes me Hawaiian," he claimed. He even made a concerted effort to live on the other side of town theoretically removed from his Negroidness. Danny, like so many misguided Negroes, little realized that such an attitude perpetuated racism as well as the strategy of divide and conquer.

Archie remembered how the group had tried to bring Danny around, but to no avail. Not even the mutual admiration that he and Archie had for their respective skills compensated for the perceived differences. While Archie admired Danny's style and class, Danny was captivated by Archie's hard-hitting, two-fisted, Joe Louis style of punching, coupled with a mimicry of Jack Dempsey's bob and weave. Archie wondered long after that experience whether Danny ever realized or, more importantly, *accepted* his racial group identity before being killed in world War II. He was a gallant fighter.

Days at the gym and nights in the bull sessions went on for about a week while Archie settled into his routine in Australia. He knew that if he trained hard, this was an excellent place to preen himself for a championship because Australians were avid fight fans and great gamblers.

In due time, Richardson lined up a fight with Ron Richards, who held the middleweight *and* heavyweight titles of Australia and for good reason. His tremendous punch could blast an opponent out of the ring in nothing flat.

"... think you can take him on?" Richardson asked slyly.

"Certainly," Archie shot back, "especially if I can condition myself properly. I need more opportunity to work out in open spaces, to smell clean, invigorating air," he said with a tinge of sarcasm.

Richardson acquiesced by hiring a trainer, a Jewish man by the name of Ike Kutner - no better choice for Archie; for what Ike wanted more than anything was to produce a winner. As a war veteran on pension, he was not looking at training as a living and this made all the difference.

Richardson established a camp at a ranch in the Megalong Valley where there were sheep and cow herders, and where people came to relax, to eat scones and drink tea. Archie was to live on the ranch with the Baptiste family and they treated him royally. He escaped from the monotony of training each day by riding into the "bush" with Bill and Red, two of the rancher's young sons who idolized him.

Roadwork extended seven miles daily from the Megalong Valley, or what the Aussies called the "bush", up a winding road to the closest town of Black Heath which had an elevation of 7,000 feet. Needless to say, the crisp, sweet morning air was exhilarating and the solitude thought provoking, giving impetus to images of Mattie. In that Archie could not change what had happened, he had the wisdom to know that he would have to defer his feelings so as not to sink into depression. So he trained furiously and even chopped wood while focusing on the money he'd make to send Mattie, of how they'd go into some kind of small business and eventually raise a family.

Sometimes, he'd drown his sorrows in ice cream which he purchased from the store at the top of the hill. He'd eat a scoop of each flavor, six in all, and then compensate for it by running and working it off with push-ups at night. Such attributes - his strong convictions and adaptability - were to become a permanent part of Archie Moore, the man and the boxer.

The age-old argument of heredity versus environment would likely receive a lively workout in the case of the beginnings and trials of Archie Moore. The kinds of problems which plagued him would likely discourage the average individual; yet he persisted in overcoming problems such as loneliness, poverty, racism, exclusion from title fights and ... WEIGHT!

It was while training in the Megalong Valley that he noticed the habits of the Aborigines, original inhabitants of Australia. They were in commune with nature though not the ruling class, treated much as Negroes in America though they were not so enslaved.

Aborigines shared their space with the kangaroos, wallabies and rabbits, the latter of which were so plentiful that the natives and others killed them for the ten pence bounty they would bring. With the proceeds, they bought *only what they needed*. This was the secret of their success at survival and the approach that Archie would direct to his problem of taking off weight: "Eat only what you need." This became his guiding principle.

He had seen one aborigine in the bush chewing on strips of meat, swallowing the juice and spitting out the bulk; yet he seemed healthy, though lean, and made long trips into the bush with no water or food.

"I decided I'd try it," he later told a reporter who inquired as to how he had brought down his weight by fifteen pounds in the span of a couple of weeks. He wanted to know why when he fought Jack McNamee, a six-foot-two-inch youngster with a furious jab, he showed no signs of weakness during that bout of March 30, 1940,in Melbourne, Australia.

"Well," Archie quipped, "it certainly wasn't epsom salts. I tried that once in a fight against Billy Sims and he almost "kilt" me. I was so weak, I could hardly answer the bell. Had I not knocked him out early in the round, I could have lost the fight." Then he told the reporter about the diet of the Aborigines.

"You might know the reporter didn't believe me," he snickered, "but as they say, 'the proof of the meat is in the chewing'. It worked for me and that's what counts!"

When the fight with champion Ron Richards finally came, Archie felt he was ready for the throng of 15,000 fans who had seen him dispose of McNamee in four, but had also seen Richards make jelly of Lesnervich. Archie relished the knowledge because Lesnervich had formerly refused to give him a fight and a chance at the championship.

The mutual ominousness of the fighters had obviously created an anxiety which had been additionally inflated by the press. They even played it up by suggesting that the two fighters were feuding; yet Richards turned out to be one of the cleanest fighters Archie had met. "He was clean and gentlemanly," he would later share with his trainer, Kutner... "and he caught me off guard."

"I literally stared up at red, white, blue, yellow and purple stars as I sprawled on the canvas where he flattened me... and would you believe in the first minute of the first round! And then hearing the boos of the crowd and the cries, 'FAKE!' 'FAKE!', jarred me a bit too! There was nothing fake about the punch that exploded in my head though," he later told another columnist "and it was all I could do to hang on, covering and clinching until my head cleared. I knew I had to save my reputation as a boxer."

"By the third round, I felt my head had cleared and I began to move in with blows to his face, slowing him down a bit. And by round seven, I knew I had him, and even before the tenth round when the fans yelled, 'STOP THE FIGHT!' 'STOP THE FIGHT' The referee declared me the victor by tapping me on the head."

Though no title was at stake in that fight, Archie had succeeded in becoming a big name in Australia as well as internationally. His reputation as a courageous fighter was established when the Sydney newspapers featured a picture of him on the canvas topped by the headline: "ARCHIE MOORE GETS OFF THE FLOOR TO STOP RICHARDS!"

Yes, he stopped Richards in ten; Sabatino in five; Delaney in seven; Lindsay in four; and Henneberry in seven; all by knockout, and all within a span of three months, an uncommon feat in the annals of boxing.

When the rematch with Richards was scheduled for July 11, 1940, in Ruschcutter's Bay Stadium, the place of the initial match, Archie was ready and taking no chances at being caught off guard this time; but he deviated from a procedure which could have caused him to lose the fight. He let Kutner tape his hands, a ritual he usually reserved for himself, and though he realized the tape was too tight, the fight was ready to begin and he felt he could manage.

By the second round, he had broken his left hand, forcing him to fake left jabs and rely on his right. Ultimately, he won the fight in a twelve round decision, bluffing his way, fighting one-handedly, a feat, which when made public, raised him even higher in the esteem of the Aussies and internationally.

Oddly enough, when some might have capitalized on the momentum, he wanted to go home; for thoughts of Mattie still filled his mind. He wondered why he had not heard from her?

Picture taken in 1940 shows Moore, who was even then carefully avoided by the champions and top contenders, with his manager Jack Richardson.

Archie Moore and trainer, Ike Kutner. What Ike wanted most was to produce a winner.

U.S. Boxer Moore "Too Good For Own Good"

The colored American middleweight, Archie Moore, who fights Ron Richards at Sydney Stadium tomorrow night week, is known as "the boy who was too good for his own good."

His manager (Jack Richardson) emphasises that this has no reference to the fact that Archie is a Sunday school teacher in his home town.

The following anecdote, published recently in an American journal, gives point to it.

Jack Kearns, who was Jack Dempsey's manager, and was the "big shot" behind the late Tex Rickard, met Mickey Walker, ex-middleweight champion, one day in Broadway.

"I'm thinking of making a comeback," said Walker.

"O.K.," replied Kearns. "What about taking on that sucker, Archie Moore?"

Walker assented, but later was told that every time Moore came to town Fred Apostoli left on a holiday.

Walker did not make a comeback.

Of course, hundreds of American fighters in Australia have claimed to have been starved out of world titles. But this story is not from Moore's scrap-book.

It was cut from an American journal by Charles Lucas when he was in America, for his own book of records. Moore is not connected with Lucas.

Little To Say

Archie Moore speaks cultured English—when he speaks.

He has been here six weeks, and has scarcely spoken a word to a single boxing writer.

His manager (Jack Richardson) is gifted with a similar reticence, but says that Moore is a better puncher than Richards.

Nobody has yet seen Moore in a gymnasium tryout.

He has been at Megalong Valley cutting logs, running behind horses, throwing boulders over the mountain side, and performing other "he-man" tasks to acclimatise himself.

He will return to Sydney tomorrow, but it is not expected that Ron Richards will leave on an extended holiday.

Richards no doubt is thinking of buying another row of suburban cottages with the takings from his fight with Moore.

In the past 12 months he has been investing his money in property. He earned £5000 in the past year.

Archie Moore is 23 years old. He was born in St. Louis, Missouri, in the same neighborhood as Henry Armstrong.

His idol as a boy was Kid Chocolate, the Cuban Bon Ton.

Early in his life Archie showed a liking for boxing, but his ma wanted him to be a minister of the Gospel.

Secret Ambition

Archie did not like to shock her, so every time his idol fought he went to a neighbor's home, and listened in to the radio broadcast of Kid Chocolate's fight.

Every penny he had was spent on pictures of Kid Chocolate, and, like every enthusiastic kiddie, he assimilated the stance and mannerisms of his idol.

It was hero worship which later played its part in developing the boxing instincts of Moore.

Moore's record as a boxer is imposing. He knocked out Johnny Romero, rated fourth in the light-heavyweight division.

He knocked out Dominic Ceccarelli, who had just previously lost on points to John Henry Lewis and Billy Conn, present light-heavyweight champion of the world.

Records of American fights do not mean a great deal now in Australia, because fighters like Richards and Henneberry have never had any trouble in beating American middleweights in Australia.

But there does seem to be a reason to respect the ability of Archie Moore.

A close-up of his ability will be provided this week when he begins to box in the gymnasium.

Q'LAND FIGHTER AT CARLTON

On Wednesoday night at Carlton, Bobby Lee, an aggressive fighter from Queensland, will meet Bill Hebberd.

Supporting fights: Mick Goldstein v. Dick Shephers, Bluey Hassan v. Bill Godfrey, Jack Marshall v. Ces. Fossey.

On Thursday night at Leichhardt, Joe Hall will meet Frank Farrington.

No fight will take place at Sydney Stadium tomorrow night.

Archie Moore was respected but avoided.

DAILY☉NEWS

Phones—Head Office: FL2631. Newcastle Office: Newcastle 1696, 1697. Corrimal: 127.

PRICE 2d.

Registered at the G.P.O., Sydney, for transmission by post as a newspaper.

SYDNEY: FRIDAY, APRIL 19, 1940.

Vol. 2, No. 433.

WHAT THE STARS SAY
on page 8

GERMANS STILL HOLD NARVIK

Stir In Hotel
Australia

MAN SHOT DEAD

Henry George Woods, 48, a city hairdresser, was found shot dead in a room in the Hotel Australia last night.

A pea-rifle with a discharged cartridge in the breech was found beside the body.

The tragedy was discovered by a maid at the hotel who, with the American wife of Woods, lived in his flat. Elizabeth Bay Road, Elizabeth Bay, and engaged the room at the hotel yesterday morning.

Found By Maid

He was seen about the hotel during the day. His body was found by a maid when she went to his room at 5.30 p.m.

Woods left his flat yesterday morning appeared to be in good spirits. He told his wife he was going to arrange the purchase of a hairdressing business.

Police found a number of notes in the pockets of Woods' clothes.

Woods and his family returned to Sydney a few months ago after a holiday trip to California.

6500 CANADIAN SEAMEN STRIKE

TORONTO, Thursday.

Our Own Cable Service.

Six thousand five hundred Canadian seamen plying the Great Lakes area have gone on strike.

A.I.F. Sister And Mascot

Australian Sisters in Palestine have made a gazelle their mascot. Sister I. McIntosh, who has been assisting with the animal's toilet, is on the best of terms with the new mascot. (Department of Information photograph).

BRITISH FIGHT FIERCELY TO RECAPTURE ROMBAK

Our Own Cable Service.

LONDON, Thursday.

GERMAN forces are still in control of the city of Narvik, in North-west Norway, according to reports received here.

This report comes surprisingly on the heels of other messages during the past days of the landing in Narvik of large contingents of British troops and violent attacks on German vessels in Narvik Fiord by the British Navy.

In an effort to hem in the Germans, entrenched on each side of Narvik Fiord, the British are stated to be attacking fiercely. Their main hope at the moment is to regain Rombak Heights, which the Norwegians, after a valiant defence, were forced to give up to the invaders.

An agency message from Sweden late to-night said that the Allies are now only 12 miles from Narvik. It claims that the landing of Allied troops in Norway was carried out in six hours, the transports immediately leaving the shores so that

Latest Cables

Claims Bremen Sunk

Our Own Cable Service.

LONDON, Thursday.

Engvard J. Olsen, a survivor of the British steamer Stancliffe, which was torpedoed by the Nazis, claims that he was aboard a German submarine when the Captain disclosed that the liner Bremen, carrying 15,000 troops, was sunk in Norwegian waters by a bomb from a Royal Air Force plane.

Big Battle

LONDON.—According to a correspondent in the Svenske Dagbladet, a Swedish paper published close to the Norwegian border, a big battle is imminent near Trondheim.

The correspondent reports that British troops are massed there and that there is considerable German activity in the area, German troops being transported there by air.

Deutschland Aground.

LONDON.—It is reported from Stockholm that the German pocket-battleship Deutschland, which has been reported, is aground off the Norwegian coast.

Archie Moore, after the fight last night with Ron Richards, which Moore won on a technical knock-out in the tenth round. (Further pictures back page. Full story back page.)

Weather Report—

"Snow on the Mountains"—

Turkish Fleet

Constable Alex Brown, 62, who was shot in the head at his home in York Street, Forest Lodge, about half an hour after Mrs. Jean Brown, 25, herself was wounded in the Royal Prince Alfred Hospital. Constable Brown, who is dying in Royal Prince Alfred Hospital, said that Mrs. Brown, his daughter, who was married to him, shot him on Tuesday night, and day. Brown has a bullet wound in the head, and another in the chest, which caused almost total paralysis. Early this morning, his condition was extremely grave.

UNI. HONORS RESULTS

HONORS results in the Faculties of Arts, Law, and Science, results in the Faculty of Architecture will be published in "The Daily News" to-morrow.

CHAPTER VIII

Together Again: Rebirth of a Family

During 1940, Hitler was at war with the allies and the world was watchful. United States citizens had been ordered home and Richardson had already taken his family back plus all but $800 of the $2500 contracted for the fights. Though Archie realized that fight purses were impacted with big expenses, he felt his share to be little to show for seven fights and a superior performance. Then too, his ambivalent feelings about what was fair were strongly tempered with Richardson's earlier refusal to have Mattie with him in Australia. What was more settling to him was that he had left a rousing reputation in Australia, one which would stand for many years.

He left again on the Monterey which went through Tahiti this time because of the danger from submarines; but it was an exotic and exciting experience. There were bare-breasted dancing girls in sarongs giving a warm and festive welcome, made even warmer, no doubt, by the value of the American dollar by contrast with the French franc.

Aboard ship were dime slot machines which Archie was not at all tempted to play with his blood money; but he was content to watch as Fighting Carlos tried his luck. Carlos had outlived his usefulness in Australia since opponents like Al, Johnny, and Danny LaVerne had left thus giving him no worthy opponents. Evenso, Carlos had seen his best days.

"Perhaps he thinks his luck will change," Archie surmised, as he observed Carlos change $100 of the $400 he had into dimes. Two hours later when Archie returned from the shower after an exhilarating game of handball with several entertainers, he found Carlos welded to the same spot. He had lost all of his money!

"Man," he complained, in his non-standard dialect, "I lose it... all four hundred." Then he took out his frustrations on the machine as though it were an opponent, hitting it with a hand that had become swollen after more than four thousand pulls on the handle.

With knowledge of the impending arrival of the Monterey and its boxing passengers, promoters in Tahiti arranged to have a main event bout between their local champion and Fighting Carlos, chosen because he was the least likely of the boxers to win. In view of his injured hand, Archie was to participate as a second for Carlos; anyway, there were no professional fighters of Archie's caliber on the island.

Round after round, he watched as Carlos took an unmerciful beating from his sober opponent. Carlos, you see, had ill-advisedly entered the ring thoroughly pickled.

After the fifth round, Archie refused to permit the well-lumped challenger to brave the sixth, though knowing that the crowd wanted to see it fought to a bloody finish. They wanted to see their champion flatten the tough, Fighting Carlos; yet theoretically, he had been flattened. He was left flat broke by the promoters who, disappointed by meager gate receipts, had absconded with the money.

Once the fight was over and he had nursed Carlos to bed, Archie decided to take a tour of Papeete, capital of Tahiti. As he strolled into the local bar, he was instantly recognized and swarmed by sailors in the bar who wanted to meet him. In that he was a tee-totaler, he didn't stay long, and as he attempted to leave, one of the sailors presented him with his own French beret as a token of his esteem.

Scarcely a block later, he was confronted by another group of not-so-friendly sailors (and not so sober either). One of them pointed to him, accusing him of having stolen the hat and an argument ensued, bringing into the melee a Tahitian arbitrator. His demand that Archie relinquish the hat was backed up by his 6 foot 4, 250 pound physique.

Realizing that he was outnumbered, not to mention impeded by his left hand, Archie repositioned himself as the "peacemaker" attempted to snatch the hat from his head. With a sharp right, he sprawled the aggressor out onto the sandy street; but to the rescue came the buddy of the peacemaker with an attempted kick to the groin. That futile effort was answered by Archie with a right to the whiskers of the buddy, dropping him in his tracks.

Between the two friends and the belt-buckle-welding French sailors, Archie kept quite busy defending himself, bobbing and weaving to avoid the deadly sabat kicks of the Tahitian style of street fighting.

It was a welcome turn of events to be rescued by another dozen or so of very rough Tahitians who, recognizing the imbalance, jumped into the free-for-all. One of them even escorted Archie out of the mob and back to the ship docked about three blocks away. And as he looked back, he could see the French sailors being outpointed by the Tahitians, making him feel quite fortunate to have escaped with only a few nicks and bruises.

At breakfast the next morning, he avoided Fighting Carlos in that he didn't want to talk about fighting so as not to remind Carlos of his own brush with near extinction the night before. He decided to keep his bout with the French navy to himself.

As Carlos ambled over to Archie's table, his bloodshot eyes and hangdog expression signalled that he was anything but on top of the world.

"How much Carlos?," Archie asked with an all-knowing look. (Once the ship docked in Honolulu, Carlos would change to a boat bound for Manila and he would need money to get from port by jitney to his up-country home some twenty-five miles away.)

"Will fifty do?" Archie whispered, as he passed the bills under the table so as to put his already downtrodden colleague at ease? He knew full well that he would never get the money back; yet this was the code of ethics among boxers. They were like nomads of the desert, where to refuse a man a drink or other assistance in time of need could sentence him to a tragic fate.

Well, the fifty dollars sure revived Carlos too, and as he palmed it, his gaze became fixed on Archie's bruises, nicks and scratches. "Hey man," he wanted to know,"what happen?"

"Oh, there's this woman I met last night," Archie grinned, "but I'm too ashamed to talk about it." And they broke into extended laughter, hitting the table and pointing out each other's battle scars until both were in tears.

At the last small port, Archie sacrificed more of his hard-won purse to purchase a bottle of expensive perfume for Mattie. He wanted so much for her to know what she meant to him during the eight months he'd been gone. He wondered whether she had received his last letter announcing his return to the states.

As the appointed day arrived, he could hardly contain himself, craning his neck to see if he could spot her as the boat pulled into the dock at San Pedro, California.

There she was, standing on the dock next to Richardson and his family. She wore a brilliant yellow dress which literally advertised the cafe au lait tones in her skin, and the neck of the dress was cut just low enough to provoke wonder; yet eight months had not dulled his memory about the shape and feel of her body. "Oh, Mattie," he uttered lovingly as he pulled her to him, "I've missed you so much."

"Ow-w!", she complained as his cast brushed her arm. "Honey, I'm sorry," he apologized while rubbing her arm and, in so doing, a tide of passion rose within him. As he held her close, he could feel her stiffen as though she resented it.

Her reaction cut like a knife and he remained speechless until Richardson, whom he had completely forgotten, broke in with, "Well, are you glad to be back?... How is Harry Miller?... Do you think they'll close Sydney Stadium now that the American calling cards are gone?" Richardson was referencing the war and the summoning home of Americans in Australia.

"Yea, un huh," Archie replied thoughtlessly without looking at the questioner, though he meant no disrespect. His gaze was on Mattie as he tried desperately to hide his disappointment at her lukewarm greeting.

"What's the matter, honey," he inquired? "Come on, tell me about it," he urged.

"Well, I've been sick, Archie," she finally gave in. "I had to have an operation."

"Operation... Operation?" he repeated, sounding like a needle stuck on a blues record. "So why didn't you write and tell me about it?"

"I asked my sister to write you," she explained. "I went to visit her in Arizona and got real sick, and besides," she added in an obviously sarcastic tone, "I didn't want to spoil your fun."

"Fun, fun!" said the broken record. "Heck, I was working hard to make a future for us and, sure, there may have been some fun along the way; but had you let me know you were sick, I'd have left everything and you know it, Mattie! Didn't we both agree that we'd need to put up with certain things in order for me to win the championship, Mattie! Well, didn't we?" Archie insisted. She followed up with a slight nod and a weak smile and allowed him to place his good arm around her shoulders and walk over to Richardson's sleek new, 1940, navy-blue Ford parked on the street near the dock.

As they rode along headed for Mattie's family's home, she and Archie in the back seat, she was virtually silent as he began to answer all of Richardson's questions and even volunteer information to fill the void.

Mattie's family was also less than enthusiastic which Archie could accept given the circumstances; so more than ever, he didn't want them to view him as a burden. In a half-ton, borrowed pick-up truck, he went grocery shopping with Mattie. With the cost of staples such as eggs at .19 per dozen, and bread at two loaves for .11, the truck was packed solid after spending $35.

While Mattie and her sisters put the groceries away, Archie conversed with her brothers about Australia. When he could control his anxiety no longer, he went to his wife, encircled her waist and asked, "Mattie, let's get a hotel room tonight, honey, so we can be alone; besides, I don't want to crowd your family."

"Oh, I don't think that's necessary," she assured, "there's a place out in back where we can sleep. There's plenty of room."

She then headed for the kitchen and one-by-one, each family member followed, not once offering Archie, the provider, to join them. "Well, that let's me know how welcome I am!" he fretted, and left the house to buy something to eat.

He went to the nearby corner of 30th and Webster to a short-order stand owned by Jim Washington, where he drowned his sorrows in two, foot-long hot dogs, a bowl of chili, and two root beers. Hopping on the stool next to him was the owners son, "J.J. Wash," about fourteen years old, and already idolizing boxing and Archie. (He later became a professional at age sixteen when in high school, winning six straight fights as a welterweight.) Archie remained with his admirer at the food stand, sharing chatter with him until closing time. When he returned home, Mattie had gone to the back house. He went to where she was....

The next morning found him engrossed in a search for a place where they could be alone; yet even this turned sour in that it was not far away enough and Mattie spent as much time at her family's home as she had before. When after a couple of days he had not seen her, he went to her house and was informed by one of her sisters that she was living in Los Angeles.

Driving a van purchased from a bread company, Archie went to Los Angeles to bring her back. He found the apartment building and a parking space near the corner and proceeded to locate where she was living. Following a knock on the door and no answer, he walked back to the van and waited in hopes that she would come home. He dozed periodically, hypnotized by a steady gaze on the apartment building.

"No wonder she didn't answer!" he said furiously, as the door opened and out of it stepped Mattie and a man in army uniform.

He bounded from the truck and headed toward them, and when he got close enough, he could see Mattie's lips as they formed words of warning to her date: "That's my husband... you'd better go!" Deliberately walking between them, he grasped Mattie's arm and moved her toward the house as the serviceman trooped swiftly away.

His feelings were an admixture of jealousy, anger, and unfulfilled love as he spoke sharply to her the words: "I don't know what kind of game you're playing, Mattie, but whatever it is, I don't like it! Go on inside and get your things together," he commanded, "I'm taking you home!"

"Listen Archie," she attempted to explain.... "I said," demanded a fierce mouth and piercing eyes, "we're going home!" And though they did, Archie knew it was over long before she left again for Arizona after about a week. He was alone again.

In that empty house with little to do besides brood over Mattie and await the healing of his hand, he determined that it was an opportune time to go and get Auntie. Looking after her, a commitment that had been sealed with the death of Uncle Cleve, was one that he took seriously, delaying only because he had been waiting for times to get better.

Auntie's recent letters provided additional reinforcement when she wrote: "I sure wish we were together, Archie. I miss you. June is growing up now and has started to go to school. When she's gone, the house is sure empty. All the old neighbors have moved and the new ones just don't act the same."

"Well, that's all I need to know. I'll drive down and get her and June and by the time I return, I'll be healed and in better shape for fighting," the faithful nephew resolved.

And what a healing it was, for with auntie's arrival, the house itself got a refurbishing and much needed warmth in Mattie's absence. Little June, Rachel's surviving twin daughter, was enrolled by her "Unka Archie" in the second grade of a nearby school. He walked her to school for several weeks to be sure she felt secure and he became quite the psychologist as he "conned" her into feeling confident.

"Boy, would your mother be proud to know how smart you are, June," he would say, "but you're just like her. Do you know that she could remember all of the states and their capitals? We used to play guessing games like, "What is the capital of Missouri? And she'd say, 'Jefferson City'... and California?... she'd say 'Sacramento'! Rachel would always say them faster than I could," Archie exclaimed with pretended frustration, an act which brought a smug grin to June's cherub-like face. And this was just what Archie wanted - for her to be proud of her mother, proud enough to want to be like her. By the third week of walking her to and from school, Archie's psychology had produced another positive side effect; because as they walked along, June began to display her new knowledge as she proudly recited: "The capital of Missouri is Jefferson City."

It was a rebirth for Auntie too as she bristled about the kitchen preparing meals and tidying up. And it was like old times again, ordering Archie to the store to get her cure-all personal staples such as Vicks Salve, peppermint candy and snuff, the latter of which was sometimes difficult to find. He also purchased epsom salts and salt which he used in hot soaks to reduce the swelling after removal of the cast from his hand.

One morning as he exercised his hand by squeezing the huge mop to clean the kitchen floor, he answered a rap at the door, smartly registered by a tattered little gnome - like man who peered up at him.

"Hey, Champ," he announced, "I'm Bevo (Be-vo), James Bevo... 'member me?" I'm the trainer for Jimmy McCracklin. Me and my fighter was on our way out here to see ya 'bout gettin' Jimmy started as a pro." Jimmy was then a fairly good middleweight amateur boxer out of St. Louis and, like Archie, had seen his share of lean times.

"Come on in and sit down," Archie invited, knowing from experience as one who had hitched a train ride from time to time, that the stumpy traveler must be famished.

As Bevo shoveled in the bacon and eggs which Archie prepared, he began recounting a very harrowing and familiar experience. "See, me and Jimmy, we hopped a freight train in St. Louis, and before we could get outta Missouri, we got caught by some railroad dicks. Dey took Jimmy to jail... he got two weeks on a work farm pickin' cotton."

"Well, why did they let you go, Bevo?" Archie wanted to know.

"Shucks," he cackled, "I had to put on one of my Uncle Thomas acts dat was hard to beat.... I bowed and scraped and even played cripple ... man, you know I had to be good to con dem peck-a-woods!"

"Yea, man," Archie echoed as a gesture of understanding; for though he had never liked this plantation - type behavior called "tomming", he knew that for some, it was a kind of survival tactic, a fearful and insecure response generated by the institution of racism. And with some, the posture of submissiveness to whites had become so ingrained as to become automatic when in their presence. As one who understood it, he was not about to take on the position of judge over the appropriateness of Bevo's actions.

"I fully understand," Archie chuckled, and they shared the laughter, prescription for a disease over which Black men had little control and are yet struggling to combat.

Becoming more settled now, Bevo laid out his dilemma: "Champ," he confessed, as though not evident, "I'm down to my last ... I ain't got no place to go. You think you could let me sleep on the flo or sup-in?"

"Oh, we can work something out," Archie assured him. Luckily, there was a room buttressed against the building on the side of a hill. Though small, it had cooking and bath facilities... "and jes big enough for me and my fighter," injected Bevo most benevolently.

By the end of the day, they had shared enough boxing lore to fill a few years and then decided to take a break between rounds. "Come on, Bevo, let's get a feel for the city," Archie suggested. So they breezed three miles downtown to Sixth and Broadway, heart of the San Diego business district. Its narrow and busy sidewalks made them hug the outer edges, out of the way of shoppers who rushed by in both directions.

Meandering through the crowd were groups of sailors, a common sight in this port city. As three of them approached to Bevo's left, one wantonly hunched Bevo as he walked by, pushing him into Archie who was forced into the street, narrowly missed by an oncoming car. As he stepped back onto the sidewalk, one of the sailors drawled, "... man can't walk the streets for these inkwells!"

"You're not talking 'bout me, are you?" Archie inquired, knowing very well that he was.

"You damn-well bet I am," the sailor sneered! "I mean you!"

But Archie's immediate focus became the silent partner to the left. He had been the one to do the pushing and had gone into his back pocket to get something, the nature of which Archie was not about to stop to deliberate.

While seeming to center attention on the middle sailor, Archie whistled a right-cross to the chin of the sailor to the left, causing the middle man to flinch instinctively and the actual target to fall unceremoniously on his backside with his feet pointing skyward. Oblivious to his lame left hand, he followed up with a blow to the midsection of the middle sailor, toppling him over the first one.

"I ain't with 'em, I ain't with 'em," proclaimed the remaining part of the triumvirate, backing up into the crowd, still encanting quite soberly, "I ain't with 'em!"

The barber in front of whose shop the incident occurred dragged the sailors inside giving them cold towels as though part of his patriotic duty. He had witnessed the whole scene from his vantage point at the window and had seen both the shoving and its aftermath.

One might speculate as to whether the sailors were of the usual aggressive variety, or whether they had been spawned from the mores of some southern towns where it was customary for Negroes to step out onto the street when white persons approached. In effect, they owned the sidewalks! Certainly Bevo had witnessed it in his neck of the woods, and he indicated his disbelief that this could happen in San Diego; yet it should be remembered that California, though not a slave state before and during the Civil War, did discriminate against Negroes and Mexicans. (One might wonder about the position of California on slavery had Mexicans not provided a significant labor force.)

As Archie regained his composure, Bevo stared at the crowd that had gathered across the street and, from the looks of things, they were undeniably hostile. "They're like a stirred-up nest of hornets," Archie noted watchfully, "ready to strike when their anger peaks. We've got to call their bluff!"

"We?" echoed Bevo, pointing to his thinly padded chest.

"Come on, Bevo," shouted Archie, dusting off his cap and putting it on rather defiantly, "let's go!" And the "hornets" were shocked if not threatened by the seeming bravado of the two.

Archie wasn't taking any chances, however. He knew instinctively that one wrong move could disturb them again; so he walked slowly and steadily across the street, looking ahead as he and Bevo stepped onto the sidewalk, into and out of the astonished group of objectors. As they walked ahead, Archie glanced at Bevo and warned, "Don't look back! Don't dare look back!"

It was only when they had walked about six blocks that Archie was comfortable enough to turn to Bevo and say, "How's about a bowl of chili?" It was a specialty of Mama San's, a popular sidewalk stand at Third and Market Streets.

As they savored their meal, a black, unmarked car slid silently into the curb. Archie recognized one of the four men as Burt Richey, former football star from the University of Southern California, (lettered in football in 1928 and 1930) and one of the early Negro lawmen in San Diego - Jasper Davis being the first.

Richey had previously been introduced to Archie by one of the brothers of the large Richey clan; but of course it was quite rare to find anyone unfamiliar with the exploits of the tough San Diego boxer. As Burt beckoned, he slid off the stool and walked over to the car, placing his hands on the car door in plain view.

"Hi, Burt," he said.

"Hi , Arch... they tell me you had a fight in town... had to take one of the boys to the hospital!"

"Is he OK?" asked Archie worriedly. "Yea, he's ok; but tell me what the deal was," Burt questioned, though seeming to know the answer in advance.

After Archie's blow-by-blow description, it was apparent that the detectives were struggling hard to contain their laughter. Burt looked back at the other detectives and then at Archie, remarking, "Go on about your business, Archie. They probably needed a good ass kicking!"

Well, Archie and Bevo breathed a sigh of relief as the car sped away, leaving behind an unfinished but clear message: "Man, those deck swabs are always messin'..."

As the two headed home, they speculated about how the sailors might treat the next Negroes they met. Archie was amused as Bevo, once a boxer himself, attempted to reenact Archie's unbelievable efficacy at punching.

ARCHIE MOORE'S FIGHT FOR LIFE IN AMERICA

Will Never Enter Ring Again

By W. F. Corbett

Solemn-faced American negro middleweight, Archie Moore, who methodically hacked through Australia's best fighters, will never slip the gloves on again.

He collapsed in a Californian street. Then followed a six weeks' fight in hospital to save his life.

Archie came out of it weighing 8st. 13lb.

His fighting weight in Australia was about 11st. 4lb.

Moore was undefeated in this country. He beat Jack McNamee, Ron Richards twice, Joe Delaney, Attilio Sabatino and Fred Henneberry.

He earned about £2000, his Sydney fights drawing gates totalling nearly £7000.

Archie was a colorful fighter. Colorful in more ways than one. His skin had a copper tinge and his hair saffron tints.

When he went back to America, he had a run of misfortune. His left hand, broken in his second fight with Richards, was fractured again three weeks before he was to meet Billy Soose, who has since won the middleweight championship of the world from Ken Overlin.

Three Operations

Then came the severest blow for Moore—"Like a shot from a clear sky," writes his manager, Jack Richardson.

"Moore fell on the street one day after coming from the doctor's rooms. Ulcers in his stomach were ruptured. He was operated on three times, and was in hospital about six weeks. The doctors gave him about one chance in a hundred to live. He finally pulled through.

"On top of the operations he had pneumonia, and blood-poisoning set in."

Moore's first fight with Richards was a gem of glove drama.

Richards waited for his left lead in the first round, and quick as the strike of an adder crossed his right, and Moore was down—and looked out.

But he got up, cut Richards about the nose and eye—and won.

It was one of the most surprising recoveries of recent times.

Broken Hand

Moore broke his left hand on the head of Richards in their second fight. And he went back to America, figuring that he would thus get the time for the hand to mend and go into another fight soon after his arrival.

He was advised not to go back to America, but to stay here while he was making good money. He was told how Deacon Leo Kelly, Kingfish Dixon and other colored folk returned to America and disappeared into obscurity.

The colored man finds it pretty tough to get along in America, unless he is a big money-spinner like Joe Louis and Henry Armstrong. Even Henry found the going hard for a time.

But Archie, in his solemn, studious way, had set his heart on going home and winning the world middleweight title.

Archie is taking a long count, now. Tough game—life and the gloves.

Archie Moore and the hand which he fractured in his second Sydney fight with Ron Richards. (See story.)

Moore against the odds.

CHAPTER IX

The meaning of "Tough": Trials and

Tribulations of an Aspiring Champion

On the following day, Bevo's fighter, Jimmy McCracklin, arrived and joined the group, one which was to become the first real family Archie had known since leaving Auntie's home in St. Louis.

Jimmy was the product of a large family from rural Arkansas and they'd had their share of problems. "There were so many of us", Jimmy joked, "there were hardly enough chicken parts to go around!"

"Yea, and I can guess what part you got!" razzed Bevo. "Aw, shut up, Bevo, Archie added, "'cause yo mama probably gave you the feet!"

It was the kind of good humored raillery that had gone on at Boonville, and though each took his turn at being the target, they really never hurt each other. Archie also admired the way Jimmy did his share of the chores though Bevo's handicraft appeared to be dodging work.

Eventually, Jimmy secured a job and contributed fifteen dollars each week, an amount which Auntie managed fastidiously in this time just before the work boom in California. He had several fights in the meantime, winning all but one, losing only to Kid Lester, a light middleweight of considerable durability.

By the year's end, Jimmy made the decision to return to Arkansas to see his mother. Before leaving, he showed his appreciation by giving Auntie two hundred of the six hundred dollars he had saved. In later years, he returned to California and rose to a position of note as a blues singer, pianist and band leader in the city of Oakland.

As for Bevo, Archie later learned he had hustled enough fighters as a trainer to leave traveling first class back to St. Louis. He must have departed before daybreak, leaving behind on the crazy quilt spread of his well-made bed, a gracious note which said:

"Thanks for your help, Champ. May good luck be with you."

Bevo

"Well, that's noble of him," chuckled the Champ as he showed the note to Auntie. "My hat's off to him!"

That "hat" was again in the ring during the winter months of 1940 and into 1941, when after six fights, Archie proved himself to be as well seasoned as before. He lost only to Shorty Hogue, and it was getting to be habit - the third time - as a matter of fact. The tough, persistent opponent had decisioned Archie, this time in a ten rounder; even though it would have been extremely difficult to win a decision over a home town hero, as early experience had taught Archie. Though disappointed, he viewed his loss to Hoague as preparation for his battle against the lightening charged fists of nationally known Eddie Booker. He was the Rocky of his day, not to exclude Charley Burley, the Negro nemesis of boxing. The latter fact notwithstanding, neither of them received the press enjoyed by the likes of Billy Conn, a light heavyweight, or Fritzie Zivic, welterweight, both of whom became champions.

Booker and Burley left a lasting impression upon Archie Moore. He would sing their praises repeatedly to the press whenever interviewed about the toughest fighters he had encountered. He would say: "I've had some rough fights in my time, some when I've even had to come from behind in order to win; but all things being equal, when I was in my prime, one of my toughest had to have been against Eddie Booker, a fighting machine, a rivet gun who shot out punches with deft precision ... and I never beat him."

"Also, there was Charley Burley whom I fought only once. He whipped me in a ten rounder, winning most of the rounds and knocking me down four times to boot. His style was "as hard as lard and as slick as grease," and I guess we must have cooked in the same skillet; because he would counter my moves, kind of forecasting and meeting them with hard-boiled defenses. Though he never made history as a legitimately crowned champion, he was to many of his contemporaries and managers, the uncrowned middleweight champion of the world."

"In order to showcase him, one manager matched him against J.D. Turner, a 225-pound Goliath, while Burley was a mere 153 1/2 pounds. Can you imagine how his jaw-rattling K.O. over Turner must have looked? This sensational victory, instead of stepping him up in the ranks, intimidated local middleweights. Those managers took their fighters and ran for cover!"

"As a matter of fact, Charley Burley, Eddie Booker, Jack Chase, Lloyd Marshall, Jimmy Bivins, Ezzard Charles and myself, were known as the "Killing Row" of Negro middleweights. When even so-called tough fighters passed through the "Killing Row," it usually lowered the guillotine on their action."

"Burley and I were viewed by some as the most evasive and hardest punching boxers in the entire middleweight division; so the matches we sought were as scarce as hens' teeth."

"Now Burley knew he'd have to have better representation; so he went to the top of Negro management. This was to no other than Gus Greenlee, owner and manager of the Pittsburg Crawfords, a Negro baseball team which played against the likes of Satchel Paige and other allstars."

"Greenlee also owned a flourishing restaurant-bar and grill, and a stable of boxers and veteran fighters such as Honey Boy Jones, Red Bruce, and heavyweight, Big Jim Thompson. Giant among them was John Henry Lewis, second Negro light heavyweight champion of the world. The first was Battling Siki, a boxer from Senegal, West Africa. He had so much courage that he actually fought a championship match against Mike McTigue in Dublin, Ireland, on St. Patrick's Day."

"Let me pause here to relate something which will point out to you the difficulties experienced by many Negro champions," posed Archie to John Steadman, columnist for the Baltimore Sun. His reference was to Siki whose beginnings were as much a mystery as the Sahara sands which produced him.

Boxing history tells us he was truly a "Desert Child"; but the popular concept of Africa as a teeming jungle might explain why he was called "Jungle Child."

Allegedly, Siki was spotted by a French actress who had been touring the colonies. It was said that she was so struck by his appearance, she took him back to her villa on the French Riviera when he was but twelve years old, making him her pageboy and naming him Louis Phal. With her accidental death, he was forced to go from town to town surviving as a busboy, turning to boxing when he was fifteen. His short string of wins was interrupted by World War I and he was drafted into the French Army, the Eighth Colonial Infantry.

Siki (or Louis Phal) learned a perplexing lesson about white men in that war of 1914-1918. "The same ones that are repulsed by me, those who see me as savage, are the same ones to slap me on the back and call me hero," was what he often sadly commented.

Siki had single-handedly wiped out a German machine gun nest, making the way for his regiment to capture a strategic enemy position. "France is proud of you,"waswhat the General said to the cold-black soldier as he conferred upon him two of France's highest honors: the Croix de Guerre and the Medaille Militaire.

Following demobilization, Siki might have had any job for the asking, being a civilian war hero; but his killer instinct led him back to the ring to advertise the awesomeness and brute strength that seemed to gain him so much respect.

His long tentacle-like arms could render a man senseless in one sweep and he rose to the top though not as a scientific boxer. He was a slugger, and he slugged his way throughout France, North America and Spain.

By 1913, he had entered the professional ranks and might have honed his natural ability had he abstained from booze. He was showy and his slap-stick style made him an audience pleaser. At 5-11 and 175 pounds, which was the maximum for light heavyweights, he terrified his opponents. His greatest victory was on September 24, 1922, in Paris, when he knocked out the famed George Carpentier in six rounds to win the light heavyweight championship of the world.

When he arrived in the United States from abroad. it was a confusing set of contradictions he met - a ban on alcohol; yet everywhere he went there were men urging him to get drunk night after night. After winning a fat purse of $2,000, he might be too broke to afford a hotel the next day. He lived high-off-the-hog, swathing his big, threatening body in diamonds and ridiculous clothes. He had been known to give away an outfit which someone admired and go home in his shorts; then he'd challenge the cab driver to a fight, betting - double or nothing - for the taxi fare.

When Siki walked along the boulevard, all heads turned toward him as he pranced along with a blond on one arm and two lions on a leash. Periodically, he fired a pistol into the air, laughing like the mad man he was thought to be. He drank more heavily, neglected his training and became fat, roamed the streets, gaining the reputation of being dangerous when drunk. His tragic end was a place in a gutter of Hell's Kitchen with two bullets in his back.

Siki was buried on December 18, 1925, and with him, one of the most problem-laden but most impressive careers of all time. He was born a Mohammedan. but he was laid to rest as a Christian. His Black brothers shouldered his casket to the grave; but they were like him only in skin color.

There was a moment of silence after Archie finished discussing Battling Siki with Steadman, as though he had just conducted a requiem for the first Negro light heavyweight champion of the world. It wasn't a good feeling to know that such a great champion had ended this way; for in some respects, Siki had been caught in a clash of cultures, and he was the victim.

After reflecting, Archie found himself resuming his story about Charley Burley with much more empathy. "Now about Burley.... He decided to try his luck with Gus Greenlee, a noted Negro sportsman; but Greenlee already had a world champion and far too many hopefuls to make room for Burley. So like me, he came west to San Diego and found work among the aircraft plants, still fighting on the side."

"I am often asked why, when both Booker and Burley beat me, neither one got to the top whereas I did. Well, I guess it's the way I sized things up. I felt I had two opponents - other boxers and Father Time. I knew I needed more than skill and that stamina and patience were required to play the waiting game.

"Discouragement, you. see, can KO a boxer even before he has a chance to step into the ring. Though I lost to Burley and to Booker, I guess you might say I staved off Father Time."

This is not to say, however, that the hands of time were entirely merciful to Archie Moore; because following the Booker fight, the clock sounded an unexpected and piercing alarm. It happened on February 2, 1941, one day after his fight with Booker. As he awaited the arrival of Catherine Turner, a girl he had been dating, he busied himself as he always did, this time raking fall leaves from the lawn.

He was gripped suddenly by a jolting pain in his stomach, as though thrust by a red-hot poker. As he fell to the ground, he broke into a cold sweat and doubled up in agony. "Call an ambulance somebody!" he heard Auntie scream, as she came to the door and saw him writhing in anguish.

Even more excruciating was the examination enroute to the hospital and the questions upon arrival in the emergency room .... "When was your last meal? What did you eat?

Have you vomited?..."

"Oh, God, I'm dying, and they're asking all these crazy questions," he agonized, though he knew the doctors were trying to help him. And after the questions which turned out to be not so crazy after all, and after test results, he heard the "awful, awful."

"You have a perforated ulcer," he could hear the doctor say, "and you'll have to be operated on right away to save your life."

"Wow, they don't pull any punches!" he thought,..."save my life? God, I don't want to die... I've got to live... I've got to live... I've got to fight!" And he became even more terrified as he glanced at the apparatus which registered his breathing.

"Doc," he moaned even in his foggy state, "can you cut me like this?" He indicated a kind of diagonal direction on his stomach. He had seen the abdominal surgery marks on another boxer who continued to box after surgery.

But boxing was not to Archie the sole consideration. The other was the plight of his Auntie and little June, then only nine years old. He continued to pray: "I've got to make it... I've just got to live... I've ... got to..." He then trailed off under the effects of the anesthetic.

When he awoke five days later, he could groggily recognize Big Al Henson, a hospital orderly who had gone by his bed each day to check on him. (Henson was allegedly related to Matthew Henson, the explorer.) "Thought we were gonna have to take you out in a basket," he said in a half smile, "but you had the fighting spirit; we knew you'd make it," Henson confided.

"What day is it?" Archie inquired weakly, scarcely recognizing his own voice. It was Thursday morning as he looked toward the window at a ribbon of warm sunlight, grateful to be able to see it. It mattered little that he was being fed intravenously; that there were tubes in his nose; that he could not even get up to see the sky. What was important was that he was alive! He had KO'ed peritonitis, very often fatal at that time, and an onslaught of pneumonia as well.

Another achievement was to be counted during this long recovery period as he took inventory of his life and what had led him to this juncture. "I should be at the peak season of my life," he said to the doctor, "and here I am, recuperating from a perforated ulcer. Why??? I've never been a drinker... lived a clean life...."

"It can also come from tension and worry," the doctor injected. "Perhaps you've done too much of that."

"Yes, I guess I have been frustrated and bitter though not always consciously. You see, Doc," he went on, "I've proven myself; but I don't seem able to get anywhere."

Well, he knew of no other reason why he should have had a hole in his stomach; so he knew he'd have to change the behavior which the doctor said could cause it. He realized that just as he could build his physical strength, so would he have to alter his mental outlook;

especially since he was determined to box again, even if against Auntie's and the doctor's wishes.

The routine of the hospital became to Archie a training ground. He took his medicine, ate the tasteless meals to build his strength and imagined himself engaged in push-ups, sit-ups and roadwork to build his endurance. It was a way of projecting onto something else to escape the wrath of worry.

He also began to relax by fixating on pleasantries, more often than not on music. He took short naps, a practice which he would later recommend with some conceit. He'd say: "I've mastered the art of taking a five to fifteen-minute nap while standing up, or even in Grand Central Station if I feel the need to. I wake up as refreshed as someone who has slept all night."

Yes, Archie had hit upon a good combination - sleep and rest, positive thoughts and a little of Auntie's special "sneaked in" chicken broth. Later it was fried chicken itself, as well as homemade ice cream. Intuitively he knew, however, that his inner strength, his will to live, had come from his faith in God.

Some said it had been a miracle. In thirty-eight days, Archie had dropped from 163 to 108 pounds; but Dr. Pollack, his surgeon, gave him a good prognosis for recovery, as did a specialist sent by Linn Platner, the promoter who had given him his first fight in San Diego. Linn had visited often, aiding in cheering Archie and building his courage. It suggested that Platner felt he still had potential as a boxer.

It was Catherine Turner who would do most to help him maintain himself both financially and emotionally. She would take him for rides in the countryside or listen to hours of music with him. He never really knew whether she liked jazz, his kind of music, or whether she listened to please him. They got on well and he began entertaining the idea of marrying her; though remembrances of his short and unsuccessful marriage to Mattie told him to approach with caution. He was developing a kind of control over himself and the things he would allow to affect him. He eventually married her, however, and began to learn what a mature woman was like.

After work, she regularly picked him up for rides in the countryside. She loved the hills which were dotted year-round with trees and flowers and it seemed Archie was seeing them for the first time. But fate was no flower. It struck him again, this time in his side, like some gnarled root or bramble bush growing within him.

"This can't be, Catherine!" he grimaced, clutching at his middle, doubling over until his head was under the dashboard of the car. She pulled to a stop and struggled to get him into the back seat and quickly to the hospital. This time it was an acute appendicitis. Talk about luck! He couldn't dwell on it, however. Had he not learned what bitterness could do?

"I guess this is life," he later related to Catherine quite calmly, as though always the possessor of positive thoughts. "I'm like one of thousands of ants working to build an ant hill, and one gust of wind can take it away in an instant.... That's fate!"

So the "ant" began the process of rebuilding after a few days of recuperation from his latest ordeal and eventually built his weight up to 155 pounds. He was definitely stronger; but what he needed most now was a job as a means of repaying Catherine and supporting himself and his household.

He was referred to Milton Kraft, a sports enthusiast who, as it turned out, was an Archie Moore fan; probably the sole reason why he got the job as night watchman. It allowed him to work at his own pace and gradually to build his strength by walking to and from work. As he passed the newsstand each night, he picked up the daily paper or a *Ring Magazine* through which he kept up with ratings and the latest boxing news.

Negro boxers in the armed services seemed to be getting a little more press since the executive order in 1941 which prohibited discrimination in the defense establishments for reasons of race, creed or color. That discrimination had existed in the armed services was both wrong and inconceivable in the light of the events of December 7, 1941, and the heroism of Dorie Miller when the Japanese bombed Pearl Harbor. Stepping out of his role as messman aboard the U.S.S. Arizona, he manned a machine gun during the attack, downed four enemy planes and won the Navy Cross.

Archie was proud and hopeful when he heard it, perhaps because of his own experiences in fighting to gain his rightful place. By the end of the year, he graduated from walking home after work to trotting, and felt that he too was ready to fill a more demanding role.

Next, Milt gave him a better paying job mowing grass which aided in building his arms and legs. Ultimately, he was rebuilding his "ant hill"; but it needed additional fortification. Though up to speed for fighting, there was some vulnerability remaining in the area of his surgery and the scar was visible just above the waistline of his boxing trunks.

"Re-enter" Felix Thurman to the rescue with the bending of a license plate, a device which Archie wore around the scar as a protector. Rather than depend on it, however, he developed strategy moves to combat the punches of those who might consider his scar area a weakness. As a matter of fact, he even learned to lure his opponents to it, trapping them with surprise punches.

In seven bouts after his comeback, Archie forged five consecutive, early-round knockouts, decisioning the wily Jack Chase and drawing with the hard-fighting Eddie Booker in San Diego, on December 11, 1942. They were not battles to be taken lightly. These were the days of fifteen- round, state title fights.

Archie Moore and young fans at Training Camp circa 1953 (*Ring Magazine*).

CHAPTER X

Match Game--Money Game:

The Politics of Boxing

It was like starting over in the forties with still no title fights. And why not, when he had knocked out top ranked Johnny Romero in 1938 and had beaten the best Australia had to offer in 1940?

W.F Corbett, internationally known writer of the *Sydney Sun* commented that Archie Moore turned boxing in Australia topsy-turvy, coming out of obscurity to spray Ron Richards, British Empire champion, with gloves; that he outfought and outboxed Richards at every point, emerging as a truly great fighter.

He had also been rated number 4 among the world's middle-weights by *Ring Magazine* of November 11, 1941; yet not even San Diego's Linn Platner could land him a decent match. The reasons were piled as high as his victories.

Firstly, managers still viewed Archie as a menace to their fighters, an odd stance to take in view of the nature of the business. It was like being an alien in his own land. Secondly, the guarantees demanded by contenders like Al Hostac, Freddie Steele and Harry "Kid" Matthews, all from Seattle, were exorbitant sums.

He was game, therefore, when Felix returned to San Diego with the suggestion that they try their luck in Oakland, then a hub city for boxing in California. With the usual scarce money between them, they purchased an old panel truck which they outfitted with an even older mattress for sleeping and an icebox for ice they could barely afford.

Once in Oakland, they looked up Mike Segal, a former boxer who owned a gas station on Franklin Street not far from a gym. Though they had made prior plans to locate a stopping place, he second-guessed them, offering his station for the token fee of one dollar per month. Here they would at least have some security, not to mention use of washroom facilities.

"We'll allow ourselves seventy-five cents each a day to eat," advised the manager to his fighter. "In the meantime, you train hard and try to get a fight and I'll get a job in the shipyard." This went on for a couple of months until the daily ration of seventy-five cents apiece was no more, used up and not to be available until Felix's payday at the end of the month.

Hunger began to set in now, and Archie was not appeased by the morsels of stale bread and water which were all they had. He salivated as he remembered the fabulous food he had had on the Monterey, the exotic tastes of the Fiji Islands, and Auntie's home cooking; but fantasizing was getting him nowhere and he was too proud to beg. Moliere might well have had someone like Archie in mind when he wrote: "A man once asked Diogenes what was the proper time for supper and he made answer, 'If you are a rich man, whenever you please; and if you are a poor man, whenever you can.'"

He knew there'd be no eating unless he found work and soon; so on a tip, he went to the train yard at the foot of Fifth Street where he found men standing in line and he fell in with them. At intervals, someone would poke his head out of the door of the employment office and yell out, "I need four number two's," or "I want three chefs." Eventually, the waiting crowd got smaller and Archie began to listen anxiously for a job he could handle. "I need a fourth cook," was the next announcement, to which Archie responded promptly though somewhat dubiously.

"I'll take it!" he bellowed. Impelled by desperate hunger, he had volunteered for something though he knew not what. And as he followed the man inside, he wondered how long it would be before it was discovered he was not a fourth cook. He figured on chancing it if only to get a few meals under his belt. Well, the joke was on him. As it turned out, a fourth cook, or "forty" as they called it, was a "pearl diver," a dish washer to be exact. "And here I am, rated number five in the world and busting suds!" was his disdainful reaction.

"What the hell," he told himself, "I've washed dishes before." Little did he realize, however, that he would be running on a troop train between Oakland and Ogden, Utah, serving soldiers who ate like horses. They left dirty dishes by the thousands for him to wash and the hot sudsy water and food residue sickened him to the point of nausea. Until he became used to it, he couldn't stomach the food; but hunger overtook him and he soon became able to gorge as much as the soldiers did.

After several runs, he quit the job on a full stomach and one hundred dollars under his belt and returned to the gas station where he had left Felix. Awaiting him was a telegram from Linn Platner announcing a fight he had arranged with his old foe, Shorty Hague. There was also a message from Felix who had decided to work in an Oakland shipyard along with his wife and daughter. They, like many others, were taking advantage of the fairly good wages that shipyards and plants were offering in exchange for work which outfitted men for war. Yes, the war had affected everyone and everything, even boxing. Civilians like Archie were unable to enlist because of health reasons. Some younger boxers were drafted, while still others enlisted or opted to work in the defense plants.

The Ring, which has reigned consistently as the Bible of boxing, left no doubt as to the posture which the industry would assume on the war issue. All "Ratings of the Month" were preceded by an edict which stated that all inactive fighters who had been rated but were in the armed forces were removed for the duration. When they resumed boxing, they would be placed again in the high position they occupied. Only active fighters, service men and civilian boxers were rated monthly. In those ratings, the position of champions in the service of Uncle Sam were frozen for the duration.

Archie fully understood why Felix would go for the stability afforded by the steady salary of the shipyard. Though he might have done likewise, he bore his injuries and followed his heart as if there had been no hunger, no mishaps, no bad times.

Returning to San Diego alone, he revenged his previous two losses against Hogue on October 30, 1942, by knocking him out in round two of the fight. He was on his way again like some fistic robot programmed for conquest. He repeated a second round victory over Tabby Romero only one week later. And though it would seem he was riding high, good sense told him not to trust his luck this time. Judging from experience, he knew the fight game was like a glass mountain where to slip could mean destruction unless he could stabilize himself, guarding against plummeting to the bottom and becoming a useless heap.

He decided to take the money from his small purses and add them to what little he had managed to save and borrow to buy a piece of land in San Diego, a place to make a permanent home for his family.

His secret coffer was a coffee can buried beneath the floor of the shed in the back yard. It wasn't that Archie mistrusted banks. It was more that he liked being able to touch the money on a whim, to count it three and four times each night, feeling a rush of growth as he watched the stack increase. No hard times, no pleasures, but nothing ever tempted him to use that precious money after he had made the decision to buy the land.

"Hope you can tough it, Auntie Willie Pearl ," he grinned saucily as he delivered his surprise announcement. "It'll be like living in the wilderness with plenty of trees, wide open spaces and a real log cabin... and on eight lots, Auntie!"

"My goodness, Archie Lee!" she gasped in amazement, holding her palm over her racing heart. "How on earth did you ever save enough? ... My sakes!"

Saving enough meant a down payment of $3,500 on an $18, 000 property. Though he knew he'd have to hump to meet the notes, he felt the responsibility would give him more drive, more hope for the future.

"I feel I'd better do it now Auntie," he told her earnestly, "'cause you never know what the cards hold for a man in boxing. Just look at my record," he reminded, as though Auntie needed reminding. Though she didn't know much about the technical end of the fight game, she had literally provided the training table as well as warm encouragement to her nephew. She knew he had done well and wanted so much for him to be a champion and this was all she needed. He had, after all, followed the four-line precept given him when he was just a little boy. And now there was a man's task ahead of him.

He hit upon using the place he had bought to open a small restaurant business which would feature fried chicken, something he loved to eat and had learned to cook at home with Auntie and during his visits to the South.

He savored his first day's small profit of $17.50 which climbed steadily through word of mouth and a bit of immodest advertising which brought customers in droves. The *San Diego Tribune* announced that Archie Moore's Chicken Shack was open to sell "The World's Greatest Fried Chicken."

When the cash register rang out a whopping $400 the next week, he paid back salaries, ordered double the merchandise, hired a college graduated maitre d' in tux to add a bit of class, and a jazz trio led by Peter Rabbit, jazz pianist. Before long, the business had hopped to a gargantuan $700-a day venture, a signal which had him standing at the crossroads. He knew he'd have to stop and plot his course: whether he was content to pursue the title, "World's Champion Chicken Fryer," or seek the world's boxing championship. He chose the latter, the task he had begun and had not yet finished.

Archie's confidence and determination to return to boxing did not sink in with the sports writers and fans, despite his favorable showing against the virtually impenetrable Hogue and the true grit of Tabby Romero. They doubted his durability in view of his well publicized and serious surgery.

"We'll put that to rest, Archie," Linn Platner decided. "I'll arrange a match against Jack Chase. If they can't buy you after spoiling his twenty-two straight wins, they never will!"

And spoil Chase he did by putting him on the canvas in "2" with a solid left hook. "His eye is hurt pretty bad and I could finish him off," Archie strategized, "but I have to avoid playing on his weakness to prove I can go all the way." And he did it, winning seven out of the ten rounds, proving ultimately that he was indeed a durable fighter.

He was to meet Jack Chase several times after this: once for the California Middleweight Championship at Lane Field, winning by adroitly maneuvering to make Chase face the sun in that outdoor match of November 27, 1942.

In the rematch, however, Chase, being a smart fighter, out-maneuvered Archie's maneuvers, winning a fifteen-round decision. They were to meet again as would many of the civilian power houses ... the Chase's, the Burley's the Booker's and others over those war years.

Inasmuch as the draft had siphoned off the eighteen year olds and volunteers from ring competition, one would have to admit that the war also had an effect on the quality of competition; for in any sport, a steady stream of talent is needed to push the cream to the top. Without this stream of life, who was there to compete, for instance, against the likes of Joe Louis?

But patriotism took precedence over expedience as evidenced by sports covers, sports articles, newsreels and newspapers. Dedicated to "Draft and Its Effects on Boxing," the March 1943 issue of *The Ring* proudly displayed a uniformed Corporal Barney Ross, replete with boxing gloves. Yes, boxing, a natural transfer into the overall goal of national defense, had entered the armed forces as had Ross, former lightweight and welterweight champion of the world. Held to have done most for boxing in 1942, he had also garnered laurels for heroism in combat against the Japanese.

Of significance is the standing of Archie Moore among selected boxers in competition as they appeared in March of 1943.

MIDDLEWEIGHTS	LIGHT HEAVYWEIGHTS	HEAVYWEIGHTS
World Champion*	World Champion*	World Champion*
* Tony Zale	* Gus Lesnevich	* Joe Louis
1. Archie Moore	1. Jimmy Bivins	1. Jimmy Bivins
2. Charlie Burley	3. Ezzard Charles	10. Joey Maxim
3. Holman Williams	9. Johnny Romero	
4. Jacob La Motta		
5. Jack Chase		
6. Eddie Booker		

It is also of interest to note that Ray Robinson was then in first place in the Welterweight Category behind the championship holder; while, as indicated before, Joe Louis or Sergeant Louis, had entered the service of his country, postponing for the duration a much publicized match against Corporal Billy Conn.

Several of the boxers previously cited were to have specific and significant effects on the life and future of champion fighter Archie More as he jockeyed for position.

A hard look at his record revealed few losses since his return from Australia and his untimely illness. "I've had about twenty-six fights, all but one in California," he explained to Platner in September of 1944. "I've knocked out opponents or won most of my bouts with little to show for it. Its time for me to move on, Mr. Platner," he announced, with the same conviction that he'd demonstrated years earlier when he left manager Cal Thompson in Indiana with Hiawaitha Gray as his trainer.

"I'm going to New York where I can get a crack at some of the big money that's floating round," Archie announced in a stiff-lipped mode, an expression which usually accompanied a pensive or decisive undertaking.

As with his previous move, this move to New York had nothing to do with his readiness to fight. It had been decided by the entanglements of boxing - the policies, the practices and mainly the politics.

Some would have preferred to see boxing operate as other sports, where regular schedules and tournaments produced the top opponents; where boards of the region, state or world unified and compelled champions to defend their titles within certain time limits, as in Europe when European or national titles were involved.

Absence of such requirements found great fighters like Peter Jackson, Sam Langford, Packey MacFarland, Mike Gibbons and Jeff Smith, going through an entire career without getting a shot at a world championship. Jack Johnson, for instance, found himself following

Tommy Burns half-way around the globe for a heavyweight title bout, finally cornering him in Australia.

In later years, Ray Robinson chased for five years like a greyhound after a decoy rabbit, seeking the welterweight crown. Potential opponent Marty Servo bobbed, weaved and dodged the issue, finally giving up the title rather than meet Ray. Ray became recognized champion after beating Tommy Bell in an elimination bout.

Without a doubt, Archie Moore was a card-carrying member of that club of perennial title seekers, now on his way to New York, sniffing the trail of the rabbit.

In recognition of the worth of his former trainer, Hiawatha Grey, he stopped in Indianapolis to see if he could convince him to accompany him to New York and again be his trainer; but Hiawatha declined in that he was training George "Sugar" Costner. Costner was later to fight Ray Robinson who decked him in round one, much to the ire of the fans who had swelled their anxiety as well as the gate to a whopping $90,000. Such gates were expected when Sugar fought. He knew it and knew the promoters knew it; so he cut himself in for the lion's share. His manager, the "Emperor", George Gainsford, had successfully engineered the "Sweet One" into being a law unto himself. It mattered little that Ray was accused of arrogance, conceit and selfishness, as Marquette pointed out in the December, 1960 issue of Boxing. As he described the "bad" in Ray, the con, the broken contracts, the bickering, the litigation, and those who despised him, they all went down the drain in memory when one of the world's greatest fighters and personalities stepped into the prize ring. And anyone within earshot of the happenings in boxing was cognizant that Ray's rise to champion status was no streak of luck. Speaking of luck ....

"Call it fate, accident, destiny or just plain bad luck," Moore confessed to the mechanic who had just checked out his car after it had thrown a rod in Bedord, Pennsylvania, "me and things on wheels just don't mix!" As the mechanic listened in disbelief, Archie recounted his four-wheeled escapades including: the trolley incident which landed him in Boonville; the truck convoy chased by irate fans out of Poplarbluff; the near-fatal blow when he hitched a ride on a freight train; now, this!

Without the $400 necessary to repair the engine, however, he was forced to leave his car, and with some trepidation, ride a bus the rest of the way to New York. Fortunately, the experience had been so debilitating that he slept through the entire trip, oblivious to whatever fate might have befallen him.

CANNON:

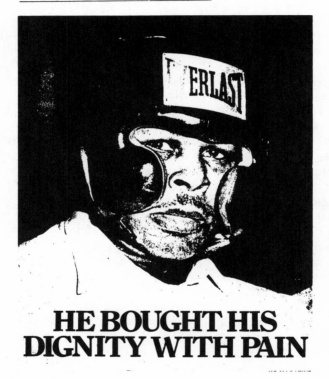

HE BOUGHT HIS DIGNITY WITH PAIN

Jimmy Cannon, sports writer of note, admired and wrote about Archie Moore's persistence and courage.

CHAPTER XI

Alien in His Own Land:

Too Good in the Ring

All eyes seemed drawn magnetically by the New York skyline as the bus pulled to a stop at the subway station. Archie stumbled as did other passengers alighting from the bus, attempting both to look upward and make their way along the crowded street to the underground people mover. "We'd all make excellent targets for a good uppercut," he laughed to himself, referring to the jutting chins of tourists who stretched their necks to see if the structures extended beyond the clouds.

He caught another bus to ride eight miles to 145th and St. Nicholas Avenue, using the last of his funds which had been depleted by the car trip across country. His destination was Strick's Bar and Grill operated by James Strickland, a sports lover. He was a drawing card for hoards of fight followers and musicians who came to mingle and absorb the latest in fistic fables, predictions and colorful street yarn.

Archie had been referred by "Black Dot" McGee who assured that Strick would give him the city. It actually wasn't an oddity that Dot would know another sportsman in the East in that he was as much at home in New York's Harlem as he was on Central Avenue in Los Angeles. The reverence for Dot's dependability and know-how would also assist Archie in establishing himself in New York.

Strick's impression had already been set by his knowledge of Archie's upsets and determination to be a champion. Even more incredible was the strong physical likeness between the two - the full faces, wide grins and tanned muscular bodies. As a matter of fact, the resemblance to Strick was also detected by the landlady of the flat across the street to which Archie was sent for lodgings. He stayed there on that first night, resting and readying himself mentally and physically for what he'd have to do the next morning. How was he to manage with no cash?

Though hard luck was by no means a new experience, he had never allowed himself to expect it and he lay there in the dark, pounding his fists against the mattress, fretting as though he had never known misfortune. "Damn it to hell," he sputtered, "I can't ask Strick for bus fare. After all, 1 am a rated fighter and I should be able to pull my load. I'm sure he'd understand if he knew about the rough time I've had; but I won't burden him with.it."

The next morning found Archie making it on foot from downtown 145th street to 42nd street, approximately six miles, pretending he was doing road work and enjoying himself. As he made the last leg of his long trek, he looked with anticipation to being booked by the Great Jimmy Johnston.

His arrival there found a cocksure, derby-wearing, Irish leprechaun with his feet on his desk. A history of experience in the fight game was etched in his face, and his mouth, "sans" cigar, turned up at the edges "...thought all promoters smoked cigars," Archie mumbled to himself.

Not this one; nor did he imbibe as Irishman are reputed to do.

Johnston was a most sociable individual who reveled in the attention he received from fight people, young and old, and with Archie's arrival, Johnston had the pleasure of both. Already in the room was Battling Norfolk, a great old-time Negro fighter who had dropped by to see Johnston.

"Moore," he began, "I want you to know Battling Norfolk, one of the best in the business. You can learn a lot from him, believe me."

"Oh yes, I know you Mr. Norfolk, mostly from what I've read; but you sure were a classy boxer," Archie commented admiringly.

"Well, Mr. ,Johnston, I'll be leaving now," announced Norfolk. Before he did, Johnston went into a metal container in his drawer. He counted out ten-twenty dollar bills on the desk and handed them to Norfolk, punctuating his benevolence with a haughty toss of his head. This generosity toward boxers was the kind of thing Archie had also seen Black Dot practice, though with much more subtlety. All Dot wanted in return for his money was to see the fighter progress.

Archie's guess was that Johnston's grand standing was for his benefit, but he didn't mind it. "At least he doesn't try to keep it all for himself," he noted.

"I'm willing to take a chance on you, Moore," Johnston announced. "I'll advance you $25 per week for food, pay your rent and give you some spending money until I can get you a fight ... Is that fair?" And as with Norfolk, he counted it out with a dexterity which could only have come from practice.

"Thank you, sir, and I hope to repay you in the very near future," promised the grateful, young pugilist.

He worked out the next morning in Stillman's gym among several of the great white hopes of the day - Jake La Motta; Melio Bettina, light heavyweight champion of the world; and two, tough heavyweights, Lee Oma and Joe Baski. Sandy Saddler was just starting out; but even then, Archie had spotted him as a future great champion. Despite being in different divisions, they worked out with each other and developed a lasting friendship.

Within two weeks and his first fight in New York on December 18, 1944, Archie was chomping at the bit, as his ten round decision over Nate Bolden confirmed. His two-fisted gauntlet brought them down one after another until he realized he was back in the same bag again. He was looking a little too good, a little too ominous, even when matched against six-foot-four, two hundred-pound, Nap Mitchell.

This became Moore's first KO since beginning his western fight crusade which culminated in 1945 with a 12-2 record. Though established by fighting against top-ranking men, this did not serve to advance him any closer to a championship bout as a leading contender might expect.

Unlike many top contenders, Archie had fought all comers - some young upstarts, other terrific hitters without science, and a lot of "Fancy Dans." He studied them all and would often share perceptions about fighting styles with Sandy Saddler, the coming featherweight champion.

"Sandy," he'd point out, "you're a natural fighter. You know how to make a man move the way you want him to. That's what feinting and precise punching are about; but as you get long on experience, you'll discover you can break a man's pace, set your own pace, pin-point your opponent's strengths and weaknesses, and it can be done within the first three minutes of a fight. A skilled boxer has got to make his opponent open up to him. He must be aggressive! To put it simply, "nothing ventured, nothing gained."

"Now take Joe Louis as an example. His reputation alone froze many a man in his tracks. He opened them up early in the fight and moved in; yet he had one flaw: he was a sucker for a right cross. He carried his left hand too low as many fighters do, mainly because they have been poorly taught or because of habit."

Max Schmeling, Hitler's fighter, took advantage of this flaw. By studying movies, he discovered that Louis would leave his left hand low after he had jabbed twice. During that famous fight in 1938, Schmeling rifled Louis with right-hand shots to the jaw until he downed the Brown Bomber. Boxing, Sandy, is a science."

As Archie moved his science lab into 1946, he was still looking for the right chemistry - a match between himself and the title holder. He had been like a huckster, peddling his skills throughout the New England states, now making his way to Washington for a fight with Georgie Parks.

Boarding a plane in New York traveling first class, he sat for a time among other anxious passengers awaiting take off. The wait was well worth it, however, when escorted into first class and seated directly facing him was none other than Mrs. Eleanor Roosevelt and three G-men, strategically positioned for her protection.

"Oh," she uttered in her familiar singing tone, "you are Achee Mooah. Come over and sit with us," she invited in a sharp but charming New England accent.

There was non-stop chatter, much to Archie's surprise, for he had expected her to be more reserved and private. She even knew a little about boxing ... "Franklin's father, Teddy, had a fling with the gloves, you know ... And do you know A. Philip Randolph?"

"Yes," Archie knew him, though he had not met him personally. He did know of his efforts in organizing maids and porters who were train workers in the '20's and '30's. They had labored long under less than equitable working conditions and wages.

Mrs. Roosevelt also left no question about her admiration for Paul Robeson and Marian Anderson. Robeson had been so embittered by racism in the American society that he found it necessary to leave it. As a champion of the underdog, he had very early developed a socialist philosophy and turned to Russia for answers. His withdrawal from his home lost to America one of the greatest baritone voices of all time.

Then there was Charles Holland, a lyric tenor who sang with jazz bands in the '30's, but who also fled the prejudice of his native land. Though Marian Anderson had succeeded in lowering racial barriers to some degree, the plight of Black males such as Holland saw little change in the operatic field.

With his flight, Holland became a successful Monostatos in Mozart's *Magic Flute*. In later years when his bell-like tones had faded, he sang Verdi's *Othello* and toured Europe in *Carmen, Boris Godunov* and *Faust*.

It was not until 1969 and a twenty-year absence that he returned to the United States. At the age of 72, he performed at Carnegie Hall. (This artistic treasure died in November of 1987 at his home in the Netherlands.)

Marian Anderson, on the other hand, stayed and fought against some of the atrocities committed against Negroes. When she was denied in 1939 the use of Constitution Hall by the Daughters of the American Revolution, a national scandal was created. There was no doubt as to the reason, given her standing as the world's leading concert contralto and the best know Negro singer in the history of music.

People in high places voiced disapproval of the D.A.R. They were joined by some 75,000 people who gathered at the Lincoln Memorial on Easter Sunday morning in 1943 to hear Marian sing. Most notable among those registering support was first lady, Mrs. F.D.R., through her resignation from the D.A.R.

As Archie looked over at her, he had the distinct feeling that Mr. Roosevelt had not done it alone; for Mrs. F.D.R. was a most influential and warm individual. She had taken him over, disarming him right in front of the G-men.

Still riding as high as though his plane had not landed, he took Georgie Parks out in "1'" ending the year with 8 fights, drawing 2, losing only to Ezzard Charles, coming champion of the world - clean cut, tough and literally down to earth. He was usually to be found at his family's homestead in Cincinnati, Ohio, except when there was a fight on the far horizon.

Though Archie's own family ties were in San Diego, he found "foster homes" in Baltimore, New York and Los Angeles. (He was eventually entered into the Boxing Hall of Fame in New York, San Diego, Los Angeles and Baltimore.)

Between 1945 and 1948, he fought 18 fights in Baltimore. It became his second home, not so much because it differed significantly from any other city, but because its Jim Crow, even if only theoretically, provided the impetus for fighting against social injustice.

Once the Baltimore and Washington areas had been exhausted, Archie decided to take matters into his own hands by embarking on a letter writing campaign urging sports editors and columnists to talk up a match with Joey Maxim, then reigning light heavyweight champion. He had the foxiest manager in the game, the great Doc Kearns.

Archie was then under management of Charlie Johnston, brother of deceased Jimmy Johnston. Though resourceful, no amount of telegrams, letters, phone calls or personal meetings by him could convince Jack "Doc" Kearns to risk Maxim's championship against Moore's lethal fists.

A sample of Moore's efforts in his own behalf consisted of messages to sports editors, preferably to those in large cities and towns. He'd write for instance to Dan Parker, sports editor of *The New York Mirror*:

Dear Mr. Parker:

Knowing of your unbiased reputation as a top sports writer, I felt I could appeal to you. As the number one contender for the light heavyweight title held by Joey Maxim, I am avoided by him. He steadfastly refuses to fight me, choosing instead men who are even in the second division. In addition to being unfair, this casts a negative light on boxing. I ask you, is boxing a game or a sport? Please use your column to tell your readers of the state of affairs in professional boxing.

Sincerely,

Archie Moore

He'd write sometimes thirty such letters a night, most short but to the point, taking care to avoid alienating anyone, dealing with fact and not personality issues. This also succeeded in making Johnston aware Archie was getting publicity on his own. Since he had gotten only two bouts for him in 1950, both of which he won, Johnston arranged for a South American package tour featuring his featherweight champion, Sandy Saddler, and he threw in Archie as an added attraction for the grand sum of $3,500.

"Wow, what a drag," he thought. "Sandy gets $25, 000 and its back to the drawing board for me; though I guess I should know how to start all over. I just can't quit!" He reasoned that no endeavor could be considered a failure until his last one succeeded. This attitude he would carry with him to South America and have one of the richest, most unique experiences of his life.

Promoters and managers arranged matches between fighters other than the logical contenders. Moore became the hound that chased the rabbit. (*Ring Magazine*)

CHAPTER XII

Argentina: The Peron Years

The Argentina to which Archie traveled in 1951 was a country of which he had little prior knowledge. In fact, he had gone to Australia knowing more, having followed the much publicized career of Jack Johnson and his fistic exploits at Sydney Stadium. All he knew or cared about was that this trip abroad would give him a chance at a little money and added recognition for a chance at the light heavyweight title in the United States. Now he had not even developed a party leaning, nor had he a real sense of politics; yet he knew instinctively that many of the entertainers who went abroad were subject to national scrutiny as Johnson had been.

The presence of entertainers, especially Negroes in countries whose class systems were not based on color, served to do two things: They conveyed the popular impression that Negroes as a whole prospered in America and that they were free and able to pursue life's offerings as well as any other American. One might say that Negro Americans in such countries were "unwitting ambassadors." (A pertinent definition given in 1612 by Sir Henry Wotten gained him the ire of King James and a storm of protest in Europe when he said: "An ambassador is an honest man sent to lie abroad for the commonwealth.")

Consider, however, that during those postwar years in Argentina, between 1946 and 1955, the official U.S. Ambassador himself engaged in relations which were fiery to say the least. This was the Peron era and a rise to power unparalleled by any leader in Argentina or even in Latin America as a whole. Roosevelt had condemned Peron in 1944 for allowing Nazi-Fascist influence and for giving refuge to fleeing axis leaders; but Peron denied this. He admitted only to embracing an idea which might also have been shared by Mussolini or Hitler.

When Roosevelt published the names of the axis in his famous *Blue Book*, it helped rather than hurt the Peronistas who viewed the U.S. as meddling too far into foreign affairs. The U.S. then ceased merchant trade with Argentina for a time during this controversy over ideaology.

It was a virtual duel between Peron and Assistant Secretary of State Spruille Braden, a factor which enabled Peron to attract Nationalist votes as champion of Argentine independence against Yankee intervention. There was, however, no Latin American bloc, since Peron also had his enemies among those countries.

Peron had risen to power and the presidency through the ranks of the military and most notably as Secretary of Labor in which position he established sweeping labor reforms. He was not, however, as adept at economics as he was at politics, accounting in part for the post war decline in Argentina. Severe droughts during this period also did much to exacerbate the decline.

Much of Peron's success was due to the passionate devotion of Eva Duarte who helped organize his return to power by promoting his release from political imprisonment for instigating class conflict and economic heresies. She had met him through her popularity as an actress and military "party girl." Using her experience as a stage, radio and screen personality, she won public support, essentially the support of the poor masses for Peron's social reforms. Ultimately, it was her own humble beginnings which aided her in communicating with and convincing the poor descamisados or "shirtless ones" that Peron was their champion, their true liberator. He would put down the mighty and exalt the meek.

Thus Peron's marriage to Eva in 1945 would have far reaching effects: it further convinced the poor masses of his sincerity despite being a man of high breeding and education. He was in sharp contrast with Eva, an illegitimate offspring who had, along with her mother, borne the disgrace of her birth. More significantly, their marriage served to unite labor with the military, enabling Peron to be all things to all people. Eva was also to become a leader in her own right, a "champion of the poor" and, though only twenty-six, half the age of her husband at the time of their marriage, a proponent of women's suffrage.

Coincidentally, 1951, the year of Archie's arrival in Argentina, was to be the first year that women cast a vote. Existing was an aura of progress aided by a kind of ideological brainwashing which tended to mask the real problem; for the country was in the midst of a deep economic depression. This factor notwithstanding, Archie was the hopeful, hungry pugilist, quite accustomed to poverty and hard times, having already lived through a depression. Conditions in Argentina, therefore, would not affect him as much as they might have some others.

They deplaned - Johnston, Sandy Saddler and Archie, meeting head-on a bevy of newspaper reporters and Ismael Pace, the fight promoter of Argentina, who was accompanied by his staff. They had come mainly to see Sandy Saddler, the headliner.

"Ain't this some shit!" Archie complained with a twinge of jealousy, "here I am on the undercard and I've even taught Sandy some of his tricks!" The latter was with no ill will toward Sandy; for they were closely knit, plagued by some of the same problems in their respective divisions. Sandy, nevertheless, was to fight the Argentine champion within the first two weeks of their arrival and Archie intended to help him wherever he could.

They passed through customs and to a waiting car which took them from the outlying airport to Buenos Aires, capital of Argentina. From the window of the car they observed what appeared to be once active work places, though worn out and idle machinery stood as epitaphs to the demise of their industries. From the front seat, Sandy asked questions of the driver as they made their way. He spoke Spanish quite well, having been born and partially raised in Cuba.

Buenos Aires by contrast was like a second class township in the United States; yet it was in sharper contrast with the scenes they had taken in enroute to the city. There were island-like street dividers decorated with arches, and park benches on which people leisurely sat reading or talking. As they passed some of the taller, twenty-to-thirty story structures, Archie pointed with amazement to his discovery... "Man," he exclaimed, "I've never seen outside elevators on buildings, and glass too!" Their hotel in downtown Buenos Aires had one such elevator; yet the hotel itself was also second rate by comparison to those in the U.S. "But what am I thinking about," Archie reminded himself, "I've never even been inside a rated hotel in the states!"

After checking in, the group was taken on a tour of the city by Roberto De Angelo, a friend of Mr. Pache's, owner of a thriving business in Buenos Aires. He sold tickets for sports events, lottery tickets, magazines and cigarettes. He spoke both Spanish and English, acting as interpreter between Mr. Pache and the group while Sandy filled in wherever he could.

As it turned out, Mr. Pache was also a personal friend of Peron's and a man of high standing and multi-millionaire status in Argentina. As such, he was a familiar visitor at Casa Rosada, the "White House" of Buenos Aires, and he would take them there at the invitation of the President himself. "Hey," Sandy whispered to Archie, "just think what they'd say back home if they knew ... a real live President!"

Peron was waiting at Casa Rosada and it was, as the name suggested, quite rose-colored and surrounded by huge guards who towered above six feet. They wore tall hats, making them resemble English castle guards. White sashes and rifles seemed to dignify their positions.

The five men, Pache, De Angelo, Johnston, Sandy and Archie, were ushered into the President's wing where they waited in an outer room to be announced. When the door opened, however, it was Peron himself, meeting his guests with open arms and a warm embrace. His firm grasp evoked a second look and the observation that he had a solid build and a height of about six feet. Meticulous grooming and the latest in military garb accentuated his good looks and youthful, trim appearance. Slick, black hair and a slightly reddened face were offset by a charming and dazzling smile.

"Won't you sit down," he invited in Spanish, as he took off his coat and hung it on the rack just behind a gleaming mahogany desk which revealed the grain of the wood. Even without the coat bedecked with medals, he left no doubt that he was still the military man, the general; for he wore rather boldly a pistol in his belt.

Still smiling, he playfully waved the other men out of the room so he could talk with Sandy and Archie and it was evident that he was no stranger to boxing.

"I was an amateur boxer when I taught at the war college," he related with pride and seeming nostalgia. "It was good for men in training for war ... and, oh, how I loved to box the American sailors when their boats docked in Argentina!" he recalled with fiendish glee, making a double jab at his imaginary opponent.

After sharing considerable views on boxing and Sandy's career, Peron turned to Archie and asked point-blankly, "Why haven't you become a champion?"

"Well, I guess it's politics," Archie answered.

"You'll have fair fights here," Peron affirmed quite seriously, "and I will be there to see them!" And before leaving, he called in a photographer and had pictures taken with both boxers and then individually, most in fighting stance.

As promised, Peron was present to see Sandy score a sensational win over the Argentine champion. He returned a week later at ringside with Eva Peron herself.

Archie left the dressing room amid cheers of the crowd in response to President Peron being introduced in the center of the ring. As he passed Eva enroute to the ring, he bowed to her and the crowd loved it, cheering loudly as he climbed into the ring with Peron and his opponent.

Peron sportingly embraced Archie and then his opponent, Abel Cestak, a handsome, young heavyweight with a classic build. Though tough and game, he was not a great fighter however, and this soon became evident as Archie unleashed staggering punches to his head and sickening hooks to the body.

By round ten, Archie had Cestak on the ropes just above where Eva sat, beautifully attired in a chic fitted suit, her blond hair pulled back elegantly in the familiar large bun at the nape of her neck. She shrieked suddenly as Cestak's blood went flying, splattering both her and the President. Cestak was stopped in "10" to the din of a crowd which told Archie they appreciated a good fight, despite seeing their champion lose to a foreigner.

The next day found Archie back at Casa Rosada by invitation of the President who praised him as the most skillful and tactical boxer he had ever seen. Peron proudly showed him a fight clipping he had saved from the newspaper dated June 10, 1951. Adding to the honor of the occasion was a request by Eva to see him.

It was an experience that he would remember vividly and recount to Sandy and others, especially after he began to fathom the power of these two individuals: "I was led down a corridor to the open door of her office and was seated opposite a large mirror facing the open door. The receptionist went in and returned telling me that Mrs. Peron would see me. She asked if I minded waiting a few moments while she attended to a matter with a gentleman who needed her help. Of course I said 1 didn't mind and I sat contemplating what I'd say to Mrs. Peron. I was so flabbergasted, you know, I didn't want to bungle it. Then, my attention was drawn to the mirror and I could see though not hear her speaking to a man. Judging from his appearance he was a working man, a common man; still she treated him with concern and respect. I could see her write something on a piece of paper which she gave him and as she stood up, she reached down and came up with what appeared to be money. As the man walked out past me, he seemed relieved of whatever burden he had brought to Eva Peron. She then paused momentarily at her desk, took out a compact and powdered her face which looked quite pale. I heard somewhere that she had been known to work through the night helping people who were in need. As she appeared in the doorway, my gaze left the mirror and I was a little embarrassed that I had watched that way. In any event, she extended her hand in congratulations to me and repeated much of what her husband had said. She further explained her work as head of the Eva Peron Foundation made possible by voluntary contributions. Before I left, I noticed that many people from various walks of life were waiting to see her. She is a most impressive woman."

This was the way of the Perons - impressive and extravagant, especially symbolized by their wardrobes. His was stacked with hundreds of suits, shoes, shirts, neckties, riding boots, caps and military hats. Eva's wardrobe bill during that time was said to have reached millions for fur, jewels and other finery. Where once, prior to becoming First Lady, her clothing was Argentine-made, her taste gravitated with her higher status to that of Christian Dior of Paris. She consistently lavished herself with riches, ostensibly to outdo the aristocrats who had once shunned her.

Eva's much publicized concern for the poor when coupled with her extravagance would seem to weaken support for her. Instead, she turned it around in her favor using it as a political weapon.

During Peron's presidential campaign, she called attention in one of her speeches to her own exquisite appearance as an indication of what Argentines could accomplish when she said: "You will all have clothes like these some day ... Some day you will be able to sit next to any rich woman on a basis of complete equality. What we are fighting for is to destroy the inequality between you and the wives of your bosses." It sounded very convincing in view of the very measurable evidence of her generosity.

Archie too enjoyed the generosity and national attention focused on him as a champion, though not solely because it was supported by the Perons. He was in essence getting accolades which were long overdue him as a champion; but Peron's attraction to Archie was explainable in the light of his unmistakable macho image and admiration for brute strength. They were seen many places together - from extended rides on Peron's yacht with Isabel, a pretty woman Archie had met - to a reserved balcony seat at the theater. And invariably, Archie would be recognized and invited to wave to the crowds.

"And I guess this might be construed as political support," he remarked to a member of the State Department who questioned his affiliation with Peron. Since Peron was campaigning and he was part of the scene, he knew how it might be viewed; but he could not concur in view of his non-political interests and the fact that other Americans had met Peron. Among them were Jack Dempsey, Sandy Saddler and Charley Johnston, not one of whom was questioned.

"Had I taken him up on his offer to remain in this country as his Minister over the Welfare of Children, I guess I'd really be in for it," he protested; "besides, it never was my intention to stay here."

Peron had gotten wind of the work that Archie was doing with children, often buying them shoes and clothing and, more importantly, building their confidence.

"I'll give you land as far as the eye can see," Peron had offered; but there was something more important to Archie Moore, who drew heavily on early character training or what some would call "mother wit."

"You've got to do two things, Archie Lee," Auntie had said. "You've got to first know who you are and then where you're going."

Well, if knowing who he was meant appreciating his heritage; if it meant exercising his will over conditions of adversity in order to succeed, then he had certainly achieved the former. Indications were that he had never looked outside himself for material things to validate himself thus not even a promise of wealth and position would steer him from the course he had set for himself when he was just a boy. He had long been convinced that anybody could succeed if he had the determination to do so. "Thank you, Mr. President, he had said to Peron; but I have some other aspirations to fulfill. I want to win the light heavyweight and heavyweight titles and then perhaps I can think about something else."

Isabel, the pretty Argentine girl, had advised him early on that Peron would eventually be driven from office and that if he stayed he would be in danger; but he didn't need convincing. He had achieved what he had set out to do. After three months and eight fights, seven of them won by K.O. and one draw, Archie Moore, as well as those who had met him, could attest not only to stellar performance as an athlete, but to the example he had set. Though not consciously, he had served as an ambassador, the difference lying in never having to debate or compromise his own or his country's policies.

He left Argentina with $9,000 earned from his fights and exhibitions, relatively rich by its standards and with an exquisite, gold, Swiss watch presented him by Juan Peron. He was richer still as a result of the good will of the people and the friends he had made. (He would return some two years later, after the death of Eva Peron in 1952, to fight in Argentina.)

Much of what Archie did not know about the Perons came later; evenso, it is doubtful that he even skimmed the surface what with the mysticism which surrounded them. Was Peron the true liberator or was he a tyrant? Was Eva the saint that some believed her to be or was she a "She-Devil?" It is plausible that their divide and conquer method of ruling - he the military, she the laborers - served to maintain an unstable equilibrium among the masses such that they were powerless to do anything about it. There was total control over every facet of their lives from the cradle to the grave, including the Catholic Church.

The much heralded Eva Peron Foundation, though dependent on voluntary contributions from the people, was tainted by allegations of coercion and threat of imprisonment. Eva herself was said to have personally ordered and overseen the torture and castration of rebel leaders and several of her husband's opponents. Their testicles were allegedly kept in a jar on the same desk where she listened to and helped the poor. Her vengeance was held to be so strong that she jailed anti-Peronist, female aristocrats along with prostitutes to make the lives of the former more miserable. Funerals of aristocrats might be delayed, it was said, until such times as their families "paid-up."

For as many such grim tales that were told, one might find an equal number to extol the virtues of Evita, the "Lady of Hope." In 1952, she and Eleanor Roosevelt were named the two most important women in the world in Donald Robinson's, *The One Hundred Most Important People In The World*.

As for Peron, he was ousted from office in 1955, three years after Eva's death, having erred along the lines of economic nationalism, his regime's most cherished principle. Oddly enough, he granted petroleum concessions to the Standard Oil Company of California.

Peron took flight, finally finding refuge in Franco's Spain where he remained until 1972, returning that same year to Argentina to the presidency. He allegedly rose again to glory on the image of Eva, whose body was brought back into the capital, to Casa Rosada.

It might also be said of Peron that he left a lasting impact on Argentina and on the world; that his major achievements might be seen in the betterment of working conditions for the Argentine laborers. The tragedy lies perhaps in what he might have done with his golden opportunity as the "Liberator."

Noticias Gráficas

Registro Nacional de la Prop. Intelectual 396.714   Bouchard 722 - T. E. 32 - 7574-73-76-77-78-79 y 7570

40 Ctvs.   BUENOS AIRES, DOMINGO 23 DE AGOSTO DE 1953   AÑO

Esta mañana el campeón mundial de medio pesado, Archie Moore, visitó al general Perón en la quinta presidencial de Olivos, para testimoniarle sus afectos y el agradecimiento al pueblo argentino

El General Perón, Aclamado en el Luna Park

Señaló un hecho poco común la presencia del general Perón sobre el ring del Luna Park. El primer mandatario, a pedido del Dr. Valenzuela, entregó a Archie Moore una medalla de oro como recuerdo de su actuación en nuestro país. El público, emocionado, aclamó intensamente al general Perón

Juan Peron admired and loved the boxer, Archie Moore. Peron had been an amateur boxer when he taught at Argentina's War College.

Top to bottom: The crowd cheers as Moore bows and presents flowers to Eva Peron.

Even as a heavyweight, Abel Cestac was no match for the scientific boxer, Moore.

Cestac's blood went flying, splattering both Evita and the president, Juan Peron. Cestac was stopped in "10".

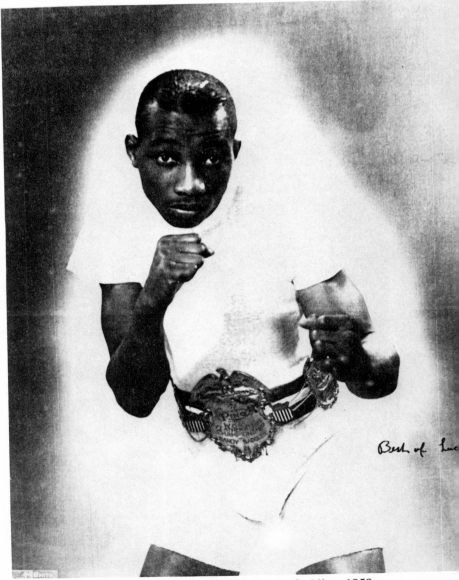

Featherweight Champion of the World, Sandy Saddler, 1950.

CHAPTER XIII

A Shot at the Title:
Moore vs. Maxim

Word had reached Archie before leaving Argentina that his long awaited crack at the light heavyweight title was finally in the offing; so why was the blood not pulsating more heavily in his veins? He became a little annoyed with himself as he flew back home gazing at the clouds through a window seat of the plane. Being so high up reminded him of his own ascent to the top. "You fight to climb and once you're there, what them?" he wondered. "Do you curse the ground? Why do I feel this way? ... Damn, what's wrong with me?" He even played the "what if" game: "What if I hadn't gotten a shot at the title, would I have gone on fighting endlessly, being the gypsy and vagabond that the press calls me?"

Perhaps he might have, since fighting to Archie also meant sheer survival. He had known nothing else. But the reasons behind his hollow feeling had to do with not knowing what to expect of a first-class opponent like Maxim. He was confident he could beat him but not sure of how. "It's like preparing for an exam," as he recalled, "confident that you'll pass because you've studied, but not sure of the questions that will be asked."

"Well, he wasn't going to curse the clouds either; and by the time the plane landed in the good old U.S.A., he had snapped back as fast as one of his own left jabs. He was resilient that way.

Before taking on Maxim between September of 1951 and the fight, Archie fought nine bouts, losing only to Harold Johnson. He bounced back, winning the return match one month later. If the past was prologue, he would surely have a good chance at the championship.

How the plot thickened as Johnston and Kearns acted out their respective roles. While they were old friends, neither had previously agreed with the other nor with Archie that a title fight with Maxim had been denied him. Even as the fight was pending, neither was in a big hurry to get it going.

Charlie Johnston was not nearly the fight man that brother Jimmy had been; however, the one thing he admitted was that Archie could have taken Maxim long before.

Doc Kearns, it would seem, had special plans. As a former scrapper himself, as tough as the Klondike which bore him, he maintained a husky appetite for making boxing deals. He was notorious for it! "Yea," Archie sneered whenever he heard Doc touted for his craft, "and he probably teethed on the same carcasses as the wolves did."

"Aw, give him a break," was Johnston's retort, "its been a long time between paydays for Old Doc Kearns." (Doc had much earlier managed ten money-making champions including the likes of Jack Dempsey and Mickey Walker.) "Besides," added Johnston as though rubbing salt in his wound, "just look at how old Walcott was when he got a title shot!" It was the well-fed man telling the hungry man to take courage. This was literally the case, since Kearns himself was actually maneuvering his fighter so as to make as much money off him as he could. As for Johnston, he was Doc's "clone," raking in as much as he could from Archie's bouts, smiling and alleging that expenses were high, banking the money while his fighter scrounged for peanuts.

Where oh where were Moore's allies in this sport of foxes and jackals? Yes, there *were* people who were adept at ducking the rules. Through clever manipulation, they arranged matches with fighters other than the logical contenders.

Such was the case when Jack Kearns arranged the surprise match between Joey Maxim and Sugar Ray Robinson, then middleweight champion. Kearns had taken a lot into consideration, as Hiawatha Gray pointed out to Archie during one of their time-outs from a sparring session. He was like a good watchdog guarding his charge, quick to unveil the tactics of shrewd managers and promoters:

"Listen, Arch, you know the score. Ray draws a big house. Besides, any way you slice it, Kearns wins. If Maxim loses to Robinson, then you an Ray would pack Yankee stadium. Then too, Kearns has wormed his way into your contract with Johnston," Gray reminded.

"Well," replied Moore with a bit of resignation, "I guess I'm tied up tighter than Dick's hatband.

I know why it was done; but I'll be dammed if I can understand why Ray would step up to another division at a time like this."

"Perhaps Kearns is on some kind of mission, Arch. You know how the guy is. Why I heard somewhere that he once visited Al

Capone in jail and got a promise from him to become an altar boy. The man is persuasive ... that's all there is to it!"

There were those in sympathy with Moore's predicament, but they were not the matchmakers; consequently for six months, the only battle waged was with disappointment. This changed to deep resentment as he digested the Maxim-Robinson outcome.

Ray, the lighter of the two fighters, easily outpointed Maxim for thirteen rounds; but he had begun to weaken under the hot lights of New York's polo Grounds and the 104 degree weather unprecedented in that city's history. With the fight virtually won, he was unable to come out of his corner in round 14 thus making Maxim the only professional boxer to score a knockout (TKO) against Sugar Ray.

This is not to say that Maxim was without impressive credentials. He had won the national middleweight Golden Gloves title in 1940; was knocked out only once in more than 350 amateur and professional fights; and he fought doggedly for nine years to get a title shot at the American light heavyweight crown which he won from the great Gus Lesnevich in 1949. He decked Freddie Mills in London for the world crown.

Following Ray's upset, Archie consoled himself with the knowledge that his sentence under Johnston would soon expire thereby freeing him up to get his own shot at the title. Though limited by the politics of boxing, He felt he could certainly do no worse than Johnston had done.

Johnston obviously must have had a sixth sense; for just when Archie had begun to make his plans, he came forward with the announcement that the long awaited fight was to take place. "No doubt you and Doc Kearns have been to the well often enough," Archie grumbled silently; though they could not have waited too much longer in view of his fight record. He was indeed a formidable opponent, as Jersey Joe Walcott, then heavyweight champion of the world conveyed. When he appeared on September 9, 1951, on American Forum of the Air with a senator of the State of Washington, he commented on the alleged monopoly of the International Boxing Club:

"Boxing is a business. A fellow has a title and there is a fellow like Archie Moore standing first in line for a crack at that title ... and to me, Archie Moore is one of the greatest fighters we have had in a long time; but in all due respect to Archie Moore, you cannot very well blame the manager of the fellow who is holding the title if he avoids men like Archie Moore."

Walcott was referring no doubt to Maxim's easy upset before the Robinson fight of Irish Bob Murphy. Though no match for the clever Maxim, he had been advanced to the championship even though Moore was the logical challenger.

Now the die was cast and the inevitable Maxim-Moore fight was to be on December 17, 1952, just four days after Moore's thirty-sixth birthday. To him, it was like an emancipation, and like that era in the history of African Americans, Archie was not really home free. There would be a few more kinks in the chain as Kearns tightened his hold. But Archie was no novice; especially when it came to weathering the storm of disappointment.

Getting here had been a long haul though he had not drawn the burden alone. From the beginning, he had had the love of a family, the help of friends like George Porter, Mrs. James, Knox and Felix. As a matter of fact, he had figured intricately into the families of all of his friends and he valued this position. As he eloquently stated:

"If support of loved ones is a must for a man's success, it is even more important for us whose families have been splintered from the beginning. Our people have survived only through coping mechanisms which we've learned over the years. For me, boxing *is* coping, though it was not the road preferred for me by my mother and my auntie. Both wanted me to be a musician and, while I've always loved music, it was not the natural thing for me that boxing was. I've tried the violin, trumpet, and saxophone. Though I didn't succeed at any of them, I've remained a student of music. Why I can even remember a few lines I learned and have found true over the years:

Music's force can tame the furious beast!
Can make the wolf or foaming boar restrain his rage
The lion drop his crested mane
Attentive to song."

"I have used music," reflected Moore, "to find peace in troubled times through Negro spirituals. Even in my training camps when I listen to jazz, it keeps me calm and relaxed so that I won't forget what I'm about. You see, if a man lets anger get the upper hand, he loses before the first round. I have rarely if ever gone into a bout with rage or anger. I guess you might say, as it does in the old spiritual, 'I live the life I sing about in my soul.'"

On this note, Archie determined to do something else in conjunction with his fight with Maxim. He wanted to complete an unfinished symphony, to strike a harmony which he had not in his lifetime experienced. It was to have his mother and father present in St. Louis to see him fight Joey Maxim for the light heavyweight championship of the world. He supposed that some would not understand his feelings about this in that he had been reared by two loving people.

Separation from his real mother and father had somehow provoked him, even as a boy growing up. He had felt a twinge of sadness, even jealousy, when he saw fathers and sons on an outing or playing "pitch-and-catch" together. He had begun to feel it more after his uncle died, when no more of his sporting friends came around to shoot the breeze or listen to a boxing match or baseball game on the radio. Archie was grateful for such precious moments; but they had long since passed. He was not robbed of the knowledge of his parents but had not since his birth been permanently united with them. He supposed his situation was better than not to have been born at all. On the other hand, he had seen far too many teenage births end in disaster for the child whose parents were ill-equipped financially and emotionally to handle the responsibility of child rearing.

What his auntie and uncle had done was a wise thing and they saw to it that he had a good relationship with his mother. He lived with her from time to time, and when Archie's step father died, Auntie then took another son, Samuel, to live with them. Though appreciative, Archie now needed to salvage the relationship with his father that he had yearned for all these years.

Acting on a tip from his Uncle Joe Wright, his father's brother, he arrived in St. Louis for the title bout with his father's address in his pocket. After settling in, he called two long-time friends - Ernest Troupe, then a detective, and his old mentor, Monroe "Munchy" Harrison - asking them to accompany him to the place where his father was living.

"You know, Munchy," he said thoughtfully, "I'll bet my dad is as sorry as I am that he wasn't around to see me grow up; so I don't want to make him feel bad." And before they walked up to the house, they planned to carry out a priceless charade.

"Open up, Wright," Troupe's voice boomed as Archie's big fist rapped loudly against the not-too-solid door, making even more noise and adding to the authenticity as it rattled.

"Who is it?" the voice inside came back rather uncertainly.

"Its the police!" Archie rang out, fighting against the urge to laugh 'less he give away the plot at the door.

Once opened, the scenario saw two very officious-looking characters with drawn badges coming face-to-face with Archie's mirror image, Thomas Wright. Though not as tall or well developed, he had the same full face and twinkling eyes, the only difference being that the eyelids lacked the puffy appearance of the fighter's. Archie had earned and even desired this trait of a boxer, one he displayed as the birthmark of his profession. After all, had not boxing marked his birth from the womb of obscurity?

They carried on the impersonation until Archie could hide his anxiety no longer. "Dad," he said with years of longing, "don't you recognize me? I'm just like you ... I'm Archie, your son!"

Not Shakespeare not Shelly, Hemingway or Hughes, nor all the writers of note, could have duplicated the poignancy of the moment when the prodigal father and long-lost son clinched in a loving union, shedding tears for years of what might have been.

"Oh, you rascal," he said to Archie when the tears had cleared, "I've heard you were quite a jokester! You really laid one on me ... but you know," he began methodically to explain why he had not contacted his son. "I tried ...

"It's ok Dad, you don't have to explain anything. We're here now and its all that matters. I want you at ringside to see me win the championship." (This writer makes no attempt to portray the subject, Archie Moore, bigger than life. Indeed, what he exhibited is the stuff of human feeling.)

Consider, if you will, a comparable scenario that occurred in the early 1900's in far-away Greenland, later revisited in the *Blade Tribune*, June 2, 1987, Oceanside, California. The article is held most significant to this account as well as to history:

Karrie Peary, half-white and half-Eskimo, and Anaukao Henson, half-Black and half-Eskimo, both eighty, were located in 1986 by Harvard professor, S. Allen Counter, a neuro-scientist and Black historian who found out that Admiral Peary and Matthew Henson, discoverer in 1906 of the North Pole, had both fathered sons by Eskimo women. But these were events which paled by comparison to their discovery. They had braved extreme temperatures and the unknown in order to get to the North Pole.

The two men had been long-time friends; yet Henson, according to Counter, was classified as a valet, a traditional position for nonwhites in that day. He was first to set foot on and place the American flag on the North Pole. That factor notwithstanding, his role was down played with credit given mainly to Peary; however, to Eskimos, Henson was a real hero. To some of the descendants of Peary and Henson, their two half-Eskimo relatives were also heroes as they were the pride of their respective fathers.

The boys spent the first fifteen years of their lives in adjacent igloos until their mothers moved in different directions. It was not until 1986 that they saw each other when Counter brought them together. Though they had knowledge of who they were, they yearned to reunite with their American relatives.

Peary and Henson's relatives from Maine and Maryland were located and, according to the report, met with the two octogenarians. There were fifty from the Henson group and about seven from the Peary family. Some disinterest by the latter group was probably due to the knowledge that both men were married to American women when they fathered the two Eskimo sons, is what Counter supposed.

Both sons, much like their fathers even down to courage, braved the 100 degree difference in temperature as well as the difference in culture. Through a translator of the Eskimo dialect, Peary was heard to say, "It is hot here ... even the wind is warm"; while Henson conjectured smilingly:

"It must be nice to be here also when you are young and strong."

Both men, their accompanying sons and American relatives visited the graves of their fathers: Peary in Arlington Cemetery and Henson in a public graveyard in New York City.

It is a very human thing to want to know one's origins and Archie Moore was no exception. He'd now have to fish one more fly out of the ointment, however, and it fell in on the night before the Maxim fight. He didn't believe his ears when he heard Johnston bring up the contract.

"Arch," he said, as though something had lodged in his throat, "Kearns wants you to sign a new agreement. He says if you don't, he'll call off the fight."

"Why that greedy mother ..."

"Take it or leave it!" he heard Johnston say as he left the room. It was evident that Kearns also had the upper hand with Johnston, a situation which never would have happened with his brother, Jimmy Johnston, Archie's former manager.

What could he do but sign the new pact thus waiving all interest in money to get the bout? He consoled himself with the thought that once he won the title, there'd be big purses down the road. He'd have to miss out on this one however - an $89,000 gate and more than $50,000 from television. Kearns had even gotten a $100,000 guarantee for Maxim. To top off this generous arrangement, he'd have none other than Harry Kessler as the referee. He knew he'd have to watch his step now!

As the odds makers would have it, many leaned toward Maxim, thought to have the endurance and vitality to go all the way; though Archie, even at thirty-six years old, had never indicated an inability to do likewise.

Maxim's style was practically all defense, with punches that seemed like powder puffs whenever he did succeed in getting through Moore's own virtually impenetrable shell- style of fighting. Moore stalked him so relentlessly that to get past him would be like sneaking dawn past a rooster. He blasted punch after well-aimed punch finding Maxim miraculously still on his feet after fifteen gruelling rounds, a credit to his ringmanship, as applause of the crowd indicated. The official decision saw Moore the top-heavy winner.

Only referee Harry Kessler, his old sore from boyhood, had seen it differently. Kessler alleged quite a bit of butting, intentional or unintentional, for which he deducted. And he knew Archie was a little provoked at him because he scored it so closely, as Bob Ortman of the *San Diego Tribune* reported.

The most stirring event of all, however, was for Archie to hear his own name followed by "new light heavyweight champion of the world"; to have his friends and mainly his parents see him realize his dream.

Archie Moore, though held one of the most dangerous men in boxing, was always anxious after a bout to know of the well-being of his opponent. His attempt to do so after the Maxim upset was met with a scowl from Kearns as he held up his hand and quipped, "Never mind the condolences, kid; we've got all the money!"

He couldn't have made a truer statement, since Archie's $800 share of the purse was not nearly enough to pay his sparring partners. "I even had to borrow money to get out of town 'cause the hotel bill had to be paid," he told the press.

Be that as it may, Moore now had the crown and there was more money to be made. It seemed, however, he still had to deal with his new "manager," the vigilant Doc Kearns. (The secret agreement concocted by Kearns and Johnston had not been recognized by any of the athletic commissions thus Johnston was still recognized as manager. Moore referred to Kearns only as his "adviser.")

Well, Ole Arch was going to give them a little more to talk about. He would fight Maxim in a return match slated for Ogden, Utah, a great fight town. And if he had to say it himself, Johnston must have had a lot of confidence in him inasmuch as he borrowed $10,000 from the International Boxing Commission against the return match which Archie again won in 15 rounds. He was in and the water was fine.

It seemed as though Johnston and Kearns were also gleefully riding the crest of a wave, testing the waters again in another South American tour in August of 1953. This time, however, Archie was not along for the ride. He was now Archie Moore, "El Champion!" He and Sandy were again a twosome, fighting in universities, in small towns and even in prisons, and Archie was the toast of the town.

Once again he was invited by his old friend, Juan Peron, to Casa Rosada; but this time, things were rather subdued. Peron seemed to lack some of his vigor and the charismatic appeal which he usually displayed.

He beamed, however, when Archie presented him with the gloves he had worn to win the light heavyweight championship. And for a moment, only the black armband served as a reminder that Peron was mourning Evita.

Eva Peron

DESERET NEWS AND TELEGRAM, Salt Lake City, Thursday, June 25, 1953

The Action Was Fast, Sharp, as Archie Retained Championship

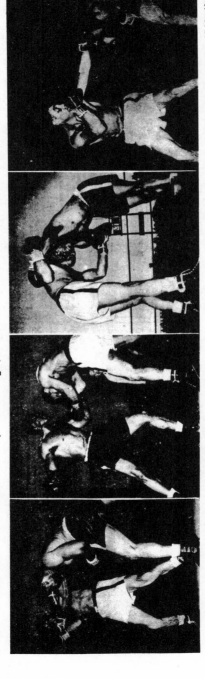

JOEY CAUGHT A HARD RIGHT HERE | AND THERE GOES ANOTHER BLOCKBUSTER | THE INFIGHTING WAS PLENTIFUL, CLASSIC | AND JOEY GOT IN SOME GOOD PUNCHES
... Moore had the heaviest artillery all evening ... But Maxim's stylish boxing stirred the fans | ... While Maxim stayed inside he retained edge | ... Maxim uncorked good blows; this missed.

(Photos by Ray G. Jones and Lionel McNeel's, News-Telegram staff photographs.)

Moore Rallies . . . Keeps Boxing Crown

Second Moore-Maxim fight.

Squeezed For Time

Favor Archie
To Beat Bobo

Challenger 2-1 Underdog
For Light-Heavyweight Crown

BY JOHN P. CARMICHAEL
Sports Editor

NEW YORK — Archie Moore and Carl "Bobo" Olson, who fight Wednesday night at the Polo Grounds for a shot at Rocky Marciano's heavyweight championship, paid formal calls on one another this noon.

Beside the official scales at Madison Square Garden. they shook hands briefly. Then Moore, the light-heavyweight titlist shed everything but shorts and socks and got on the scales.

There was some whispering and a few grins and finally Moore's weight was announced as 175, exactly the limit he had to make.

Actually the figure was 174 and 15-16ths and Archie, all smiles, pointed a finger at Julius Helfand, chairman of the New York Boxing Commission and said: "See. I told you."

OLSON, shedding his socks but slim and straight in his underwear. was caught at 170¾. In contrast to Moore's smiling recognition of shouts and waves, the middleweight champ- presented a poker face. nodding his head slightly at friends and well-wishers around the ring.

Dr. Sam Sherman, personal physician to Olson, made a request to use oxygen between rounds, if necessary. But chairman Helfand ruled it out.

He referred to it as a "gimmick" and suggested that if this were permitted, fighters would think up other media of assistance in future bouts.

MARCIANO'S manager, Al Weill. pin-pointed as to how Moore and Olson will fare, said: "I lean to Moore . . . heavily." Jack Kearns, who watched Moore defeat Joe Maxim three times, said: "How can you go

TIME is running out on Archie Moore. At 38, when most professional athletes are over the hill. Moore is risking his light-heavyweight title Wednesday night against a man 12 years his junior. The time squeeze is even greater in Moore's pursuit of Heavyweight Champion Rocky Marciano. Moore has to beat Olson to get a September shot at Marciano.

How They Compare		
ARCHIE MOORE		CARL "BOBO" OLSON
38 Yrs.	**AGE**	26 Yri.
6 Ft.	**HEIGHT**	5 Ft. 10½ In.
175 Lbs.	**WEIGHT**	170½ Lbs.
40 In.	**CHEST (Normal)**	39 In.
43 In.	**CHEST (Expanded)**	41 In.
18 In.	**BEACH**	70 In.
17 In.	**NECK**	16½ In.
16½ In.	**BICEPS**	13 In.
12½ In.	**FOREARM**	11¾ In.
32 In.	**WAIST**	31 In.
12 In.	**FIST**	12 In.
21 In.	**THIGH**	22 In.
13 In.	**CALF**	13 In.
7½ In.	**WRIST**	7¼ In.
11 In.	**ANKLE**	10 In.

Facts and Figures

PRINCIPALS — Light-heavyweight champion Archie Moore of San Diego. Calif. vs. middleweight champion Carl "Bobo" Olson of San Francisco.

TITLE AT STAKE—Moore's light-heavyweight championship.

DISTANCE—15 rounds.

PLACE—The Polo Grounds.

PROMOTER—Jim Norris.

EXPECTED CROWD—35,000.

EXPECTED GATE—$330,000

TV-RADIO FEE—$100,000

FIGHTERS' PURSES—Moore gets 30 per cent of all net receipts. Olson' ret, 27½ per cent.

TIME OF MAIN EVENT—9 p.m. (CDT).

TELEVISION—Nationally to homes over ABC network with 60-min. blackout in New York area. Chicago outlet, WBKB, Channel 7.

BROADCAST—Nationally over ABC network

BETTING—Moore favored at 2-1.

WEATHER — Somewhat cloudy, warm, humid.

17 RAIN: Postponed to Thursday night.

RETURN BOUT—If Olson wins, contract provides he give Moore a return title bout within 90 days.

WINNING STREAKS — Olson has 21 straight victories. Moore. 20.

"Squeezed For Time".

SPORTS ARENA — LOS ANGELES

RAY ROBINSON

"Pound for Pound" considered one of the greatest fighters in the history of boxing. Joey Maxim became the only professional boxer to score a knockout (TKO) against Sugar Ray as Middleweight champion.

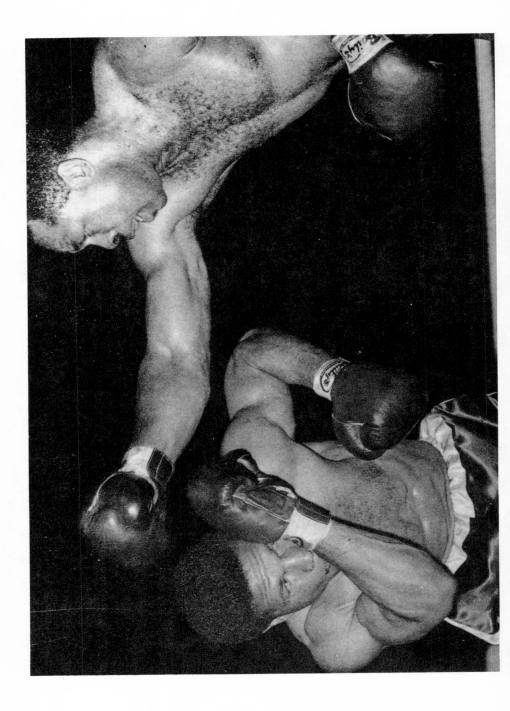

CHAPTER XIV

Legend of the "Mongoose":

A Diligent Press

Champion Archie Moore's return to the United States in 1954 heralded a third Moore-Maxim bout. It was the same year of Brown vs the Board of Education by which decision segregation in public schools was declared unconstitutional. This did not, however, affect public gatherings which remained segregated. This was also the first Black-white, American championship match to be fought in the state of Florida.

Even the unbelievably talented "Step Brothers," the toast of Paris, had been confronted in earlier years in Miami with signs which warned, "No Jews, Dogs or Niggers Allowed!"

Only Gavilan, the Black Cuban, had fought Bobby Dykes a few years prior to this in Florida. Archie so wanted, therefore, to be at his best. There was just one thing that he had not counted on. His gypsy-like existence had already seen the failure of two marriages including his marriage to Kay. He was now married for a third time to a school acquaintance whose name shall remain anonymous. As someone he'd known, he felt there would be mutual understanding by virtue of her knowledge of his earlier struggles. He had left her in San Diego when he went to New York and to other places to fight.

Even before this, however, the familiar signs of drifting apart had surfaced. And, as he would later admit after four marriages which did not work, "I blame no one. Its like a job - you have to work at it." But Archie was a globe trotter and he was hardly around. To a woman married to a budding world champion, boxing could well have been viewed his mistress.

He embraced boxing, loving her for sticking by him when no woman would, for allowing him to use his hands to fondle and flirt with success, to kiss the mouth that opened the way for him to move out of unfulfilled desire to a delirious climax. Boxing was his everything! He often wondered why he continued to try the institution of marriage; though in some cases he had powerful urging (a statement which will no doubt evoke criticism from women who persist in believing that it is a man's pursuit).

Moore was not against marriage by any means. He had witnessed some which worked: Auntie Willie and Uncle Cleve, Felix and his wife, former manager, Cal Thompson, and his wife. At least in those instances, he had seen give and take relationships. Each time he took the step, he also hoped and believed it was the right woman.

It was also a matter of wanting children and a conviction about fatherhood which grew out of his own longing for his real father who, for most of his life, resided but five hundred miles away from Archie. With the former knowledge acutely stamped in his memory, he tried very hard and often pondered the failure of his marriages. To marry or not to marry; whichever he did, it seemed he regretted it.

Just prior to the Maxim fight, Moore had gone to Toledo to pick up James "Cheerful Norman," (not aptly named since he was quite a somber individual, rather rigid and a no-nonsense gambler).

He arrived at the home Cheerful occupied with his wife, Lucille. As the men talked about things in general, they could hear voices coming from the downstairs living room.

"That's my wife!" announced Archie, her arrival surprising both men since she had to have driven non-stop to get there.

"Damn," remarked Cheerful, she's a strong woman (though strong willed might have been a better description)!

"I'm happy to see you," Archie offered; "but I wasn't expecting you. Is anything wrong?"

"I just thought I should be here," she declared, despite their prior discussion about why he had to go alone.

"The fight is in another couple of weeks," he told her, "and you know we can't afford it financially, nor can I afford to worry. It would be distracting, honey. You know what training is like."

Reluctantly, she left the next morning headed back to San Diego, refusing to leave the car and get a flight back as Archie suggested. He drove behind her to be certain she would not miss the trail going south.

To his utter shock and irritation, she showed up in Miami on the day before the Maxim bout, pursuing a line of questioning which indicated her distrust. Such feelings surfaced when she made public allegations that Archie had failed to give her financial support. Her protestations found a willing ear with the authorities; especially since she seasoned it with allegations of "affairs with white women." Now if the former charge was to stick, she used the right glue, considering conditions in Florida and this Black-White, precedent-setting championship match.

There it was on the front page the next day: "Archie Moore Behind Bars." "They attached my purse and treated me like garbage," he exclaimed bitterly. "If it hadn't been for Doc who convinced them otherwise and posted my bail ..."

With access to both fighters, Jack Doc Kearns was a familiar visitor at both camps. And though the old guy was a pest, Archie liked him. On the morning before weigh-in, however, he had his doubts. He puzzled as he stepped on the scales to see the needle register five pounds overweight. "How can this be!" he wailed. "I've weighed several times this week and earlier today" Archie knew something was amiss because he had followed his diet religiously. Fifteen days before the fight he was weighing 183 pounds and was rounding into shape. Where had he gone wrong?

Moore's pre fight schedule had never included strenuous roadwork on the day preceding a fight; but there he was in the broiling southern sun trying desperately to make weight. When he returned and weighed, he knew he'd been "had". Doc Kearns, it seemed, had played with the scales, supposedly as a practical joke. "Some joke ... and what if I had weakened myself in the effort?" he fumed, though finally laughing at himself.

Miami provided a great setting for this rematch, attracting avid fight fans and celebrities such as Lena Horne; Errol Garner; Art Tatum; Humphrey Bogart and Lauren Bacall; Burt Lancaster and the suave, supersportsman, "Black Dot" McGee from Los Angeles.

Not the least of them was one whose presence gave Moore one of the greatest honors he could have received. Thurgood Marshall, one of the sharpest constitutional minds of the century, had come to see him fight. "You are the only reason why I'd come here and sit in this segregated arena, Archie Moore! I want to see you whip him," he said quite soberly.

He did it a third time in a fifteen rounder; but this time, he truly flaunted his boxing skill by decking Maxim twice, a feat not easily accomplished. (Years later, Maxim would describe Archie Moore as the greatest fighter of all time. "He fought all the tough ones," he admitted.)

After winning the fifteen-round rematch, Moore felt like a true champion. Seventeen years of seasoning had finally paid off. His skills as a scientific boxer were amazing and even considered phenomenal by some in view of his ripe age of 38, held as old for the ring.

Jack Murphy, sports editor for the *San Diego Union Tribune* explained it effectively and almost poetically when he wrote that Archie Moore still would not turn the page on the calendar. He fought, wrote Murphy, as though it were the springtime of his life. According to Murphy, the only month he seemed to recognize was May.

It wasn't easy to survive the fight game as Moore had for over a quarter of a century; but he managed it with strength of character, a glib tongue, a "secret diet," and most of all, with a pair of lethal fists. Not to be overlooked above all is the game he played with the press. They followed this pied piper of fistdom, lured by his prowess and unique ability to manipulate words. He was capable of sopping up a few paragraphs of ink wherever he went.

It was just about this time and the Maxim fights that the press began tagging Moore with the title "Mongoose," a name he had chosen for himself. In explaining the reason, he advanced what sounded like a page from the *National Geographic* when he explained:

"The mongoose is a cagey and fierce animal, so fierce that he will fight the dreaded cobra, depending on technique to combat the cobra's swift and deadly blows. But the mongoose is faster and he can feint the cobra out of position by waiting until the very last moment to move, making the cobra miss and miss and miss until he fails to retract effectively. The mongoose then moves in for the kill, seizes the cobra under the throat and crushes his skull."

Hence the origin of the nickname, and it was one with which few argued, least of all, the men he had whipped. As one Langdors has said, "Nicknames and whippings, when they are once laid on, no one has discovered how to take off."

Accounts of Moore's exploits read like adventure. He sparred with the press like no other boxer of modern times. He accomplished it with the style of a professor, often concocting his own terms and varying the pronunciation of words with great aplomb. Reporters grabbed at the bait as would catfish to worms after a good rain. Each one attempted to "out-name" the other, laying monikers on the champ which razzed him about his weight, his secret diet, but mostly about his age.

Thus to "Mongoose" was added "The Old Mongoose" and other creative titles which were sprinkled throughout the accounts of Moore's escapades. They were creative to say the least...

MOORE'S PRESS TAGS

Ancient Arch
Old Arch
The Ancient One
Childe Arch
The Venerable Vagabond
Ageless Archie
Merry Methuselah
The Antique
The Relic
The Old Ring Master
Amazing Archie
The Ageless Phenomenon
Graying Gladiator
The Genial Gypsy
Bearded Patriarch
The Amazing Antique
Fallen Arch

The Elderly Pitchman
The Old Gentleman
The Aging Tiger
Captivating Con Man
Pugilistic Antique
Old Gray Fox
The Artifact
The Maestro
Agile Archie
Magnificent Faker
San Diego Square
Traditional Con Artist
The Elder Statesman
Old Philosopher
Bearded Prince
Ancient Gypsy
Fistic Fable

Impenetrable Legend ...

Heat's On

Moore sparred with the press as no other boxer in history.

From left to right:
Joey Maxim, Manager of Rocky Marciano and the "Foxiest" manager of them all, the great "Doc" Kearns.

Archie Moore and Rocky Marciano weigh-in, New York, 1955 (*Ring Magazine*).

CHAPTER XV

Coming Close: Moore vs. Marciano

"Moore Lore" has been voluminous, stacked with events in the career of a man of courage, undisputedly one of the greatest boxers and most colorful personalities of all time. A vivid description of Moore's press pageantry was given by Dick Beddoes of the *Vancouver Sun* May 6, 1958. In a column entitled "From Our Tower" he conveyed that more stories had been told about "Childe Arche" than about any man in his field, living or dead, including John L. Sullivan; that both lies and fiction surround him, but as honor and tribute. He contended that Archie Moore was even better than Paul Bunyan.

An avid reader himself, Moore's attention was drawn just after the Maxim fight to a news headline which read: "She Can See If She Can Get $800." It was a tear-jerking account of the plight of Cora Lee Hunter, a five-year-old blind girl whose sight in one eye was able to be revived while one eye had to be removed. Offering his services free of charge was a vacationing master surgeon. Money was needed only for Cora Lee's pre and post-operative care. This grabbed at the champion.

As Archie crossed the swimming pool area of the Moulin Rouge after breakfast that morning, he ran into Howard Moore, one of his jazz cronies who had seen the same article. "Man, just look at this," Howard spouted excitedly, "Wouldn't it be great if we could raise the money? With all the celebrities down here, this is a cinch ... and with your name behind it too!"

The champ began by putting up the first $200 of what he had and he hadn't much. His purse had been attached due to his wife's allegations of nonsupport; therefore, they literally begged from door-to-door the two's and few's from neighbors and merchants, the sum of $1100. Inspired by this accomplishment, they decided to sweeten the pot for whatever other needs might arise. He went on local radio and television with Cora Lee to make an appeal to the general public.

He even visited the great Lena Horne, then appearing at one of the big clubs. She gladly gave Archie one of her sizeable residual checks. It would seem her goodness matched her beauty. Thus with such cheerful giving, the goal was met and by the time the scheduled operation arrived, the sum had swelled to $11,500.

Returning to San Diego, Archie anxiously awaited results. After two weeks, he received a letter from Cora Lee's grandfather who sent a news clipping with the headlines, "She Can See!" It was this kind of humanistic endeavor which gave a counterbalance to Moore, the pugilist. He was as merciless in the ring as he was sensitive to human feeling outside of it. He was a man of many dimensions, not the least of which were courage and a dogged persistence.

After his third defeat of Maxim in 1954 and three additional KO's - Bob Baker, Bert Whitehurst and Harold Johnson, Moore, according to the San Diego Commission doctor, had developed a heart problem, a palpitation or uneven beat which would prevent him from fighting until it was treated.

The legitimacy of that finding notwithstanding, Moore was more than a little vexed even years later in 1986 when he met Dr. Dan 0. Kilroy at a Rotarian function honoring Nick Taviglione, prominent businessman of Riverside, California.

"I know you were put out with me," volunteered the white-haired Kilroy who had aged less graciously than Moore the Mauler, "but I couldn't have done otherwise. I didn't want to risk your life .... You were a great champion."

"Uh-hmm," grunted Moore with a still unconvinced response, an attitude perhaps left over from his many experiences with those who had put so many blocks to progress in his way.

In any event, medical treatment and an additional shot of will power paid off when Moore was matched one year later against big, rough, Nino Valdez, a real test for his ticker. After a clear-cut, fifteen round decision, it was on to New York for a bout with Bo Bo Olson, the arrangement of which was as engaging as the bout itself.

Enter again Doc Kearns, management magician, master of the slight of the mouth. What Kearns was about was inching Moore closer to a title fight with Rocky Marciano, then heavyweight champion of the world. Olson was a willing accomplice, due in part to the convincing argument made by the Doc who presented a bill of goods which might have outsmarted a super lie detector.

Writers such as Alan Goldstein of the *San Diego Sun* revisited the charade as late as 1985, following up Moore to hear him spin amusing anecdotes about the infamous Jack "Doc" Kearns. Doc was described to Goldstein as so convincing he could sell Willie Shoemaker a dead horse. His eyes danced when he discussed money, spending it faster than his fighters could make it.

"Speaking of robbing Peter to pay Paul, he borrowed $10 from me to catch a cab bound for wherever he could find Sid Flaherty, Bo Bo's manager, and the "luck of the Irish" couldn't have helped him elude the Doctor," alleged Moore. in his familiar half-joking manner, a characteristic which left reporters either scoffing at him or believing enough of his yarn to write it.

Like a Philadelphia lawyer, Doc began making a case for why matching Bo Bo with Moore would be almost charitable, as Goldstein's article reported. He wept and moaned over Moore's bad ticker, alleging that Bo Bo would be a cinch to win, and then command a million to fight Marciano. In the meantime, it would give Moore a chance to make one last badly-needed payday, the article went on to relate.

With that last saga of "Les Miserables," Flaherty dabbed at his eyes and threw in the towel and a $30,000 advance to sweeten a pot from which Doc and Moore dipped equally. The next order of business was to attend to weight and training for the fight scheduled June 22, 1955, seven weeks away. Moore had to take off 20 pounds, having fought Valdez at 193 pounds. The plot was complete when after three rounds, Bo Bo was out cold and Doc began yelling for a shot at Marciano. (The humor in that saga was evidently not lost on Goldstein.)

Let it not be assumed, however, that Doc was like some "'Lone Ranger," singlehandedly lassoing the public with his convincing schemes; for Moore had also dogged the trail in a publicity campaign which soon made the Marciano-Moore match the one that everyone wanted to see. "Wanted: Reward For Capture And Delivery Of Rocky Marciano To Any Ring In The World ... Advise Sheriff Archie Moore," read one of the posters. It aided in building during that era, the largest financial gate since the advent of television.

According to Arthur Daly of *The New York Times*, Moore used a match of nimble brain and tongue as few challengers had done. Daly admitted that the Ancient Gypsy was cute and clever, predicting, on the other hand, that Rocky's ruthless pounding would pick Moore apart. He held to but one certainty: that if winning was dependent on conversation, Rocky wouldn't have a chance.

One day before the fight found champion and challenger in the office of the New York State Boxing Commission to discuss the rules agreed upon by the commission and managers, Al Weil and Charlie Johnston.

"They'll be no mandatory-eight count in the fight," instructed Jules Helfand. "A fighter is fair game once he is on his feet." Yes, each heard it ... the smooth-looking, skillful artisan, Moore, and the non-stop slugger and slam-bang, "any punch" wrecker, Marciano.

Moore felt the rule to be clearly in his favor since his plan was to knock Rocky down and, if he got up, to rush him for a knockout. Presumptuous you say? Not with due consideration for a style which made Rocky easy to hit, as Walcott had already proven. Walcott had been the first to accomplish it; but Rocky had the stamina and recuperative strength of a rhino.

First round ... zeroing in on an edge-of-seat audience, eyes fixed on two proven champions refereed by Harry Kessler. "Who taught you how to box," taunted Moore in the first round? "You fight like a washer woman!"

On to round two and a red-faced Rocky who needed no invitation, coming out swinging in the familiar Marciano "rush 'em" style - all offense. Pete Coutros of the *New York Post* labeled Moore's detonating delivery as the "sucker right" which drove Marciano to the canvas early in the second round. Moore explains it in graphic detail:

"After he got up and Harry Kessler ... had counted "4", Marciano staggered to the ropes as I was sent to the nearest corner and watched in amazement as Marciano places his big forearms over the ropes and stares out at a throng of over 60,000 fans as though apologizing for getting hit. Barely audible over that screaming sea of people, I could hear my cornermen yell, 'Hit him, hit him' ... there's no mandatory - "8" count!" (Moore becomes quite demonstrative and emotional as he continues this account.) "As I go toward Marciano to take advantage of my edge, Kessler steps between us, turns to me and begins wiping my gloves. Why, I'll never know. I hadn't hit the deck, so there was no rosin on my gloves. He then turns to Marciano, wipes his gloves and gives him a jerk which brings him to his senses ... and with the bell signalling the end of the round, Marciano is on the road to recovery.

The rest is history, one that might have been different if not for Kessler."

While some have not concurred with Moore's version, written fight accounts abound with controversy regarding one man's victory over another. Jim Bailey of the *Little Rock Gazette* commented on the 1927 Dempsey-Tunney return match in Chicago and the infamous long-count of anywhere from 14 to 20 before Tunney got up. The referee's attention was split between counting and making Dempsey stay in his corner to prevent his standing over Tunney to hit him when he got up.

Oscar Fraley, writing for *Boxing*, September, 1957, explained that by the time Dempsey moved to a neutral corner, the count had reached "5". But Barry's next count, which should have been "6" by the knock--down timekeeper's toll, had started over at "1" from the time Dempsey reached the far corner.

While the account reveals that Tunney consistently maintained he knew what he was doing and could have gotten up at any time, millions felt Dempsey had won by knockout thus making him even more popular than Tunney. In the dollar market, however, Tunney reigned supreme as a millionaire, champion fighter.

"I've heard all the stories," Moore reminds. "But at the risk of being labeled a sore loser, my own near victory has always made me wonder why the fight film of the Marciano-Moore confrontation contained none of Kessler's moves after the knockdown."

Why had Johnston not objected in the first place to Kessler as the referee? Would it have been different had Moore been able to rush Marciano for a KO as he had planned? The knockdown had not been just a lucky punch; for Moore had proven himself the more scientific boxer, able to maneuver his opponent into a vulnerable position. But Rocky's science was his strength and he used it in most of his KO victories to wear down his opponents with an accumulation of punches before the hay-maker. He literally broke the blood vessels in the arms of Roland La Starza who attempted to use them as armor against the rain of punches he brought down on him.

Daly reinforces this in his description of Rocky's strength in a *New York Times* article (1965) when he said Joe Louis couldn't raise his arms above his head for two weeks after taking a pounding from the ceaseless fire of the Block buster.

Victory had been close, "but close only counts in horse shoes", Moore reflected. "I carried a grudge against Kessler until he died in

1987; but when I heard of Marciano's untimely death in an air crash, I was deeply grieved. He was a great champion and a truly nice guy."

(Moore was later in 1988 to receive the Rocky Marciano Award. He was flanked by his oldest daughter, Rena, and young Rocky Marciano Jr. During the same year, he was named by *Ring Magazine* as the "Greatest Light Heavyweight in the History of Boxing.")

What is it that lures a man long recognized as the best in his division to cross over into the heavyweight class? One answer is found in Moore's description of himself: "I've always been curious ... I like to experiment," he confesses. And there would be additional opportunity to do so in the heavyweight category.

Marciano was reported to have said when he hung up his gloves: "If an old man like Moore can give me that much trouble, it's time for me to retire." That decision left the heavyweight title vacant, giving Moore a shot at Patterson, the logical contender.

Moore's conviction about winning was bolstered by the knowledge that Patterson had been decisioned only by Maxim and his own three-time victory over Maxim was now stamped in everyone's memory. But there were still some reservations.

Was he too old by some predictions to fight the young and also scientific Patterson? Regardless to the answer, Moore knew he had to continue fighting to keep in shape as well as for the money.

His concentration had recently been wavering, however, between fighting and his other fixation - that of jazz and some of the colorful personalities it produced. They were men and women who, like Archie Moore, had persevered despite the odds. Though unrewarded except by the beauty they created, they also went on fighting so to speak. It is perhaps the reason why he gravitated toward them.

In a kind of traveling-road-show fashion, Moore teamed up with Lucky Thompson, a great tenor sax man. He felt his own reputation as champion might attract a following for Lucky as well as for the jazz which they nurtured. Lucky featured Horace Silver on piano, Kenny Clark on drums, and Beverly Peer on bass. They appeared in small towns in shows which proved enjoyable though not financially rewarding. (Lucky's recording of "Just One More Chance" cut around 1947 eventually became a collector's item.)

The team effort had to be scrapped though not because of Moore's lack of interest. It was mainly because his activities had meant late hours and neglect of training. "Cheerful Norman", then his trainer, had been on a tirade regarding this new regimen, to which Moore's reaction was, "Everybody's got to take time out now and then, Cheerful." But he was anything but cheerful and after much nagging, Moore entered into rigorous training to gear up for Patterson who had come up through the ranks and was himself a swift-punching fighter whose style Moore knew very well.

"I trained harder than ever before," he recalls, "boxing six rounds a day, doing three-to-four miles of road- work a day, and even after getting in trim, Norman continued to work me, or rather overwork me. I proved no match for Patterson. As I worked around him, it felt as though I was moving about on foam rubber; but it was my legs that were weak. Finally, I couldn't avoid his punches and he knocked me out in round four."

"Excuses you say, ... "an old man ... 'too old to fight a young champion like Patterson?'" He had proven recently to many that age was no barrier. His body was not the same as most at age 36; yet two unsuccessful efforts signalled that he should not pursue the heavyweight title further.

He had not even fleetingly, however, entertained leaving boxing altogether. It would seem also that his persistent, curious nature filtered into his personal life; for he decided to tie another knot in a string which had already broken four times in unsuccessful attempts at marriage. In 1956 he married Joan Hardy, a young woman he had met some seven years prior.

As the daughter of industrious Marie Hardy, Joan was the logical choice to show off the creations which her mother produced. She was all of 5-feet-10 inches tall, young and pretty. She and other young Black women had organized a group which regularly modeled at places like Small's Paradise on New York's lower east side. Another of the Hardy offspring, Juanita Hardy, dancer by profession, would marry actor Sidney Poitier, though that marriage is now dissolved.

Creativity was literally a strong thread within the Hardy family starting with the father, Ed Hardy, a master brick mason. He applied his artistry to veneering the Archie Moore home which has become a San Diego landmark. Its winding chimneys visible from freeway I-15 stand as testimony to the skill of Black men like Hardy. Such trades were handed down along with those of iron workers, cement finishers, plasterers and even morticians, most of whom emerged out of the Jim Crow South.

Example: Since at least the mid-19th century, the trade of brick masonry has passed through four generations of the descendants of Eloi

Darensbourg of St. John Parish, Louisiana and Philomene Sorapuru, niece of Thomy Lafon (educator, entrepreneur and philanthropist). The brick trade journeyed through sons, grandsons and relatives to New Orleans, Chicago and Los Angeles where it is currently practiced by the Douroux brothers and their offspring. Yet the pressure placed upon individuals, especially Black professionals in the world of entertainment and industry, has made success difficult to achieve.

Perseverance was decidedly the stuff of success in New York, where, even at the turn of the century, there was focus on social culture and fostering of the Negro's artistic genius. This became known as the "New Negro Harlem Renaissance," a cultural nationalism out of which emerged individuals who achieved in music, in poetry, oratory and painting.

Paul Lawrence Dunbar, noted for using Negro dialect within the formal structure of his work, gained national recognition as a poet. Born in 1872 to former slaves, he came into literary prominence in 1896 with one of his best - *Lyrics of a Lowly Life*. Before his death in 1906, he had published not only numerous dialect poems which had become his trademark, but many more in conventional English, still popular and yet in print.

James Weldon Johnson's love of New York and New Yorkers is a well-recognized phenomenon in his works as a writer. His novel, *Autobiography of An Ex-Colored Man*, first published anonymously in 1912, described passing [for white] and life on Manhattan's West Side with special focus on sports and theatrical people.

Most illustrative of the new racial consciousness was that exhibited by R.H. Boyd, Baptist leader and owner of *The National Doll Company*. Using the National Baptist Convention as a platform, he urged all Negro Baptists to buy Negro dolls for their children. In a publication, *The Crisis*, he called for initiative to "help in the Christian development of the race."

It was Booker T. (Tagliaferro) Washington, former slave, who dominated the public life of the Negro community for the last quarter of the nineteenth century. Gaining prominence as an educator, he became the spokesman for millions of American Negroes, urging them to acquire vocational skills and basics necessary to perform in an industrial society and eventually become a viable part of the economy. This approach, though satisfying some of Washington's Negro and white contemporaries, provoked discontent among the younger Negro leaders not satisfied "to take one job or title less than their full political and social right."

W.E.B. Du Bois, often contrasted with Booker T. because of their opposing views on education and the way to equality for Negroes, began writing in 1887 as editor of *The Herald* at Fisk University. He published in 1909, the same year as the founding of the NAACP, the Biography of John Brown, by his account, one of his best works. Until his death in 1963, he continued to produce and espouse the value of higher education for the Negro race.

The accomplishments of these and a multitude of Black pioneers must be seen in the light of the arena in which they operated. Consider that it must have been difficult to be creative and imaginative when the real world promised little for the Negro American.

Conditions of inequality are what produced a migration enthusiasm which centered chiefly on Northern cities. By the early 1900's for instance, New York had three-fourths as many Negroes as New Orleans. By 1913, there were over 35,000 within about eighteen city blocks; but after 1900 as the recognized leaders passed away, there seemed to be an emphasis on cultural Pride with an increasing stress placed on Negro self-reliance and on building politically the strength of the Negro community.

This group support for individual effort extended through the forties and fifties in New York, perhaps best exemplified in entertainment at the Apollo Theater about five blocks from where the previously mentioned Hardy family resided on 125th Street.

The Apollo was the birthplace of a plethora of super and lesser known talents. It boosted the careers of individuals such as Erskine Hawkins of "After Hours" fame, its piano rendition played by Avery Parrish. It has often been referred to in Black social circles as the "Negro National Anthem"; though "Lift Every Voice" by James Weldon Johnson more officially claims that title.

Comics such as Pig Meat Markham, Moms Mabley and Nipsy Russell used the Apollo stage as a training ground. It was where a hopeful could be made or broken, "thumbs up or thumbs down," in Roman gladiator style.

The famed Apollo was not without its royalty. It enjoyed appearances by "Lady Day" [Billy Holiday] and by Ella Fitzgerald with Chic Webb. Their "A Tisket - A Tasket" made Ella the household note of the decade, segueing her into a career yet unparalleled in popular music. She was a versatile performer, as much at home with Louis

Jordan and "Stone Cold Dead in De Market" as with symphony orchestras across the globe.

If Ella was queen, then part of her royal family must include Duke Ellington of the swing era; Count Basie of the "big band" forties era and Nat "King" Cole, the balladeer of "Mona Lisa" and "Route - 66" fame. Among countless princes and princesses were Lionel Hampton, genius on the vibre harp rendering tunes such as "Midnight Sun"; Illinois Jacquet doing "Flying Home"; and "Saucy" Sarah Vaughn whose rapid vibrato literally massaged the "Body and Soul". Her royal siblings, Billy Eckstine and Arthur Prysock, were part of the same style and quality of that era in Black music. The school of talents spawned by the Apollo was taken upstream in a lively current of competition and stardom.

The foregoing description has not been a departure from the life of Archie Moore. It was an integral part of his life as it was that of many city dwellers across a nation whose Black populous derived its sense of being and, in some cases, actual survival from its groupness.

Moore fraternized with many personalities in the music world; but after the Lucky Thompson tour, he knew he had to give quality attention to fighting to make a living in order to raise the family he was so eager to begin.

The Moore family was to grow into five children from his marriage to Joan: daughters Rena and Joanie; sons Hardy, De Anglo, named for his Argentine friend; Anthony, and adopted son, Billy. There are two children from a former marriage, Archie Moore Jr. and Betty Moore.

Auntie Willie died on November 8, 1988 in her late 90's. Moore's mother, Mrs. Lorena Reynold still lives at the age of 91. "They are my life," he was quoted as having said, much to the surprise of some of the press who long viewed him as a vagrant and wanderer; but public knowledge of Moore "the man" had not yet surfaced.

Auntie Willie

WANTED   WANTED   WANTED

REWARD

FOR CAPTURE

AND

DELIVERY

OF

ROCKY MARCIANO

To Any Ring in the World for the Purpose of Defending His Heavyweight Championship Against the LOGICAL contender ARCHIE MOORE.

REWARD: the Boxing Public Will See a Great Fight and Witness the Crowning of a New Champion.

ADVISE

(SHERIFF) ARCHIE MOORE

The kind of publicity waged by Moore himself aided in building, during that era, the largest financial gate since the advent of television. Moore wept when Rocky died.

Moore is the second man in the world to knock down Marciano. (Jersey Joe Walcott was the first). Kessler's actions perhaps changed

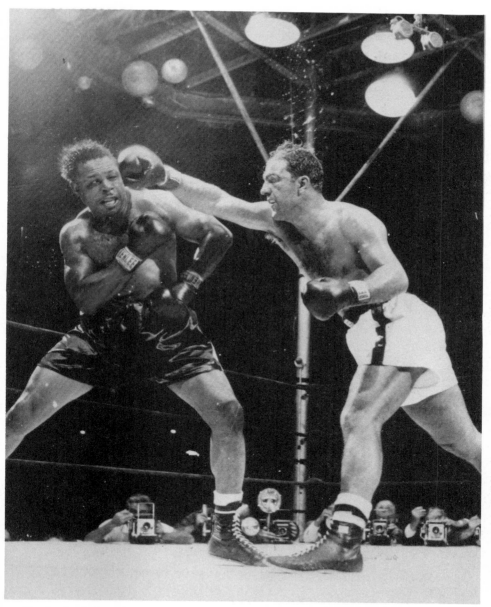

Rocky had the recuperative strength of a rhino. (*Ring Magazine*)

New York Amsterdam News

Vol. XLVII — No. 34   SATURDAY, AUGUST 25, 1956   Entered as Second Class Matter, Bridgeport, Conn.   CITY EDITION — 15c

Archie Moore Weds

MAN AND WIFE—light-heavyweight champ Archie Moore and Harlem model Joan Hardy flew out to the coast Monday and then rushed down to Mexico by auto to get married in a secret ceremony. Amsterdam News Woman's Editor Betty Granger was one of matrons of honor.

Jackson-Baker Winner May Meet Moore

PATERSON, N.J., Aug. 22 —Abe J. Greene, commissioner of the National Boxing Association, today specified that Archie Moore should get the first crack at the heavy-weight title, whether it be against Floyd Patterson or the Hurricane Jackson-Bob Baker winner.

Greene, up from his return from the annual NBA convention in Havana, where he was re-elected commissioner, made a statement to clarify confused reports emanating from the conclave that Moore would have to fight an "elimination" match before gaining his shot at Rocky Marciano's vacated title.

Confused Picture

In his efforts to clear up the confused heavyweight championship picture as far as the NBA is concerned, Greene stated that:

1—Moore is recognized as the No. 1 heavyweight contender (if a title bout is 'right behind him.'"

2—Patterson will be asked about the condition of his in-

NBA's Greene Says Archie to Get First Crack at Title

ARCHIE AND HIS BRIDE — Archie Moore, light-heavyweight champion, and his bride, former Joan Hardy of New York, smile for photographers in San Diego before they were married Monday in Ensenada, Mexico. They were married in Winnetka.

OF KINGS AND RINGS — Archie Moore, self - declared heavyweight champion of the world, and his bride, the former Joan Hardy, 24, a New York model, display fists and wedding bands. They were married in Ensenada, Mexico on August 20.

Joan Hardy Of Harlem New Bride

By BETTY GRANGER

ENSENADA, Mexico—World's light-heavyweight champion Archie Moore was married to curvaceous New York model and designer Joan Hardy here Monday after a thrilling coast to coast race between cupid and a United airliner DC-7.

The beautiful Mexican civil ceremony was witnessed by the bride's mother, Mrs. Edward D. Hardy, Mrs. Evelyn Cunningham and this reporter who flew here with the couple after being sworn to secrecy. This writer and Mrs. Cunningham, close friends of the bride, served as matrons of honor for her.

In one of the best kept secret moves in many a moon we slipped out of Idlewild Airport at 4:15 Saturday afternoon for a fast flight across the nation to the _____ plane's $80,000 San Diego, _____ home, pausing every- _____ to be joined by the groom's _____, Mrs. Willie P. Moore.

We also paused to pick up a $2,000 wedding band set with diamonds which the groom had ordered made up from New York by telephone. Monday morning the six of us motored across the border and 60 miles into the beautiful and colorful town of Ensenada where the couple's duet became a solo.

Mom Designs Gown

For the rites, the tall, beautiful bride wore a gown and jacket created by her mother, made of white embroidered satin and

CHAPTER XVI

Great Confrontation: Moore vs. Durelle

Though the Maxim fight might have provided a convenient place for this account to have stopped what with Moore's quest for the championship, it was the Moore-Durelle "Great Confrontation" which would lock him into the minds of fight fans as a one-of-a-kind fighter, a boxer emeritus. His performance in that fight could only have been described by two kinds of columnists: those who knew him and those who thought they did.

The mounds of press articles generated by that bout make description in this work manageable only within the context of a cursory analysis of some of that coverage. It has the support of first-hand accounts by the pugilist himself.

In the former case, some of the information used is without precise date or title, having been collected by Moore over half a century. He has outlived some of the very media men who counted him out; yet he has preserved his records and himself remarkably well.

New York columnist Jessie Abramson warned that Moore, whose age he guessed was 44 or something, would need to defy Father Time, old bones, graying hair and youthful, 27-year old Yvon Durelle in order to win. Bill Lee on the other hand conveyed in his column, "With Malice Toward None," that Moore must have been relying on some kind of heavy fire power to risk his title against the young French-Canadian, and in Montreal at that. There was, to say the least, much speculation over the outcome.

Gene Ward, predicting "Ancient Archie, 14-5 Choice to Whip Yvon in Montreal," reminded what a victory over Durelle would mean in terms of Moore's standing. A knockout, he pointed out, would give Moore the all-time kayo mark all to himself. He and Young Stribling, former light heavy and heavyweight contender, were even at 126 kayoes.

Moore wanted to leave a contribution to boxing as had Joe Louis as a 13-year title holder and Ray Robinson as a boxing stylist.

When urged to pick a round, however, Moore said only that his goal was to beat Durelle in the best way he knew how and many of the press underscored the know how. Eric Whitehead's "Moore the Merrier After Eyeing Durelle," predicted that Durelle would provide a virtual chopping block for the Ancient One. This prediction was no doubt prompted by Durelle's meager showing against Clarence Hennant, a second-rate fighter out of D.C. Durelle had gotten no better than a draw against another of Moore's old foes, a fact about which Moore commented with a tinge of sarcasm:

"Keep in mind that I had already taken Tony Anthony out in "seven" a year ago. And while we're on that subject, Tony Anthony seems to have some notion that my "ol gray head" will exit the ring in "five" this time as I pit myself against youth. I'd like to remind "Timid Tony" that its not my old gray head they respect, its my old, gray fist! Never under estimate your opponent, I always say; but you have to give it to Durelle. He's only 27 years old, a game Nova Scotia fisherman who is evidently confident enough to think he has the right bait to snag me." (Little did he suspect that Durelle would get an early bite.)

Lawrence Dayton described round one in "The Night Archie Moore Refused to Lose." He saw Durelle miss a few roundhouse hooks as he attempted to bob low as though to throw a left hook; but Durelle threw a right which collided with Moore's chin, sinking the old man to the depths like a stone.

Melvin Durslag of the *Los Angeles Herald Examiner* asked Moore to relate his experiences in terms of what his column labeled, "A Freak Accident."

Reconstructing in his mind just how the thing happened was reportedly how Moore first reacted to being knocked down. Secondly, as he explained, he had to make a conscious effort to get back on his feet. He further related to Durslag that a second knockdown was a sure sign that the man had found a weakness in his defense. Thus the knockdown was no accident.

He later recapped the melee for this biographer in his usual vivid pattern:

"Not since Lloyd Marshall sixteen years before Durelle had I been floored four times in a fight. If it weren't for the shock of Durelle's punch, I guess I would have been embarrassed. I knew the newsmen had already run to the phones to conjure up a headline like, "Old Man of the Sea Gaffed by Fisherman". "I just couldn't let that happen, not with so many people depending one me ... my wife out in the audience expecting our second child, my Auntie who had invested her life in me and most of all, my people. My win was their win. Even as Sharkey counted after each knockdown, I never lost my determination. Someplace in the back of my consciousness, I heard a voice ... 'When a task is once begun ... do it well or not at all.' As I got up and went to my corner, I was jarred by still another directive. It was the divisive Doctor Kearns telling me to look over at my wife and smile. I didn't understand it at the time; but as I smiled and winked, I could see Durelle staring at me in open-mouthed astonishment. He had thrown all 172 pounds behind those punches; so I guess he wondered what the hell he'd have to do to keep me down. Between the illusion and clinching, I was able to hold on; but by round five Durelle had hooked me again. Had gaining and losing sometimes 40 pounds between title fights weakened me? Was it true what they alleged - that Marciano had taken everything out of me?"

"As I got up this time, I determined to break Durelle's winning streak. No more clinching! I became Moby Dick, turning the harpoon on Captain Ahab, driving it home in round eleven! It was my clubs to the head and final left hook which set Durelle afloat on his back. He lay there belly up, taking "10" from the Shark!" (Jack Sharkey).

Sports writers went ape after the fight, trying to get an interview. While the Graying Gladiator spent the night in a steamroom, some camped on his doorstep. The next day saw a flood of national as well as international coverage.

"Archie Displays Amazing Courage," wrote Braven Dyer in "Sports Parade." As a 40-year, veteran sports writer, he commented that he had never before seen such a display of courage laid out for the world to see; that the test of courage is not to die but to live. Moore had unequivocally passed with the highest honors.

"Old Pro Archie Employed Left Jab to Trap Durelle," was the title employed by Bill Lee of the *Courant*, which labeled it a blood-curdling battle to end all battles in which champion and challenger were knocked down four times each. Though the challenger was seen to have punching power and tremendous strength, these were held no match for Moore's experience and the class derived from some 200 career fights.

Moore could finally appreciate the struggle and reflect by saying:

"Though everyone knew why it had taken me so long to get to the top, it didn't help me accept it since, as a KO artist, I was what the crowd wanted. Not even Dempsey, for whom I have a great admiration, was able to make the "All-Time Top Twenty" list in the KO department. He fell short by six percentage points."

"It is still the heavyweights who dominate the KO ranks. They just about double the percentage of light heavyweights; but in any case, it is the puncher and not the Fancy Dan who builds the gate. As a matter of fact, the record books show that punchers were featured in 99% of all fights when gates reached the $100,000 mark. Consider just a few - Tyson, Ali, Sugar Ray, Louis, Dempsey - as examples. Consider also the purses of today's champions by comparison. For the Durelle fight I got a $100,000 guarantee with a 20% option. ABC got its cut from the television end of it."

"My, how things have changed. Why I remember the time when I sparred with three-crown champion "Hurricane" Henry Armstrong for .50 a round. After a total of nine rounds and three days work, my total pay amounted to $4.50, an amount I never collected. Can you imagine by today's standard, including interest? Henry would owe me approximately $300,004.50. I can laugh about it today and I took pleasure in razzing Armstrong whenever I sawhim, threatening to sue him to collect what he owed me. But seriously, I guess money is one of the biggest motivating factors in the fight game for the men who fight as well as for those who wager. After the Durelle surprise action, they were definitely betting that a rematch would see me in trouble again."

Speculation actively ran the gamut as even Sugar Ray Robinson was reported by the press to favor Durelle to win, probably due in part, as Dink Caroll of *Gazette Sports* explained it, to Moore's refusal to fight him before the Durelle return match. Though a Moore vs. Robinson match would have proven a profitable sell out, Ray the challenger was demanding the big end of the purse from the title holder, an arrangement to which Moore logically objected.

What had Ray to lose in another division anyway? Perhaps Moore's tough time with Durelle had signalled to him that he'd have an easier time beating him than he would Carmen Basillio whom he'd dodged for some time. (This resulted in Ray's being stripped of his middleweight title by the New York State Athletic Association and it took legal action to get it back.) Perhaps Ray might also have considered himself a better finisher, as Carol conjectured, not likely to have let up on Moore once he had decked him three times in the first round.

Actually it was quite unusual to find the "Sweet One" out of the driver's seat. Goodness knows he had tried to maneuver Moore into his way of thinking by extending a dinner invitation to his own home in New York. It was cordial enough with both wives present; but the creole shrimp dinner proved tastier than the deal Ray cooked up.

To Moore, it had seemed more sensible to accept less from the promoters and hold out for a percentage from the televised fight. And as it turned out, he had correctly estimated the financial potential of TV sports even at that early stage of the game. (Companies such as Pabst Blue Ribbon and Gillette were among the early TV sponsors of "Friday Night Fights on the Air.")

What Ray proposed at his home, splitting a million dollars down the middle, again ignored that Moore was indeed the title holder. Thus demanding the big end put Ray in the position of the dog who thought he saw a bigger bone reflected in the water. He had literally opened his mouth and lost his chance as did the public who might have witnessed a fight to end all fights. The Moore vs. Robinson spectacular would never come about. Ray would still have Basilio and Moore would again face Durelle while making verbal overtures for a fight with heavyweight, Ingemar Johanssen. In addition, he had recently hit a new streak of luck.

With wide media exposure resulting from his phenomenal defeat of Durelle, Moore had not escaped notice of TV director, Norman Lloyd. He knew of Samuel Goldwyn's search for someone to play Jim, runaway slave in the movie version of Mark Twain's "Adventures of Huckleberry Finn."

According to Jack Stone of the *American Weekly* (1960), Goldwyn and Lloyd had discussed casting while taking a breather between tennis sets. There seemed to be some difficulty in finding a suitable actor for Jim. The character had to be sweet and simple yet sly and cunning. "Like Archie Moore," asked Lloyd?

"Precisely," echoed Sam Goldwyn!"

Lloyd saw Moore as having some of the same additional characteristics as the cunning and crafty Jim. Both were alike in physical strength, mental alertness and determination, not to mention a lively imagination and hope for a better life.

Even renowned Louella Parsons had seen some good emoting from Moore in the ring, according to her comments in the *Los Angeles Herald Examiner* ('59). She felt Moore had chosen an appropriate time to accept Goldwyn's offer considering the Floyd Patterson - Ingemar Johanssen fight talk in the air.

She had also been duly impressed by Moore's TV speech after the Durelle fight and was confident he could easily handle the part of Jim.

And so it was that Goldwyn himself called Moore in San Diego with an offer to read for the part. It was just before tearing down his training camp to depart for Montreal, with time to do little more than get a tour of the MGM Studio and a quick briefing. Just as quickly, the news of Moore's interest in the part spread with the general reaction that "he'd been acting all his life anyway." In truth, he'd been a showman in the ring, gregarious and loquacious without benefit of a script. He was well read in the boxing world but had not since school days been one for reading the classics or participating in the arts.

"My stage debut," he relates with a smirk, "had to have begun when I was about eight years old and in the third grade. Can you imagine me in a Maypole dance? For some reason, we had to practice at the "Star Theatre" on Market Street in St. Louis, a place regularly featuring Black vaudeville."

"I can remember that we walked in pairs carrying the colored streamers which would be wrapped around a pole. Even then, I felt kind of excited at the idea of performing before a crowd though a little embarrassed at having to hold the hand of a girl."

"We all sat for a time waiting for an adult dance group to complete its rehearsal. The headliner was Miss Josephine Baker, rising star in the field of entertainment. She was exotic and leggy, wearing dance tights which fit as well as her skin."

"After rehearsal, she came down to where we were sitting and asked, 'Who are these beautiful children? ... Do we have some dancers out here?' But of course no one volunteered. We were awe struck by this pretty and vivacious lady who seemed so interested in us!"

"When our teacher told her we were from Touissant L'Ouverture, Miss Baker indicated she knew who he was [a Black revolutionary from Haiti]. Little did I know that she would also find her way into the history books."

Accounts reveal that Josephine grew up quickly, working by the age of eight to help support her family in St. Louis, the place of her birth. She became a chorus girl while still in grade school and by age seventeen, she was dancing in Noble Sissle's "Shuffle Along." Her Paris debut in "La Revue Negre" (1925) led her to international fame as did performances in "Dark Star" of the Folies Bergere"; Black Shadows" (1923) and "Moulin Rouge" (1944).

She was awarded the French Legion of Honor in recognition of her efforts during World War II. Such efforts took her away from show business for a time, but she was prompted to return in order to support a number of racially different, orphaned children she had adopted. Her return performance was the starring role in "Paris, Mes Amours", a musical based on her life.

Her childhood was perhaps her biggest motivator, much like Archie Moore who never forgot that childhood experience with Josephine Baker. Never in his wildest dreams, however, had he imagined himself on a stage as an adult. But here he was, about to get his feet wet. First however, he had to attend to a bit of unfinished business in the prize ring.

The sixteen-page script was sent by Goldwyn to Montreal where Moore was to fight the return match with Durelle. He set it aside and focused on his real job; yet the acting opportunity gave him added impetus for a victory.

As the fight drew near, the press became a beehive of activity. Opinions were teetering indecisively between Moore's proven ability to win and the possibility of defeat due to age. They were writers such as Nat Fleisher, "Mr. Boxing" of *Ring Magazine*; Pete Waldmeir of the *Detroit News*; Bill McGoogan of the *St. Louis Post Dispatch*; Jesse Abramson of the *New York Herald Tribune*; Red Smith, syndicated columnist, and Jack Murphy of the *San Diego Union News*.

General anxiety over the bout became more acute with speculation over who was to be third man in the ring. Would it be Sharkey, held to have done a commendable job of refereeing in the first bout, or would it be Ruby Goldstein or Harry Kessler?

In the case of Sharkey, the Durelle camp yelled loudly, alleging that Moore had gotten the benefit of a long count in two of the three first-round knockdowns. By contrast, the Moore camp left no doubt as to its objection to Goldstein due to what it considered a poor job of refereeing the Johanssen-Patterson fight.

Of course everyone within shouting distance was aware of Moore's vendetta against Kessler as a result of the Moore-Marciano rumble.

In the end, it would be Sharkey for the return match which saw Moore favored to win by a 3-1 margin; whereas the first fight had favored him 5-1.

It is a foregone conclusion in the fight game that some one has to be the boss in the ring, as Jack Murphy of the *San Diego Union News* reminded. It was a factor that was to emerge early in the first round as Moore signalled that he was there to fight, not to defend himself. He would have none of the crowding and back peddling; nor was he going to expose himself to Durelle's haymakers as he had the first time around.

Letting loose with a barrage of sharp punches and lightening combinations to Durelle's head, he twice flattened the challenger in the first round. Thus it was already evident that like most rematches, this one would not live up to the original. Durelle, a seeming shadow of his old self, was knocked to the canvas a final time in round three.

Had the old Durelle actually been lucky in the first bout or was he encountering a renewed Archie Moore? It would seem the latter was the case as the jubilant veteran retained his light heavyweight crown, seeming not to mind as his wife, Joan, defied custom and climbed into the ring to share her husband's victory.

Moore had also contradicted the status quo; but the question was, how long would he continue to play his "September Song" after 23 years in the ring? He had come into his own in the boxing autumn of his life, nearly the "longest autumn" in the history of boxing.

His reply to the hounding press was that he would step down as soon as he had a son who could take his place at 16 (a statement definitely done in the Moore comedic style, hedging because of a decision he had not seriously considered). The latter consideration is not uncommon in the fight game where, for myriad reasons, the champions do hang on. Do such men have something to prove either to themselves or the public? Is it the money or just plain glory seeking?

In the case of Moore, he did not fit into the destitute category by the standards of that era; nor was he bereft of self confidence. What was certain was, as he was often heard to declare, "I love to fight!" It is for the latter reason that he did not retire from the ring as have some others before he reached his goal, only to find the fight still rumbling in his belly, urging return to the ring. Such decisions have often ended in defeat or even worse, in injury.

Regarding comebacks, there are those who say for the sake of Ali's posterity and his well being, the Ali-Holmes fight should never have taken place. While defeat was inevitable, it was an ending to a brilliant career wrought by Larry Holmes on October 2, 1980, and the old adage, "You can't go home again," appeared to ring true.

A match most nearly paralleling the former, though even out-grossing that bout, was the Haggler-Leonard fight of the century. Ray, the idol of millions, had already reached his zenith in achievement and acclaim in addition to earnings unprecedented in the middleweight category. Not even the original Sugar Ray could boast of raking in 11 million dollars for 12 rounds or less.

Leonard's comeback was viewed as crazy by a concerned public because of his already injured optic nerve. Thus it was anxious and hyped-up fight fans who saw him out-maneuver and decision the fearsome Haggler. Yet Leonard was smarter than most in his "one-time comeback" as he strategized through twelve power-packed rounds with the notorious, "Hag", to prove to the world that he was more than America's darling.

More recently, Michael Spinks, WBA Champion, was reported in the *Los Angeles Times* ('88) to possess some unusual ideas about boxing and the money element. Though having been an Olympic champion, he had allegedly been willing to return to a regular job in St. Louis and be content without fighting or money. It was the persistent urging of manager Butch Lewis which, according to Spinks, made him return to the ring though reluctantly. He compared fighting another man to having all of his teeth pulled, saying that anyone claiming to enjoy fighting would have to be "crazy!" (His showing against "Iron Mike" Tyson might be explainable in the light of his feelings.)

No doubt strange things go through the minds of champions at the apex of their careers. To fight or not to fight, is the all important question. In Moore's case, it was as though he had made a comeback or, in his words, "like being a new, young star."

"... kind of funny when you think about it," chuckled Moore, "a star after 205 fights and 43 years of age before being discovered! Imagine being invited to recite a ballad on the Ed Sullivan Show, a two-week engagement at the Apollo Theater and a chance to up-stage Ray Robinson in a rope-jumping demonstration in Las Vegas."

And as he arrived to a hero's welcome at the airport in San Diego and a motorcade down Broadway which was lined with cheering citizens, he had to convince himself that he was the same guy who, 22 to 23 years before, had worked on a WPA job on the St. Louis levee for $14.20 a week.

"I was between a rock and a hard place," he recalled with a tell-tale glint of suffering in his twinkling eyes. "I worked days and had an occasional fight worth about $25 and my manager took $13 of that; but when the foreman of my job proved so inhuman, I forgot poverty. Can you imagine standing around the fire because the weather is five degrees above zero and having the foreman get mad and kick out the fire?

Needless to say, the fire was rekindled in me and I threw in my shovel and quit! I guess I might have dug another hole for myself. But you see, I had pride *and* faith!"

Moore has maintained a lasting friendship with former opponents Joey Maxim and Bo Bo Olsen. Seen here on the occasion of the World Boxing Hall of Fame event of 1989.

Archie Moore vs. Yvon Durelle, one of the greatest fights of the century.

CHAPTER XVII

Reflections of Life: Prelude to Acting

If there was such a thing as being on top of the world, then this was true of Archie Moore, finally having proven to the world that Old Arch, the Ancient One, could hang with the best of 'em. He had also succeeded in puffing up his souffle of accomplishments with this new-found opportunity as movie actor.

Columnists hardly knew which to focus on, the beakbuster or the actor, as their news and magazine articles abounded with Moore lore. He recalls it vividly: "I had spent two whole days embellishing the script, trying to sound less like a reader and more like an actor. I was actually intrigued at the idea of making myself into another person. And I guess I was literally about to do just that since I had allowed myself to taste of the good life, expanding to 200 pounds, 25 pounds over my normal weight. So I figured, what the hell, its my best acting weight!" (Presumably also for fighting Johanssen.) Sure, thinking I could really act might have sounded a bit presumptuous on my part since I was fully aware that my name as a boxer had been exploited; but I was prepared to give it my best shot. I even made a sacrifice and shaved my beard and the goatee some claimed was my security symbol."

Here he was, as Jack Stone reported in the *American Weekly*, a middle-aged Negro graying at the temples, now stepping before a camera to play a part that was second only to that of young Eddie Hodges, the movie's Huck Finn.

As a hush fell over the sound stage, the staff listened as Jim confessed to being a sinner and that he had slapped his little girl before he knew she was deaf. He spoke ever so softly and sincerely in an effortless Mississippi-Missouri accent.

"You can almost hear what he is thinking," marveled Goldwyn. "His naturalness and sincerity shine through. Hmm, an athlete as an actor - it's a situation I should pursue more often." (Though "showman" was the word used by Al Goldfarb of the Stockton California Record

('59), reminding readers of the light heavyweight champion's flair for dramatics.)

He lingered there under the lights, still standing on the marks which had been made for him, not at all in unfamiliar territory. Consider that in the fight game, he knew exactly how far it was from the center of the ring to the corners; how many side, backward or forward steps to take to be where he wanted to be. It was a kind of ring geometry which served him well.

As he stood there, he felt as naked as he would have in his boxing shorts as he finished the soul-stirring lines and awaited the decision. The reaction to sixteen pages of emotion-packed drama was a burst of applause and the misty eyes of an astonished Moore who smiled and nodded his thanks. It made him feel good to see the cameramen, propmen, technicians and scene shifters applaud him. "I guess they do this for everyone," he thought aloud, falling on the ears of Johnny Rothwell of the MGM staff.

"Not them", Rothwell retorted, ... "They see so much of this stuff.... If they cheered, they meant it!"

It would seem the only thing left to do was sign a contract; but there was a glitch in the script, one with which Moore was uncomfortable. He had already been very aware of the Black public's feeling about playing the part of a slave, an awareness he shared with Hollywood columnist, Bob Thomas:

"I have asked to have some of the lines changed, especially the ones which use the word, "nigger," he told him. As Moore describes one scene, "I am chopping wood outside the house of the woman who owns me and overhear a conversation between Huck's pap who is trying to get $500 from my owner. When she refuses, Huck's pap says, 'You've got that nigger there. Sell him!' This further motivates me to escape to a free state where I can make enough money to buy the freedom of my wife and child."

"In still another scene, the steamboat picks Huck and me off the raft and the first mate exclaims, 'It's mighty strange - a Nigra'. These were the two remaining uses of the word left in the script, and they were part of an historical classic, part of the racist vernacular of that time. They were used descriptively and not directly to me; so I accepted the script over some remaining objections by Jet Magazine."

"Who more than I had known the degradation of Black men, personally as well as what I had seen on the screen during those few times when I could afford a movie? There were all those early "colored" actors like Mantan Moreland; Step'n Fetchit; Lightnin' and Amos and Andy; Eddie "Rochester" Anderson; Butterfly McQueen and women who were made to wear mammy kerchiefs; those hungry, aspiring thespians who were told to cringe at the sight of a graveyard or a black cat, drag their feet, roll their eyes, and say, "Yassuh Boss!" Can we criticize them for playing such parts without blaming the kinds of mentalities which created and maintained this image?"

"I didn't feel the part of Jim was demeaning. I rather thought he projected a certain dignity and strength as he proved time and again his ability to cope with the inhumane set of circumstances thrust upon him."

"I enjoyed every minute of it, meeting for the first time people I had seen on the silver screen - people like John Carradine, Andy Devine, Buster Keaton, Mickey Shanghnessy, Tony Randall and others who helped me and made me feel comfortable. Man, did I need comforting to attempt two songs in the movie! Luckily, jazz pianist Eddie Beale served as my coach and performed a near miracle."

"Then upon completion of the film, there were the reviews which I drank in with some immodesty." Moore's reference was to such reviews as these:

Columnist Sam Balter said the Mongoose was better than any boxer had the right to be.

Bud Furillo's "Steam Room" posed that the light heavyweight's performance was worthy of an Oscar (though he criticized Moore's postponement of a world title defense against Eric Schoeppner, originally scheduled for July 18, 1959).

Al Goldfarb's "For the Record" predicted an Oscar for Moore's performance with no surprise that he could pull it off. Goldfarb cited Moore's patience with all the repeat shots as consistent with how he kept on fighting for the championship. Moore had probably not fallen as much in the ring as he had in perfecting a fall for the camera however.

While Goldfarb reported only admiration for Moore by everyone on the movie set, he found but one "bad rap" against the "Old Faker": He made a liar out of his own mother when he differed with her on his date of birth. Moore's standard reply to this alleged discrepancy was, "So I guess I was three years old when I was born. I was there too ... I oughta' know!"

There was Bob Shafer, who literally counted the calories Arch took in at restaurants like Chasen's where the movie crowd gathered.

He criticized Archie's seeming disinterest in his impending fight. He admitted, however, that while Arch was no Barrymore, he had done a commendable job as Jim.

Moore had crossed over into another realm, as much enjoying the movie jargon at Chason's as the actor's enjoyed the fight side when some dropped by the Beverly Hills Chateau Marmont where he was living, close to the Sunset Strip. His jazz buddies regularly popped in and played a few sets or saw him on the movie set. Even Ingemar Johanssen dropped by to take publicity shots with Moore and John Carradine. Ingemar was then doing a bit part in a war movie.

No visit was more settling, however, than that of Doc Kearns. He had to have enjoyed the attention he got when he arrived on the set, this legend in his own time who had made a Hollywood serial with Dempsey years before. By Doc's account, it held a record as the worst picture in history. Ultimately, Doc was still unimpressed with Hollywood and, as he bade goodbye, he pulled Archie aside and whispered behind the shield of his hand: "Hurry up and get this foolishness over with. We still have some fighting to do!" What a character!

The "foolishness" as Doc labeled it, continued into the '80's with guest shots and bit parts by Moore, among which were "Heartbreak Ridge" with Charles Bronson, a few westerns with Clint Eastwood; several parts on "Wagon Train"; a part in the play "Carmen Jones" and others. There would be more awards and achievements (some of which are listed at the end of this biography), but his finest hour had not yet come.

Perhaps some of the significant commentary on Archie Moore came in the form of accolades and honors received the year of the Durelle fight and into ensuing years. Jack "Doc". Kearns, not inclined to give undeserved compliments, put it this way to Jack Liang of First in Sports": That Archie Moore was a thrill fighter just as were Dempsey, Ketchel and Walker; that every fight of Moore's was unique, a quality which brought fans flocking. Not only was Moore amazing, he acclaimed, but phenomenal in his ability to make weight with seeming ease.

Moore's much published propensity for weight loss through the "secret diet" was finally published and received a most humorous evaluation by Melvin Durslag of the Los Angeles Herald Examiner. Like most, he had waited with bated breath for the secret. Moore, it seemed, began the day with 4 ounces of sauerkraut juice with a teaspoon of lemon juice - "heated"! Just the thought, resolved Durslag, would be enough to make one choose death from obesity!

Dining was ostensibly one of the pleasures to which Moore gave special attention, most often chewing and not swallowing. Dining was also the order of the day when one month after the December fight, diners were on hand for the annual event of the New York Boxing Writer's Association. They gathered to see Moore receive the James J. Walker Memorial Award and acclaim him "Fighter of the Year."

As principal monarch of the occasion and with no show of false modesty, Moore shared with the audience the awareness that without Durelle's actions, the fight, his victory not withstanding, might not have been as spectacular as it was. (As the poet Pope put it, he conquered but "felt his captive's charms.")

The audience was warmed by the recognition of Durelle, and Moore sketched out a plan which revealed his continued interest in the heavyweight division; especially a shot at Ingemar Johanssen, then champion of the world. It was a match which never materialized.

The fight which seems to stand out in infamy, despite having beaten other heavyweights in his career, was the Cassius Clay - Moore fight. Moore relates it thoughtfully:

"After making a name for myself with the Durelle fight, I was approached while in Canada by promoter Eddie Quinn with an offer to fight heavyweight George Chuvalo for which Doc got a $25,000 advance. After Doc took $10,000, I had to spread out the rest on immediate debts. With me was trainer Dick Sadler and my sparring partner, Junius Washington, and another big heavyweight from Mississippi. Lo and behold, Quinn decided he wouldn't pay the $100,000 guarantee; so the fight fell through with not enough money to afford return fare for Sadler and the others. Talk about sing for your supper! Sadler, also a song and dance man, had to get a booking playing boogie woogie and tap dancing in a supper club."

"After returning to Los Angeles, promoter Ilene Eaton of Olympic Auditorium fame saw an opportunity and got me to fight Cassius Clay for the paltry sum of $35,000. I accepted it because I had to repay my part of the $25,000 advance."

The fight actually began before round one with Cassius coining the phrase "Moore shall go in four." It was a practice for which he had already become quite famous, especially since his predictions came true. Such bluff and bluster or verbal sparring was, quizzically enough, borrowed from Moore, the man he was getting ready to demolish.

Their association had begun several years before when Cassius, fresh from the Olympics, was sent by seven businessmen from Louisville, Kentucky, to Moore in San Diego. They wanted him to be trained by someone who knew how to refine the skills Cassius already possessed.

Cassius, all of 19 years old, lived with the Moore family and adjusted fairly well. What impressed him most was the environment of Moore's Ramona, California, "Salt Mine." the training camp which stretched across 120 acres of green hills and winding roads. Both trainer and his young charge drank in the early morning air as they ran up and down hills straining every tendon in their legs and thighs, building muscle and endurance. Young Cassius looked with disdain, however, on Moore's assignment of dish washing and mopping floors, considered as discipline.

"I didn't come out here to wash dishes and mop floors," "spake" young Cassius, though with no intent at disrespect. "I came to box and, so far, I haven't done much of it," he protested!

"I know that," admitted the Old Master, "and I also know you are burning up inside; but you need to know that throwing punches is not all there is to boxing. You have to follow instructions! What will you do when your trainer and cornermen advise you in the ring? Will you move in when you should stall, deliver one punch when a flurry of punches to the body would be more effective? You see, people on the outside can see what you often can't.

Clay, then a much lighter man, had modeled moves of many of the stylized boxers. About this Moore gave what he considered sage advice:

"You're eventually going to be a heavyweight, Cassius, and I want you to be a devastating puncher. If you can knock a man out early in a fight, why go the distance and unnecessary wear and tear on your body?"

Cassius had other ideas, however; especially regarding being isolated in order to train. He rather thrived on and loved affiliation. And though he left the Moore camp, it would seem he used some of the teachings and much of his own natural ability and drive to become one of the most skilled and charismatic boxers of modern times. His jeering and taunting of other fighters, while seeming as buffonery to some, succeeded in putting life back into boxing.

When he fought Sonny Liston whom he labeled the "gorilla," it was for just cause. He had been one of the most awesome hit-men in ring history, terrifying even boxers like Floyd Patterson. As a matter of fact, neither of his two title bouts preceding the bout with Clay had lasted more than a round; but on February 25, 1964, Liston faced a new foe who met his psychological, fear-provoking stares with leering, dancing and name-calling like the "Bear" and "Chump!"

The weigh-in was a near prelim with Clay described as acting demented, harassing an almost unrestrainable Liston.

Despite this psych, Clay's blood pressure which registered 200/100, was attributed by the press to stark fear!

This brash young challenger was to defeat Liston not once, but in a return match in Maine in '65. It was a bout which left many questions unanswered in that no one ever saw the blow which knocked Liston to the canvas in "2". It was the shocker that caused even referee Walcott to delay counting.

As a booing crowd yelled "Fix," the victor, now Muhammed Ali, the "Greatest," became the new heavyweight champion of the world. In truth, he was, as Moore put it, "the goose that laid the golden egg."

Had Liston taken a dive? Was he older than alleged, just looking for a quick way out? Were such allegations due in part to suspicion because of a prison record and the patronage of mobster Frank Palermo, known to have influence in boxing? Or was it that Liston, like Dempsey, Louis, Walcott, Frazier and even Muhammed Ali, had to face the day when it was time to exit the ring. It is plausible, however, that public speculation over why champions lose is due in part to the public's very adulation of them. So closely are emotions tied to some champions that their defeats are not acceptable. Such was Moore's loss to the young Cassius Clay, once his pupil. While the fight throng screamed to Moore, "Shut him up!" ... there were jaded hints of "fix" in one of Moore's few poor performances in a 28-year stint in the vicious circle.

"I sank into a kind of depression after the Clay fight," confessed Moore to one columnist, ... due less to having lost and more because of some of the unkind things that were said about me." He went to say, "I don't believe I deserved that nor did my record support it. As a matter of fact, the Clay fight was hardly the time for anyone to have approached me with throwing a bout since the odds favored the younger champion. The time to have submitted to temptation, if I were so inclined, would have been in my prime when I was knocking out anything that came my way for mere moving around money. Yet not even then was I approached or tempted. Everyone knew how hungry I was for the championship."

As Bill Lee described it, Moore had the ambition and pride to shoot for the top, losing only to heavyweights Patterson, Marciano and Clay. Had he remained in the light heavy class, he was doubtful that Moore could have been beaten in his heyday. Certainly no one has bested his all- time knockout record of 140 KO's in 234 bouts.

It is perhaps his loss to the more publicized Marciano which would lead some to believe that Moore had been destroyed by that fight. In fact, he fought and won fights thereafter, most notably, the Durelle spectacular which continues to serve as an exemplary display of courage.

Let it also be said that it took a genuine respect for the sport of boxing for Archie Moore to finally bow out as the Undefeated Light Heavyweight Champion of the World. He did it as quietly and as gently as an autumn leaf which turns to gold, descending from a lofty place, yet providing fertile ground for new growth.

Archie Moore as Jim, the slave, in Huckleberry Finn, produced by Samuel Goldwyn Jr..

Appointed by President Regan, Moore served as youth boxing instructor for HUD. Here he is with Don Newcomb and HUD Secretary Samuel

Moore with George Foreman in the '90's.

Moore is Technical Advisor to George Foreman, former Heavyweight Champion and strong contender for the championship again in the 1990's (photo courtesy of Bruce Bennett, Houston Post).

Archie Moore was one of 32 stars entertained by U.S. President Dwight Eisenhower during his 50's drive for fitness.

EPILOGUE

ABC

ANY BODY CAN*
Working With Youth

"Think about it," speaks Moore the philosopher, "with the exception of perhaps Alexander The Great or Joan of Arc, few are able to leave a meaningful legacy before they've reached a considerable age."

"Aging"... this is an accomplishment in itself, but one very often overlooked. For whatever reasons, older people are not asked to share the wisdom acquired over time. They are often counted out and forgotten."

"It reminds me of what Jack Drees announced to the world from Montreal, Canada, in 1958. It went something like this... '"Durelle charges, throwing bombs from every angle, and Moore seems unable to defend himself.... Moore goes down again.... Moore is badly hurt! Well... Father Time has finally caught up with The Old Mongoose.'

"Yep, they've been counting me out for the last thirty years or so, and they're quite benevolent about it too. 'Let's do something before it's too late', they say. Now don't get me wrong. I've appreciated the gestures; but you see, I look at life a bit differently from most. I am not time conscious, which is probably why I haven't worn a watch in years."

"Clock watchers are folks who forget that time doesn't really move. It is we who are doing the moving; so you see, I don't exactly relish keeping count of how fast I'm leaving this life."

"I guess its a habit I acquired in the ring. Sure, I realized I had just three minutes to do what I had to do; but I found it better to concentrate on what I was doing rather than how fast, boxing as though I had no time limit. When the bell rang, it caught me fighting my best fight. This after all is all that anyone can do ... fight his best fight."

* Initially known as Any Boy Can.

"When I hung up my gloves in 1963, I decided not to lie down and be counted out, not to lead a sedentary life which can do little else but get you used to the grave."

"What did I think I would do at my age? How old was I when I retired? How old am I now anyway? Well, I guess you might say I'm old enough to leave a legacy."

So speaks Archie Lee Moore, who began fighting in 1936 and retired in 1963 as the Undefeated Light Heavyweight Champion Of The World.

After retiring, Moore was certain he had more to count than age, especially since he was in amazingly good physical and mental condition. Although he hadn't hit immediately upon just what he would do, he knew his work would be with youth. He'd hoped to train another champion such as Cassius Clay; however, few came to him for advice. It would seem an old man's ideas just did not fit into the modern scheme of things.

"Have the rudiments of boxing changed?" Moore queries with a degree of sarcasm. "Not in my book. A left jab properly delivered is still a boxer's best weapon; but how many are there around who have really perfected it?" he asks.

Moore has certainly proven himself in that arena as the world's KO king, a record of which he can be proud. He also feels deeply about the quality of boxing, lamenting that not enough people care about it.

"If", he points out, "boxers were truly recipients of quality training, there might be less injuries, not to mention altering the view of boxing as a violent sport. But then, what contact sport is there that doesn't have the possibility of injury?"

"Has anyone seriously looked at the survivors in boxing or, more importantly, why they have survived? One would think even the American Medical Association would be beating a path to my door!"

Moore set about extending to others the knowledge he had acquired. He merged the militaristic training he received while in the CCC with his scientific skills in boxing. Further, he could certainly share the art of perseverance developed as a result of three decades of gypsy-like wanderings around the world, bidding for a shot at the championship. It all boiled down to skill, wisdom and discipline. These were three of the many strengths he could offer and he had a captive audience.

"Training begins at home," Moore asserted, underscoring the tenets of the program which would actually begin in his own backyard with sons Hardy, De Angelo, Anthony and Billy. "I'm determined that my sons won't repeat my mistakes. With the proper guidance, they should be able to do as well or even better than I. As a matter of fact, "Any Boy Can," he professed with conviction. And "Any Boy Can" has been the driving philosophy of his life as well as of the program which began in 1965 in San Diego, Archie's town.

"Gradually, I took my ABC program to the streets," says Moore, "where I would be sure to find likely candidates - Black, Brown and poor and headed for trouble."

"At times, I'd begin instructing eight students and after awhile they might dwindle to four. 'Sissy Stuff'! they'd call back over their shoulders, swaggering as they left."

"Fine", I'd say. "You won't miss me and I won't miss you!" I'd face the remaining students and in the voice of a drill sergeant I'd yell, ... "Alright students... ATTEN-SHUN!"

"My name is Instructor Moore. I'm here to teach you how to step off in life with your best foot forward."

"By the end of the lesson", Moore explains, "each student would know how to assume a stance and hold his guard. With some, it might be the first time they realize the importance of listening and following directions, not to mention the virtue of patience. They'd come to me as feisty, young bantam roosters eager to hit the bag or each other."

"'When can we fight?'", is their standard question, and my answer is always, "when you are ready!" You see, I know when they're ready. By the end of six weeks, I can and have produced students who are disciplined, confident and knowledgeable enough to pass on the lessons of self-defense, self-respect and self-motivation."

"They recite and commit to the creed, 'When a task is once begun, never leave it til its done', and to a litany of do not's. They must say, "Good ABC students do not lie, cheat, steal, smoke, drink, or gamble". It is under this kind of instruction that for twenty years, I've taught boys, and occasionally girls, to practice their jabs while scoring points in character building."

"Body and mind must work together in order to do anything well", advises Moore. "You have to think on your feet, be flexible and open to challenge."

For the former reasons, an important part of the ABC approach has been to engage students in fast-paced word games and decision-making activities which relate to real life. It makes sense when you consider that one's decisions spell the difference between success or lack of it, not to mention recognizing opportunity when it knocks.

Moore has consistently espoused the belief that his program is good for anybody and that becoming a boxer is not necessarily the outcome.

"If an individual can learn self-reliance," Moore affirms, "he cannot be forced into crime or drug usage. He can walk with poise and confidence, the self-same qualities needed to walk into an establishment and land a job."

The ABC philosophy has been applied wherever the winds have blown the Old Ring Master ... to boxing gyms, to small clubs, at PTA's, to parks and housing developments in St. Louis, Missouri; Montreal, Canada; Lagos, Nigeria, or Los Angeles, California, to name but a few.

The concept has been extended to young adults, also to military men and men in prison, heralding the message Moore considers his most important life's work.

"Who says I'm too old?", he smiles, shooting his left about as fast as he ever did. "It's like being champion again, grabbing headlines through the ABC way of fighting."

The following are samples of headlines appearing in various publications over the years:

Columbus, Ohio:
"MOORE HEADS ABC DRIVE TO PREVENT DELINQUENCY"

Lewiston, Idaho:
"SIX YOUTHS GET BOY OF YEAR AWARD"

Sacramento, California:
"ABC BOYS SHOW ARCHIE MOORE'S WAY TO FIGHT TO-WARD GOOD LIFE"

Canton, Ohio:
"A FIGHTER FIGHTS FOR BOYS OF U.S."

Boy Scouts of America:
"ARCHIE MOORE WINS BOYS WITH 'THINKING GAMES'"

San Diego, California:
"MOORE SAYS GOLDEN RULE FORMS BASIS FOR HIS AC-
TIONS"

Jefferson City, Missouri:
"BOXER RETURNS WITH MESSAGE"

Seattle, Washington:
"CURE FOR VANDALISM BY AN ELOQUENT SPOKESMAN"

Tipton, Missouri:
"EX-BOXER VISITS STATE CORRECTIONAL PRE-RELEASE
CENTER INMATES"

Los Angeles, California:
"EX-CHAMP TO HELP CHILDREN FIGHT DRUGS"

Washington, D.C.:
"MOORE INTRODUCES HIS ABC TO D.C."

Vallejo, California:
"ARCHIE'S BOYS MAKE THE GRADE"

Sacramento, California:
"LETTERS, CALLS HAIL ARCHIE MOORE–LT. GOV. FINCH
CALLS STAND AGAINST DRUGS EXCELLENT!"

Truro, Canada:
"DAY OF CHALLENGE: THE MESSAGE OF BOXER ARCHIE
MOORE"

   If additional indication of Archie Moore's ABC success is needed,
it may be observed in chance meeting with former students, now
successful adults who recognize and respect him:
   "Remember me, Instructor Moore? I'm student Mallory Flournoy.
I was in your ABC Program in San Diego. I'm now a boiler repairman
on a ship ... been trouble shooting in the Philippines."
   Or there might be a Dwight Calloway, early junior instructor in
the Vallejo, California, ABC Program, now employed in government
service.

Ultimately, no more graphic success of the program can be noted than in this letter from Nigeria, West Africa, where Moore was hired by that government to teach boxing to the Army, to youth in detention homes and in schools.

6 January 1988
Martins N Wagobe
Imo State Sports Council
Oweri H.Q. Nigeria, W. Africa

Dear Instructor,
  I hope this letter will reach its destination with my thanks in billions. Happy New Year to you and your family. I would have replied your letter and your instruction note earlier than this time but due to the fact that I was engaged in national and West Africa competition tournaments, by that time I could not get enough chance to reply early. I hope you won't hold some resentment about it.
  In that competition (i.e. in all African games hosted in Kenya), I was the only Nigerian pugilist to qualify for the finals during the tournament. After the fight, I won but I was robbed due to I met the host country (a Kenya boxer) then because of that I won silver instead of gold. Last year, December, I won the Belt for Champion of Champions in Nigeria which was donated by Eagles Oil Company.
  Still last year. I won the President Cup donated by Gen. Babomgidas of Nigeria in the light middleweight class. As of now, I'm preparing to go to another national festival which is going to be held on the ninth of this month (Jan.) and will last until 27th which is going to qualify me for the South Korea Olympic Games. I am inviting you to come and watch how an ABC student will snatch the South Korea Olympic Gold in boxing.
  I will like you to stay by my side by me during the fight. Instructor Moore, after the Olympic, I will turn to pro. I would like to stay with you in the U.S. And as a matter of fact, you are the one that brought me up in career and you are going to be the one that will end my career also.
  I need. only the invitation letter from you which I will use to meet the American Embassy for my Visa. I will be 21 years in August. Instructor, this is where I'm going to end my story and I will be more happy if you will come and watch me in South Korea and if my request to come to the U.S. to turn pro is granted.

Have posters and my personal pictures as a token of love. I will like you to put more instruction notes when replying this letter, that will carry me through in South Korea.
Have a good time.

Your Student of ABC

Martins N Waogbe

Students for almost three decades have called him "Instructor". Hometown folk, among whom he has resided for more than half a century, have dubbed him "Mr. San Diego." Moore, already referred to by much of the press as [the] Elder Statesman, truly earned that title. His profound statements urging a national effort against drug abuse and violence are now part of the Washington Congressional Record.

It was during one of those times when he was in D.C. that Moore would have a chance meeting with the Elder Statesman of considerable renown. Throngs awaited his passage along the parade route and, like everyone who loves a parade, Moore and the great Willie Mays were no exception.

As the black convertible limousine carrying the president came into view and headed for the White House, they heard, "Hey Willie, Archie, come on over here!"

It was the undeniable sports buff, Ronald Reagan, President of the United States, standing and waving to the crowd, causing a nightmare for Secret Service men who ran alongside the car.

"How are you doing Archie, Willie?... come over and see me," he trailed off...

Thus in 1981, Moore became the Presidential Appointee of Ronald Reagan to work under Samuel R. Pierce, Secretary of Housing and Urban Development (HUD). Under the national heading, Project Build, Moore has taught boxing to underprivileged youth in and around the housing projects of California. This has become his finest hour. He has applied the philosophy and mechanics of his own ABC program and in the 90's, he still believes that *any body can.*

"The housing project life can be mean," says long-time friend, Adrian Dove, also in government service; "but the Champ is no stranger to hard knocks. He actually rides it out, living among the people, subject to the same stresses that compact living can bring about."

"Champ has never really allowed himself to forget poverty," reflected Dove, obviously referring to Moore's habits and modest mode of dress - the prized knitted tam of the type worn by his idol, Jack Johnson, and a jumpsuit which might be sported any place from a businessmen's luncheon where he serves as speaker, to a guest appearance on a talk show.

Moore drives a red Toyota pick-up truck specially fitted with a rig of his own design to hold regulation punching bags. His ingenious device can convert a park or city street into an outdoor gym in minutes.

"So I bring the mountain to Mohammed," laughs Moore gingerly, his golden brown skin yet unmarked by age or boxing. "Perhaps I owe my good health to heredity," he says in answer to questions about his lasting prowess. "But, as I've always said, body and mind work together. When you mingle with kids as I have for all these years, it keeps your old body and brain from collecting sludge."

It was his imaginative and active mind which earned him the tag, "The Sweet Scientist", used by Jim Murray, noted sports columnist for the *Los Angeles Times*. His reference was not to any of Moore's fix-it abilities, for he has none; but it was to his approach to his job when he stepped into the ring. Much as a mechanic, as Murray so eloquently put it, Moore sized up his opponent methodically, deciding just which of his tools he could best use to exact defeat. In Murray's words, he was like a "well-oiled machine."

While some of the old prize fighters have been forgotten, those historically motivated sportsmen who know the value of empirical knowledge still seek out the opinion and wisdom of Archie Moore.

Why do you pick Jack Johnson and Joe Louis as your all-time favorites?" the eager press might ask... or... "Who's got the best left jab today?... or... "Who will eventually emerge as the undisputed heavyweight champion - Douglas, Tyson, Foreman or Holyfield? ... and eventually, some inciteful reporter will get around to asking how he overcame the odds to become a champion. His answer ... "With skill and will, Any Body Can!"

Archie Moore and Art Abrams of "Cauliflower Alley" stand beside Moore's "portable gym"--a Toyota truck outfitted with specially built frames to hold heavy punching bags.

Archie with five year old Kyle Douroux. "Never too young", he says.

"Moore" admirers.

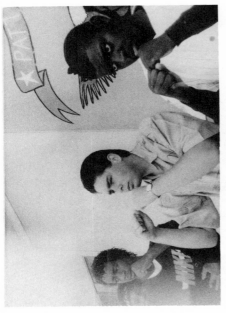

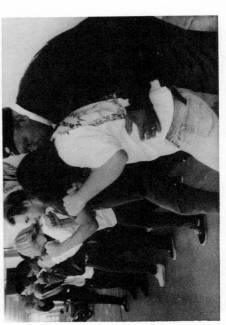

Moore believes that character training and discipline are necessary

ARCHIE MOORE

NOTES, QUOTES AND ANECDOTES

This biography has taken approximately five years to complete, partially because of the long time span to be covered and the large volume of information on the subject. Moore is a complex individual. His profound statements about boxing, his humanistic approach to life, his views on fatherhood are all likely to evoke from those close to him a wide range of reactions from empathy to amusement. He is often humorous without meaning to be, not to mention testy and unpredictable.

The following notes have been gathered by the author to bring the reader even closer to the man who happened to become a boxer.

I listened to Moore's "godson," Charles Lloyd, colorful and successful Los Angeles criminal lawyer, affectionately describe Moore, his "godfather". As graphic outside the courtroom as he is when defending a client, Lloyd presented a vivid picture regarding a unique incident:

"We were on our way back from D.C. where Godfather and I had attempted to see Richard Nixon regarding help for the ABC Program. Since he was unavailable, we decided to accept an invitation to a poolside party from Elkin Brothers, former Moore sparring partner who lives in Maryland just outside Washington, D.C.

"As is apt to happen when there are sports people around, things got lively and Elkin playfully tossed a screaming woman, a non-swimmer, into the deep end of the pool. She began to thrash and fight the water, drifting to the other side."

"Always quick to react, Godfather raced around to the other side of the pool as others froze to their spots, seemingly confident that the champion would save her. He began screaming, 'Come on Charley', you hold my feet while I reach out after her. Goodness, I hope she's not wearing a wig!'"

"The panic was in his face as he attempted and finally succeeded in grabbing the hair of her head which had already bobbed for the second time."

"Believe me, it wasn't at all funny then. But the panic really set in when everyone, including Elkin, discovered that neither of us could swim. We looked at each other and cheered, 'Rock On!' We were like Caesar and Anthony. We had conquered!"

"Seriously, it says something about the confidence people have in a champion of this magnitude. Once the Godfather gets into your bloodstream, he's with you for life," says Lloyd in earnest.

"I was privileged to see him honored by Juan Peron, his long-time admirer. He had just returned to Argentina as president and as promised, he gave Moore one of the most impressive receptions Washington had ever seen. We were welcomed to the Argentine Embassy by Peron's diplomats, a tribute to the Peron-Moore friendship," says Lloyd.

* * *

The late Roscoe McCrary, once owner of a thriving barbecue business in St. Louis, was asked by Moore to accompany him in a search for Miss Mosby, his former ninth grade teacher. It was around 1983 and he was in St. Louis on HUD business. Here he was some five decades later, still ruminating about the day she punished him unjustly, changing his outlook on school. He wanted to show her what he had become. Talk about long on memory ... ! Moore relates thoughtfully:

"'Yes she's still alive,' McCrary told me, 'living at a senior citizens hotel in the downtown area.'"

"We found the hotel and approached the manager who recognized me instantly and pointed out Miss Mosby to me. There she was, sitting on the porch among several other seniors all of whom were rocking, all except Miss Mosby that is. She had been eroded by time but was still determined enough to be unconventional.

"I approached her ever so gently, calling her by name ... Miss Mosby, Miss Garnetta Mosby?"

"'Yes, I am, and who are you?' she shot back. She asked it as sternly as she had asked who yelled out in her classroom many years ago. And for an instant, I imagined I could still feel the stinging slap which embarrassed me in front of the class."

"Remember me?" I asked, moving around in full view. "I'm Archie Moore. I was once your student. I left St. Louis and became a prize fighter, a boxing champion."

"'I don't know you,'" she answered crisply. "'I don't know you!'"

"After all these years," I thought, and then I turned away quite dejectedly, feeling as though I had again been punished. "You would think she might have heard of me through the years in the news, a hometown boy who won the championship," I said to Roscoe.

"'Well Archie,' Roscoe said to me obviously attempting to lessen my pain, 'perhaps she's just too old to remember. Come on Archie,' he told me, 'let's go by my place and get some ribs.'"

***

Joe Kellman was eternal friend of the underdog. One would think as owner of over fifty glass manufacturing outlets nationwide he could literally see into the problems of youth. He was also originator of BBF, Better Boys Foundation, a thriving youth club in Chicago.

As a long-time friend of Archie's, he was genuinely concerned about his welfare, noting that he had since his last fight added considerably to his girth. He offered to send Moore on an all-expense paid trip to a North Carolina fat farm where he had also been.

Without a doubt, public knowledge of this would surely increase the business of any fat farm which could beat the reducing system of the great Archie Moore. Sure, they might be using him; but he went mainly to humor Joe Kellman, hoping that not too much ado would be made of his going elsewhere to lose his excess suet. Between fits of laughter, Moore relates it point-by-point:

"The farm was a pleasant enough place just on the edge of town, a few miles from where I'd be staying. I went first to the farm, discovering that my well-guarded secret was out. There, waiting with cameras, note pads and pens in hand were the hungry reporters, scurrying to take my picture as I arrived. I noticed too that the proprietor was not a bit camera shy."

"Well, what the hell, I decided, publicity is publicity."

"I arrived each morning and assembled for the lecture with about eighteen other participants and the doctor who conducted the program. Everybody seemed pleased at the weight they'd already lost, a process which was monitored by the amount of food minus salt intake."

"The rule was that participants should consume only what was prepared by the program. This included a prescribed amount of water."

"The morning fare was hot lemon water and a bowl of white rice - no butter, no gravy."

"Lunch was a saltless chicken broth through which a chicken had probably briefly waded. No doubt their guilt was eased somewhat by providing us with another cup of lemon water - no sugar, no spices."

"Supper...you guessed it...another bowl of rice and a hot lemon tea that China would frown upon."

"Well, mine became a special case, a case of pure starvation. Each night, I'd be so ravenous, I'd salivate and even fantasize eating a medium-well steak, baked potato and a cob of corn saturated with butter, chased by a sourdough roll."

"I just couldn't take it anymore; so I'd walk down to a small store each evening and purchase a box of crackers [salted] and a can of sardines on which I dined royally, slooping them into my mouth with sheer pleasure. I'd wash this down with a Hires Root Beer, then ready myself for the morning weigh-in and blood letting. With a careful regimen of calisthenics and several trips to the John, I had lost weight by weigh-in time and became rather receptive to swallowing the broth with the fowl aroma."

"The doctor eyed me suspiciously, seemingly disturbed to the point of frustration when I showed weight loss, though maintaining a high salt level in my blood."

"I can't understand it," he was still uttering even on my last day in the program, having lost a total of seventeen pounds."

"Though he smiled pleasantly upon my leaving, a sixth sense told me the doctor was saltier than my sardines. I guess he didn't know that I was undisputed champion of the secret diet."

***

There had always been something sacred about Archie Moore's "Salt Mine", his own special training camp at Ramona, California. It had all the components to set the mood for shared work and serious training, as the name suggested.

He equipped it with reminders of how he had climbed from obscurity to the championship, crediting the press with a large part of his ascent.

On each step leading up to the cabin where he and his training entourage lived were inscribed the names of various sports columnists and editors who had aided him in securing the bouts which he needed to get his chance at the title.

There was Red Smith, Jack Murphy, Sid Ziff, Melvin Durslag, Arthur Daley, Nat Fleisher, Brad Pye, Jim Murray, Dave Gregg, Dan

Parker, Roger Pippen, Don Freeman, Carol Oats, Earl Gustkey and Bud Furillo, to name but a few.

The schedule of the Salt Mine was rigorous and systematic - six miles or so of roadwork before breakfast, then breakfast, sparring, hitting the bag, and rope jumping as an afternoon activity.

It was after the evening meal when there was nothing to do but relax that the conversation got going and sometimes games of cards or checkers. But no matter what, there always seemed to be a profusion of profanity.

"I had to stop it", Moore explained, apt to use a little himself here and there.

"It serves no real purpose," he said to the crew - sparring partners, Dale Hall and Junior Washington and the "Big Bopper" and trainer, Richard Fullylove. "We've got to stop it...it's getting to be a distraction!"

So he hit upon an idea to which he added strong motivation: Each use of a profane utterance carried with it a penalty, the listing of which was tacked on the door:

IF YOU SAY, YOU PAY!

MF	$1.00
F	.50
S.O.B	.25
S	.10

"Well," explains Moore, "at the end of one week, there was no one including myself who had not reached into his pocket for at least $10. Even when they ran or worked out in two's, the pot got fed because they penalized each other."

"It had begun to hurt too. By the end of four weeks, the Salt Mine could have qualified as a monastery and the gallon can was nearly full."

"I took.the money, about $250, and purchased some of the things everyone enjoyed eating and drinking. While it might sound corny, it kept things clean and our minds on the business of training."

"I shared my idea with Lefty, manager of the University Pool Hall in San Diego. He can sure use it!"

***

Moore's press has been like "Ol Man river". It has kept on rolling along through men like Bud Furillo and Mel Durslag, who still consider the Old Mongoose "good press" in the '90's...

Bud Furillo
The Steam Room

Moore's memory is testimony to his ability to dodge punches

Archie Moore was the greatest defensive fighter of all time.

This is because he was smart enough to keep his gloves up in front of his head, not at his sides. Punches ricocheted off his gloves, not his head.

The Ol' Mongoose admits to being 71. He's sharp as Eddie Murphy. Well, almost. Oh, the Ring Record Book says he'll be 75 in December. But, when you have spent a lifetime of fibbing about your age, just to get fights, that's how it was.

Moore fought from 1936 until 1963. He had 215 professional fights. The entire light heavyweight division hasn't had 215 fights.

Arch was 38 before he got a shot at the title, when they had only eight, and one champ to a division.

Doc Kearns entered the ring in 1953 as the manager of Joey Maxim. He left with the new champion. Doc always liked winners. He had Dempsey.

Moore was standing with Los Angeles Athletic Club Vice President Duke Llewellyn and Herald Examiner alum Larry Stewart when I walked into the LAAC to introduce people attending a Special Night For Jimmy Jacobs.

"Do I know Bud?" Moore asked, and answered, "We go back a hundred years." We embraced, sat down and he asked for my address. "I think it's time I sat down and wrote letters to those who helped me," he said. "Would you like that?" Who wouldn't?

His favorite columnist, Mel Durslag, will be receiving one. Mel loves Arch. The feeling is mutual.

MOORE TOLD ME he had just returned from New Brunswick and a reunion with French-Canadian Yvon Durelle, whom he fought twice. The first was an unbelievable fight.

Durelle floored Moore five times. Archie won by KO in the 11th. I'll never forget watching it with a great number of people at a bar off the Sheraton-Town House. Whereas the crowd started out cheering for the Canadian, suddenly, I began to hear, "Get up, Arch!" Moore became a national television hero that December night in 1958.

He entered the ring wearing a robe that read on the back, "Nat Rosenburg's Diamond Palace, San Diego." This robe inspired Muhammad Ali to advertise "Williams Furniture, London," on his trunks, where one is accustomed to seeing Everlast, when Ali defended his title against Bob Foster.

It was Moore who planned the strategy for George Foreman to wrest the heavyweight title from Joe Frazier. He was Director of Strategy for Foreman. Arch taught Foreman how to hit without hurting his hands. He told him to punch down on the top of Frazier's head when he rushed in. Manager Dick Sadler objected strenuously, fearing Foreman would hurt his hands.

"George could break a hand hitting Frazier on top of the head," Sadler said. Archie said, "There's nothing on top of a man's head except skin, a little bone and fluid."

Foreman knocked Frazier down six times in two rounds in Jamaica. Smokin' Joe was actually terrified. He tried to run on one occasion, but where could he go, to the Bahamas?

"I wish George would get in touch with me," said Moore. "I think he has the style to beat Mike Tyson, who reminds me of Frazier. I like Evander Holyfield's chances, too."

MOORE WORKS for HUD under Samuel R. Pierce Jr., a black cabinet member. Arch tried to shoot down the drug problem around San Diego in the '60s. He formed a group called ABC, or, Any Boy Can. Everyone thought he was funded. He spent his own money for the most part, except for contributions that came in because of columns written about his dedication to youth.

He'll be at the Irvine Marriott tomorrow for an amateur boxing show for charity. He still cares. He was driven to make something of himself from the time a teacher slapped him in elementary school for saying "Ouch!" when a classmate stuck a splinter into his right thigh.

"I drank the tears from the humiliation and never went back to school," he recalled. He told his aunt, Willi Pearl Moore, whose house he was born in Dec. 13, 1913, in St. Louis, that he would be a fighter. And he lived by a poem she recited to him.

When a task has once begun,
Never leave it until it's done,
If the labor's great or small,
Do it well or not at all.

Willi Pearl is in a convalescent home in town. The 98-year-old is visited religiously by Arch.

Durslag remembers a morning when Moore asked Doc Kearns if he could order room service. "Just coffee," said Kearns, the slipperiest manager of them all. Soon as Doc left, Moore reached behind the bed for something he had bought doing roadwork. He winked at Mel and dunked a dozen doughnuts.

Let me leave you with this thought. How many great defensive fighters do you know with total recall at 74? Get the picture? ∎

Hear Bud Furillo and Peter Vent on "Sports Time" on KFOX-FM (93.5) weekdays from 4 to 5 p.m.

Los Angeles Herald Examiner
Friday, September 2, 1988

Melvin Durslag

Archie Moore, adviser: Give Foreman a chance vs. Tyson

Archie Moore, master of sports, serves George Foreman as Donald J. Trump serves Mike Tyson, which is to say Archie is an adviser.

Trump, of course, lacks the savoir faire and cultural refinement of Archie, who, tolerant of these deficiencies, still is willing to tender a magnificent proposition to the champion's camp.

Archie is proposing that Foreman, who is only 40, fight Mitch Green, the Boutique Bomber, in an elimination producing the next opponent for Tyson.

"It's a natural," says Archie. "And both are as qualified as any of the others around today."

"What does Foreman weigh these days?" Archie is asked.

"He goes 250, down from 300. But, a punch mechanic of distinction, I am teaching him to throw a body blow to which Mr. Tyson might be very vulnerable. In his last fight, Foreman delivered this body blow to an opponent whose innards got very shaken. The man thought the bottom of his body had detached itself from the top, like a freight car uncoupling."

Having studied, close up, Rocky Marciano — he even floored him in a title fight — Moore is asked how Tyson compares.

"Tyson has faster hands," responds Archie. "He dishes it out big. Like Rocky, he is a great fighter. But Rocky proved he could take it and come back. We still wait to see if Tyson can. How will he react when the punches are bouncing off him?"

ONCE A PRACTITIONER of note and sometime champion, Archie was known for his unconventionalities. But never, during his stretch of 212 professional fights, did he try on a jacket at 4 in the morning.

"My tailor worked by appointment," recalls Archie. "But never did I go for a fitting between midnight and 8 a.m. If I was up during those hours, I was engaged in pursuits more meaningful."

It was at the boutique that Tyson's fitting was interrupted by a visit from Green, who, sizing up the garment, may have criticized the cut, resulting in a knuckles explosion.

"I always made a practice," says Archie, "of never fighting beyond 10:30. Anything later is so uncivilized."

Living in New York at the time, Archie used to take fights in Baltimore, to which he traveled back and forth on the same day to save a hotel tab.

"I had a bout with a Lloyd Marshall," he remembers. "I also had a reservation on the 11:02 back to New York. What I pictured as an easy fight turned out to be nasty. Marshall knocked me down four times. I said to myself, 'My word, if this continues, I'll miss my train.' I knocked him down three times — and then knocked him out. Pulling on my pants over my trunks, I rushed for the station. It was a boiling summer night. At the station, I grabbed a grape soda and gulped it down. I got such cramps I couldn't stand. I laid down on the platform, waiting for my train."

But Archie reminds us he never engaged in evening fisticuffs without getting paid.

"That's the professional way to proceed," he says. "Tyson will learn that with experience."

"WHY DO YOU FEEL Foreman is qualified to fight for the title?" Archie is asked.

"Foreman is a puncher," he answers. "A devastating puncher. A puncher always has a sucker's chance. And if George could get by Mitch Green, as Tyson did, I would say he has a little shot coming. George was once champion. Tyson would owe him a shot. Is there no such thing anymore as professional courtesy?"

"How would you get Foreman down to fighting weight?"

"The same way I got myself down. My weight category as light heavyweight champion was 175. Between fights, I usually soared to 219. Now, you ask, how did I shed 44 pounds? I did it with boiled chicken."

Few have stopped to realize the utilitarian value of boiled chicken.

"When you boil chicken," explains Archie, "you can eat it as such and then use it to make chicken salad. Boiled chicken also produces chicken soup. So what we have is the perfect foodstuff for the fighter combating weight."

"And after the fight?" he is asked.

"After the fight, he can go to fried chicken, which is more caloric, but offers greater flexibility. One can eat fried chicken hot or cold. One can slip a piece in one's pocket, or in one's briefcase. One can eat it on a street corner, waiting for a bus."

Listening to Archie, you can't help believe that everything is looking good for Foreman, who never has engaged in a fight in a haberdashery, but who, on occasion, has had his measure taken elsewhere. ■

***

The columnists were keepers of the Archie Moore fight record. They followed him around, even noting his choice of meats and cream sauces. They noted the Petracelli suits he purchased, as well as his modeling of the new Air Force uniform in which he took a constitutional walk down 5th Avenue in New York.

Time, however, does have a way of altering one's tastes; for the aesthetic preferences of the Champ are currently to be found in second hand stores. It is after work or on his lunch hour that he loves to go "junking".

Last month, he purchased a vintage saxophone to add to about a dozen other musical instruments which he cannot play. This includes a bongo-drum which he claims should propel him into a side man's position with noted New Orleans - Los Angeles drummer and band leader, Earl Palmer.

"One day I'm going to play that thing," he promised jazz great saxophonist Plas Johnson who has called Moore's bluff, offering to give him saxophone lessons privately.

"Yea, Plas, I can make my debut with you and we'll call in Diz and Lateef and make them jealous!"

Though not a musician, the Champ does have an ear for the sweet sounds, especially when they're made by saxophones. After a few bars, he can usually identify the artist. He particularly likes James Moody's "Moody's Mood for Love," Coleman Hawkins' "Body and Soul", Ben Webster's "Time After Time," Lester Young's "D.B. Blues" and Plas Johnson's tenor solo on the original "Pink Panther" theme, a classic in American music. Moore has the greatest hope that Jusef Lateef will one day be able to perform his own symphonic composition.

"The tones of a saxophonist," he says, "are as tell tale as fingerprints." Moore is a man with an active imagination.

***

The following vivid narrative gives a clue to Moore's humanism and humility, not to mention his unique taste.

"Wait 'til you see what I bought," he announces with obvious satisfaction. "But first, let me tell you about a woman I met. She's a little short lady named Mrs. Johnson who owns a second hand shop on Broadway near Slauson in Los Angeles."

"As I entered the store, I spied a lamp. The tag on it read $20; so I did what any smart junker would do and proceeded to convince her to lower her price."

"'I'll see what I can do,'" she said as she removed the tag. Then, she left to meet the truck which had just arrived with more junk."

"'Hey... mind helping me?'" she asked me. It was more an order than a request. She was sure a feisty little thing."

"It's funny too how she manages to look - like a four foot-five inch sausage in a jumpsuit, tied between links." (And the "sausage" wore a long, black, flowing wig which trailed regally behind her.)

"'Here, catch these first... put these over here,' she ordered, officiously directing me in the proper placement of her new treasures."

"I was very amused at the license Mrs. Johnson was taking with a mere customer; but after all, hadn't she promised to give me a break on the lamp?"

"'I tell you what I'll do. You still want the lamp?'" she asked me. 'Hmn, there's no tag on it.... Tell you what; since you were so nice, I'll let you have it for $20.' I guess you might call her a "junk store liberal."

"Would you believe," shared the genuinely disappointed customer, "that the damned thing has faulty wiring? It is quite unique, though."

The lamp was different alright, like someone's feeble attempt at a prank. Imagine an armadillo, badly in need of a taxidermist's overhaul with a curious, paisley-printed ruffled lampshade affixed to its back.

Yep, the Champ got his lamp and...

TIME ... MARCHES ... ON!

ARCHIE MOORE
AWARDS AND COMMENDATIONS

1954 Spotlight on Harlem - ABC TV
1955 Baseball Fans of Toledo, Ohio Award
1955 Battling Nelson Memorial Award - New York City
1957 Award of Excellence
1958 Edward J. Neil Memorial Award - New York City
1958 Boxer of the Year
1959 March of Dimes - Sportwriters of N.Y.C Award
1959 Honorary Parade Marshall - San Diego, California
1959 Clem Mc Carthy Award - New York City
1960 Lions Club - San Diego Award of Merit
1961 Outstanding Father - New York City
1961 Southern California Boxing Writers Association Award
1962 Archie Moore Day - Los Angeles, California
1962 Supreme Award of Merit - Carver Institute
1963 Optimist Club Award - Fresno, California
1963 Dr. Robert F. Hyland Award
1964 San Diego Veteran Boxers Association Award
1967 Optimist Club Award -.San Diego, California
1967 California Senate Commendation - Sacramento, California
1967 Public Service Award - Insurance Brokers of San Diego, CA
1968 Santa Clara Exchange Club Award, San Diego, California
1968 "Mr. San Diego" - San Diego, California
1968 Key to City - San Diego, California
1969 Boy Scouts Appreciation, San Diego, California
1969 Pro American - La Jolla, California
1970 Palm Spring International Hall of Fame
1970 Man of the Year - *Listen* Magazine
1970 Key to the City - Sandpoint, Idaho
1971 Wings Over Jordan Community Service Award
1971 5th Annual Victory Awards
1972 Western Canada Native Winter Games Recognition
1973 Sons of Union Veterans of the Civil War Award
1978 Yarmouth Boxing Club Award
1979 The Students - Staff - Antigonish High Award, Canada
1979 Appreciation - Vasquez Defense Fund
1979 Renfrew Boxing Club - Calgary Mounted Police
     Association Award
1980 World Boxing Hall of Fame - New York City
1982 Archie Moore Boxing Tournament, San Diego

1982 Afro-American Achievement Award
1983 International Shrine of Boxing Award
1983 La Colonia Youth Boxing Club Award, L.A., California
1984 YMCA Olde Tymers Inc. - St. Louis Pine Street YMCA Award
1985 Missouri Training Center for Men Award
1985 NAACP Award
1985 SEA - TAC Tuskegee Institute Award
1985 St. Louis Boxing Hall of Fame
1985 Missouri State Penitentiary - Honors
1985 City of San Diego Testimonial - 50 Years
1985 Key to City - Hillsdale
1985 Old Time Professional Boxers Award
1985 1ST Annual "Archie" Awards - San Diego, California
1986 IWWP - Boise, Idaho
1987 San Diego Community Award
1987 Rocky Marciano Memorial Award, New York City
1988 WBA Legend Award - New York, New York City
1988 Ring Magazine: "Greatest Light Heavyweight in Boxing History"
1989 Ramona, California, Site of the "Salt Mine Training
      Camp - Names "Archie Moore Road"
1990 World Boxing Hall of Fame, Canastota, New York
1990 President of "Cauliflower Alley", Los Angeles, California.

CAULIFLOWER ALLEY CLUB.

A NON-PROFIT CORPORATION

Ring of Friendship

*An association of past, present and future
champions, contestants and allied personages
joining in recognition and celebration of fellowship
within the boxing and wrestling world.*

President Emeritus
IRON MIKE MAZURKI

President
ARCHIE MOORE

AN INVITATION TO ALL

Join Cauliflower Alley Club and its world-famous *"Ring of Friendship"* —
now you can be associated with ring legends, film and television "reel"
members, civic and social leaders — in the most unique ring organization.

With over 1200 international members you participate in club activities
to attend annual nostalgic reunion banquets and area chapter luncheons.
The club's communication center and newsletters link old and new friends,
bringing together champions and fans, forgotten legends and celebrities of
ring history for a renewed interest in honoring their past accomplishments.

Annual dues $15 (tax deductible for any and all donations)

Send for an application form now and receive your inscribed embossed
parchment membership certificate and card. You will receive all future
quarterly newsletters and access to communication with other members.

Charter Chapters have been formed in California and Florida, with others
planned by our rapidly growing membership in 40 states and 16 countries.
Souvenir "ear" logo pins, patches, T-shirts, caps and jackets are available.

For information and applications write or call:
CAULIFLOWER ALLEY CLUB
5221 SIERRA VILLA DRIVE, LOS ANGELES, CA 90041
(213) 466-1021

Note: "Iron Mike" Mazurki has been a champion wrestler and actor of
the highest caliber, appearing in movies such as *Some Like It Hot*
starring Marilyn Monroe.

Muhammed Ali and Archie Moore sign autographs for "Sports Collec-"

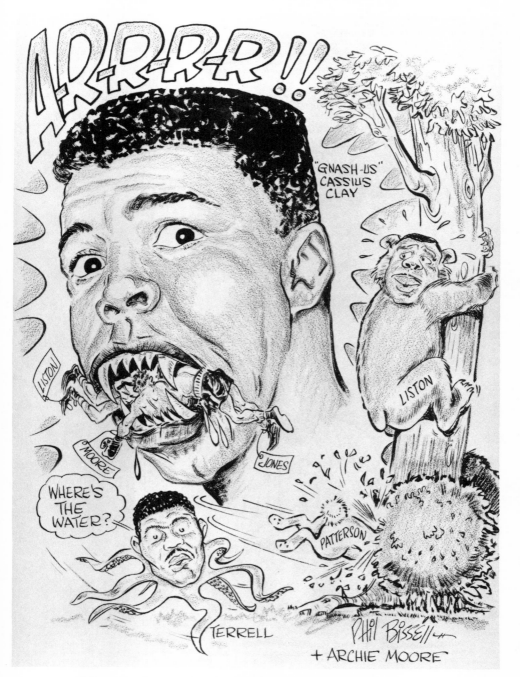

"You see, I never fought Ali; I fought Cassius Clay!"

Moore was a master of determination, a thrill fighter. His unpredictable nature brought fans flocking.

ARCHIE MOORE'S
BOXING RECORD

1936

Jan. 31	Poco Kid, Hot Springs, AR	KO 2
Feb. 7	Dale Richards, Poplar Bluff, MO	KO 1
Feb. 18	Ray Halford, St. Louis, MO	KO 3
Feb. 20	Willie Harper, St. Louis, MO	KO 3
Feb. 21	Courtland Shepard, St. Louis, MO	L 6
	Kneibert Davidson	KO 2
	Ray Brewster	KO 3
	Billy Simms	KO 2
	Johnny Leggs	KO 1
April 15	Peter Urban, Cleveland, OH	KO 6
April 16	Frankie Nelson, Cleveland, OH	L 6
May 4	Tiger Brown, St. Louis, MO	L 6
May 18	Thurman Martin, St. Louis, MO	W 5
	Ferman Burton	KO 1
	Billy Simms	KO 1
July 14	Murray Allen, Quincy, IL	KO 6
	Julis Kemp	KO 3
	Four H. Posey	KO 6
Oct. 9	Sammy Jackson, St. Louis, MO	W 6
	Dick Putnam	KO 3
Dec. 8	Sammy Jackson, St. Louis, MO	D 6
	Sammy Christian, St. Louis	KO 6

1937

Jan. 5	Dynamite Payne, St. Louis	KO 1
Jan. 18	Johnny Davis, Quincy, IL	KO 3
Feb. 2	Joe Huff, St. Louis, MO	KO 2
	Murray allen, Keokuk, IA	KO 2
Apr. 9	Charley Dotson, Indianapolis, IN	KO 5
Apr. 23	Karl Martin, Indianapolis, IN	KO 1
	Frank Hatfield	KO 1
	Al Dublinsky	KO 1
Aug. 19	Deacon Logan, St. Louis, MO	KO 3
Sept. 9	Sammy Slaughter, Indianpolis, IN	W 10
Nov. 16	Sammy Christian, St. Louis, MO	W 5
	Sammy Jackson	KO 8

1938

Jan. 7	Carl Lautenschlager, St. Louis	KO 2
May 20	Jimmy Brent, San Diego, CA	KO 1
May 27	Ray Vargas, San Diego, CA	KO 3
June 24	Johnny Romero, San Diego, CA	L 10
July	Johnny Sikes, San Diego, CA	KO 4
Aug. 5	Lorenzo Pedro, San Diego, CA	W 10
Sept. 2	Johnny Romero, San Diego, CA	KO 8
Sept. 20	Frank Rowsey, San Diego, CA	KO 2
Sept. 27	Tom Henry, Los Angeles, CA	KO 4
Nov. 22	Ray Lyle, St. Louis, MO	KO 2
Dec. 7	Irish Bob Turner, St. Louis, MO	KO 2
	Bobby Yannes, San Diego	KO 2

1939

Jan. 20	Jack Moran, St. Louis, MO	KO 1
Mar. 2	Domenic Ceccarelli, St. Louis, MO	KO 1
Apr. 1	Marty Simmons, St. Louis, MO	W 10
Apr. 20	Teddy Yarosz, St. Louis, MO	L 10
July 21	Jack Coggins, San Diego, CA	NC 8
Sept. 22	Bobby Seaman, San Diego, CA	KO 7
Dec. 7	Honeyboy Jones, St. Louis, MO	W 10
Dec. 21	Shorty Hogue, San Diego, CA	L 6

1940

Mar. 30	Jack McNamee, Melbourne, Aus.	KO 4
Apr. 18	Ron Richards, Sydney, Aus.	KO10
May 9	Attilio Sabatino, Sydney	KO 5
May 12	Joe Delaney, Adelaide, Aus.	KO 7
June 2	Frank Lindsay, Tasmania, Aus.	KO 4
June 27	Fred Henneberry, Sydney, Aus.	KO 7
July 11	Ron Richards, Sydney, Aus.	W 12
Oct. 18	Pancho Ramierez, San Diego, CA	KO 5
Dec. 5	Shorty Hogue, San Diego, CA	L 6

1941

Jan. 17	Clay Rowan, San Diego, CA	KO 1
Jan. 31	Shorty Hogue, San Diego, CA	L 10
Feb. 22	Clay Rowan, San Diego, CA	KO 1
Feb. 26	Eddie Booker, San Diego, CA	D 10
	(Retired because of extended illness)	

1942

Jan. 28	Bobby Brit, Phoenix, AZ	KO 3
Feb. 27	Guero Martinez, San Diego, CA	KO 2
Mar. 17	Jimmy Casino, Oakland, CA	KO 5
Oct. 30	Shorty Hogue, San Diego, CA	KO 2
Nov. 6	Tabby Romero, San Diego, CA	KO 2
Nov. 27	Jack Chase, San Diego, CA	W 10
Dec. 11	Eddie Booker, San Diego, CA	D 10

1943

May 8	Jack Chase, San Diego, CA	W 15
	(Won California Middleweight Title)	
July 22	Big Boy Hogue, San Diego, CA	KO 5
July 28	Eddie Cerda, San Diego, CA	KO 3
Aug. 2	Jack Chase, San Francisco, CA	L 15
	(Lost California Middleweight Title)	
Aug. 16	Aaron Wade, San Francisco, CA	L 15
Nov. 5	Kid Hermosillo, San Diego, CA	KO 5
Nov. 26	Jack Chase, Hollywood, CA	W 10

1944

Jan. 7	Amado Rodriquez, San Diego, CA	KO 1
Jan. 21	Eddie Booker, Hollywood, CA	KOb8
Mar. 24	Roman Starr, Hollywood, CA	KO 2
Apr. 21	Charles Burley, Hollywood, CA	L 10
May 19	Kenny La Salle, San Diego, CA	W 10
Sept. 1	Battling Monroe, San Diego, CA	KO 6
Dec. 18	Nate Bolden, New York City, NY	W 10

1945

Jan. 11	Joey Jones, Boston, MA	KO 1
Jan. 29	Bob Jacobs, New York, NY	KO 9
Feb. 12	Nap Mitchell, Boston, MA	KO 6

Apr. 2	Nate Bolden, Baltimore, MD	W 10
Apr. 23	Teddy Randolph, Baltimore, MD	KO 9
May 21	Lloyd Marshall, Cleveland, OH	W 10
June 18	George Kochah, Baltimore, MD	KO 6
June 26	Lloyd Marshall, Cleveland, OH	KO10
Aug. 22	Jimmy Bivins, Cleveland, OH	KOb6
Sept. 17	Cocoa Kid, Baltimore, MD	KO 8
Oct. 22	Holman Williams, Baltimore, MD	L 10
Nov. 12	Odell Riley, Detroit, MI	KO 6
Nov. 26	Holman Williams, Baltimore, MD	KO11
Dec. 13	Colion Chaney, St. Louis, MO	KO 5

1946
Jan. 28	Curtis Sheppard, Baltimore, MD	W 12
Feb. 5	George Parks, Washington, DC	KO 1
May 2	Verne Escoe, Orange, NJ	KO 7
May 20	Ezzard Charles, Pittsburgh, PA	L 10
Aug. 19	Buddy Walker, Baltimore, MD	KO 4
Sept. 9	Shamus O'Brien, Baltimore, MD	KO 2
Oct. 23	Billy Smith, Oakland, CA	D 12
Nov. 6	Jack Chase, Oakland, CA	D 10

1947
Mar. 18	Jack Chase, Los Angeles, CA	KO 9
Apr. 11	Rusty Payne, San Diego, CA	W 10
May 5	Ezzard Charles, Cincinnati, OH	L 10
June 16	Curtis Sheppard, Washington, DC	W 10
July 14	Bert Lytell, Baltimore, MD	W 10
July 30	Bobby Zander, Oakland, CA	W 12
Sept. 8	Jimmy Bivins, Baltimore, MD	KO 9
Nov. 10	George Fitch, Baltimore, MD	KO 6

1948
Jan. 13	Ezzard Charles,Cleveland, OH	KOb8
Apr. 12	Dusty Wilkerson, Baltimore, MD	KO 7
Apr. 19	Doe Williams, Newark, NJ	KO 7
May 5	Billy Smith, Cincinnati, OH	W 10
June 2	Leonard Morrow, Oakland, CA	KOb1
June 28	Jimmy Bivins, Baltimore, MD	W 10
Aug. 2	Ted Lowery, Baltimore, MD	W 10

Sept. 20	Billy Smith, Baltimore, MD	KO 4
Oct. 15	Henry Hall , New Orleans, LA	L 10
Nov. 1	Lloyd Gibson, Wash., DC	LF 4
Nov. 15	Henry Hall, Baltimore, MD	W 10
Dec. 6	Bob Amos, Washington, DC	W 10
Dec. 27	Charley Williams, Baltimore, MD	KO 7

1949

Jan. 10	Alabama Kid, Toledo, OH	KO 4
Jan. 31	Bob Satterfield, Toledo, OH	KO 3
Mar. 4	Alabama Kid, Columbus, OH	KO 3
Mar. 23	Dusty Wilkerson, Phila, PA	KO 6
Apr. 11	Jimmy Bivins, Toledo, OH	KO 8
Apr. 26	Harold Johnson, Philadelphia, PA	W 10
June 13	Clinton Bacon, Indianapolis, IND	LF 6
June 27	Bob Sikes, Indianapolis, IND	KO 3
July 29	Esco Greenwood, No. Adams, MA	KO 2
Oct. 4	Bob Amos, Toledo, OH	W 10
Oct. 24	Phil Muscato, Toledo, OH	KO 5
Dec. 6	Ooc Williams, Hartford, CT	KO 8
Dec. 13	Leonard Morrow, Toledo, OH	KO10

1950

Jan. 31	Bert Lytell, Toledo, OH	W 10
July 31	Vernon Williams, Chicago, IL	KO 2

1951

Jan. 2	Billy Smith, Portland, OR	KO 8
Jan. 28	John Thomas, Panama City, PAN	KO 1
Feb. 21	Jimmy Bivins, New York City, NY	KO 9
Mar. 13	Abel Cestac, Toledo, OH	W 10
Apr. 26	Herman Harris, Flint, MI	KO 4
May 14	Art Henri, Baltimore, MD	KO 4
June 9	Abel Cestac, Buenos Aires	KO10
June 23	Karel Sys, Buenos Aires	D 10
July 8	Alberto Lovell, Buenos Aires	KO 1
July 15	Vicente Quiroz, Montevideo	KO 6
July 26	Victor Carabajal, Cordoba	KO 3
July 28	Americo Capitanelli, Tucuman	KO 3
Aug. 5	Rafael Miranda, Argentina	KO 4

Aug. 17	Alfredo Lagay, Bahia Blanca	KO 3
Sept. 5	Embrell Davison, Detroit, MI	KO 1
Sept. 24	Harold Johnson, Philadelphia, PA	W 10
Oct. 29	Chubby Wright, St. Louis, MO	KO 7
Dec. 10	Harold Johnson, Milwaukee, WI	L 10

1952
Jan. 29	Harold Johnson, Toledo, OH	W 10
Feb. 27	Jimmy Salde, St. Louis, MO	W 10
May 19	Bob Dunlap, San Francisco, CA	KO 6
June 26	Clarence Henry, Baltimore, MD	W 10
July 25	Clint Bacon, Denver, CO	KO 4
Dec. 17	Joey Maxim, St. Louis, MO	W 15
	(Won World Light-Heavyweight Title)	

1953
Jan. 27	Toxie Hall, Toledo, OH	KO 4
Feb. 16	Leonard Dugan, S. Francisco, CA	KO 8
Mar. 3	Sonny Andrews, Sacramento, CA	KO 5
Mar. 11	Nino Valdes, St. Louis, MO	W 10
Mar. 17	Al Spaulding, Spokane, WA	KO 3
Mar. 30	Frank Buford, San Diego, CA	KO 9
June 24	Joey Maxim, Ogden, UT	W 15
	(Retained World-Light Heavyweight Title)	

1957
May 1	Hans Kalbfell, Essen, GERMANY	W 10
June 2	Alain Cherville, Stuttgart, Ger.	KO 6
Sept. 20	Tony Anthony, Los Angeles, CA	KO 7
	(World Light-Heavyweight Title Bout)	
Oct. 31	Bob Mitchell, Vancouver, B.C.	KO 5
Nov. 5	Eddie Cotton, Seattle, WA	W 10
Nov. 29	Roger Rischer, Portland, OR	KO 4

1958
Jan. 18	Luis Ignacio, Sao Paulo, Brazil	W 10
Feb. 1	Julio Neves, Rio de Janeiro	KO 3
Mar. 4	Bert Whitehurst, S. B., CA	KO10
Mar. 10	Bob Albright, Vancouver, B.C.	KO 7
May 2	Willi Besmanoff, Louisville, KY	W 10

May 17	Howard King, San Diego, CA	W 10
May 26	Charlie Norkus, S. Francisco, CA	W 10
June 9	Howard King, Sacramento, CA	W 10
Aug. 4	Howard King, Reno, NV	D 10
Dec. 10	Yvon Durelle, Montreal, Canada (World Light-Heavyweight Title)	KO11

1959

Feb. 2	Eddie Cotton, Victoria, Canada	EXH5
Mar. 9	Sterling Davis, Odessa, TX	KO 3
Aug. 12	Yvon Durelle, Montreal (Title Bout)	KO 3

1960

May 25	Willi Besmanoff, Indianapolis, IN (Non-title)	KO10
Sept. 13	George Abinet, Dallas, TX (Non-title)	KO 4
Oct. 29	Giulio Rinaldi, Rome, Italy (Non-title)	L 10
Nov. 28	Buddy Turman, Dallas, TX (Non-title)	W 10
Oct. 25	N.B.A. withdrew recognition from Moore.	

1961

Mar. 25	Buddy Turman, Manila (Non-title)	W 10
May 8	Dave Furch, Tucson, AZ (Non-title)	EXH4
May 12	Cliff Gray, Nogales, AZ	KO 4
June 10	Giulio Rinaldi, New York, NY (Title Bout)	W 15
Oct. 23	Pete Rademacher, Baltimore, MD (Non-title)	KO 6

1962

Feb. 10	NYSAC and EBU withdrew recognition from Moore.	
Mar. 30	Alejandro Lavorante, Los Angeles	KO10
May 7	Howard King, Tijuana, Mexico	KO 1
May 28	Willie Pastrano, Los Angeles, CA	D 10

Nov. 15   Cassius Clay, Los Angeles, CA   KOb4

1963
Mar. 15   Mike DiBiase, Phoenix, AZ   KO 3
Retired in 1964 to enter Cinema and Television Fields.

1965
Aug. 27   Nap Mitchell, Michigan City, MI   KO 3

Note: KOb10 means Archie lost.

ARCHIE'S BOXING RECORD

TOTAL BOUTS	228
TOTAL KNOCK OUT	140
WON BY DECISION	53
WON BY FOUL	0
DRAW	8
NO CONTEST	1
LOSS BY DECISION	17
LOSS BY FOUL	2
KO'D BY	7
NO DECISION	0
NO CONTEST	1

ARCHIE
MOORE
LIGHT HEAVYWEIGHT CHAMPION
OF THE WORLD
1952 TO 1962

Index

MacFarland 114
Madler 68
Mannone 73
Marciano 160-164, 175, 192
Markham 167
Marshall 67, 100, 153, 174
Mattie 60, 70, 71, 74, 78, 90, 105
Maxim 114, 121, 137-139, 141, 143, 152, 153, 164, 173
McCoy 55, 58
McCracklin 93, 99
McCrary 212
McDaniel 57
McGee 57, 117, 153
McGoogan 179
McNamee 81
McQueen 187
McTigue 101
Miller 106
Mills 78, 139
Mitchell 119
Moran 34
Mosby 14, 24, 212
Motta 114, 119
Murphy 140, 154, 179, 214
Murray 214
Nixon 211
Norfolk 118, 119
Norman 152, 164
Oats 215
Olson 160
Oma 119
Ortman 144
Pabst 177
Pache 127
Paige 101
Palermo 191
Palmer 61, 219
Parish 78
Parker 122, 215
Parks 37, 38, 43, 120, 121
Parsons 177
Patterson 164, 177, 190
Pearl 112
Peary 142
Peer 164

Peron 125, 126, 128, 131, 132, 145, 212
Petracelli 219
Phal 101
Pierce 205
Pippen 215
Platner 51, 58, 105, 109, 111, 113, 114
Poitier 165
Polee 59
Pollack 105
Pope 189
Porter 31, 32, 39, 48, 59, 68, 69, 72, 140
Prysock 168
Pye 214
Quinn 189
Rabbit 112
Rachel 16
Raft 58
Randall 187
Randolph 120
Ray 139
Reagan 205
Reynold 168
Richards 79, 81, 109
Richardson 69, 71, 77, 79, 87
Richey 95
Robeson 120
Robinson 57, 78, 114, 115, 138, 174, 176, 177, 181
Romero 48, 59, 69, 109, 111, 114
Roosevelt 33, 120, 121, 125, 132
Rosenblum 59
Ross 113
Russell 167
Sabatino 82
Saddler 119, 122, 127, 131
Sadler 189
Salve 93
Sanford 5, 32
Satchmo 57
Schmeling 120
Schoeppner 187
Segal 109

Archie Moore's "Salt Mine" Training Camp in Ramona, California.

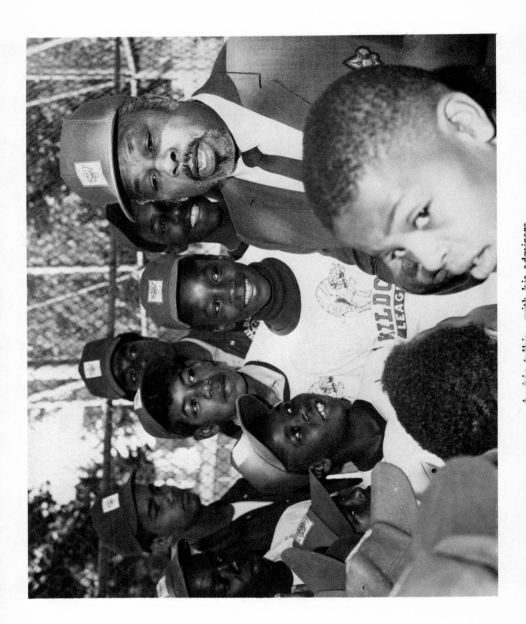

A friendly visit with his admirers.

A happy Archie Moore with sponsors and students.

Archie being interviewd for television.